DAILY ENCOURAGEMENT IN THE
CHURCH PLANTING JOURNEY

DAILY
ENCOURAGEMENT
in the
CHURCH PLANTING
JOURNEY

365 Days of Wisdom, Inspiration, and Courage
for Church Planters by Church Planters

Edited by Jim Carpenter

Foreword by Paul Becker, President and Founder
of Dynamic Church Planting International

Oceanside, California

Published by Dynamic Church Planting International
PO Box 4119, Oceanside, CA 92052-4119

ISBN: 978-1-935221-01-2

Design and layout by Melanie Myers Design
www.melaniemyers.com

DYNAMIC CHURCH PLANTING INTERNATIONAL
www.dcpi.org

To Jesus,
the Lord of church planting,
who by His precious blood
seeks and saves the lost,
who builds His church
and the gates of hades will not prevail against her,
who intercedes for us
and keeps us for Himself,
the One we love the most.

FOREWORD

As a pastor, I had been planting my first church for about two years. I sat in my living room at home. Some of the church leaders were in conflict with me and didn't want to follow my leadership. As I thought about my vision for the church, all I could see was a big, black emptiness about six months into the future. I had no vision for the church plant beyond that time. I walked out the front door and sat on a concrete step. And I wept.

I was drowning in dis-courage-ment. Satan, the Enemy, was sucking the courage right out of me and replacing it with discouragement.

Church planters desperately need courage. And we need it every day.

Now, I serve as the President and Founder of Dynamic Church Planting International (DCPI). We love church planters at DCPI. We want to see you become all you can be. We want you to serve God courageously your entire life until you die or Jesus comes. We want you to see God do miraculous work in your church planting. We want you to live happily with your spouse and children.

One of the great miracles of DCPI is how the Lord has brought together thousands of incredible church planting leaders from all over the world to serve our God together. What a great privilege it is for us to serve together to expand God's Kingdom around the globe, in every country.

Our mission statement is: "Equipping leaders to plant five million dynamic churches to reach this world for Christ." That is the vision that the King of Kings gave to me during a Prayer Retreat in 2008. The world needs five million new churches to disciple hundreds of millions of people for Jesus! To give them a church home where they can grow in the Lord! To complete the Great Commission! To transform our world!

The world needs five million new churches. There are not enough churches to win and disciple Christians in this world. Since 1970, the number of Christians has increased by almost one billion. That is an increase of more than 83%. But the number of churches has only increased by 19%. As a result, many new believers are not getting discipled…they are not experiencing the life of Christ! They have no church!!! Heartbreaking!

There is a training famine in many countries. In some *first world* countries there are many options. But in many *third world* countries, there is a massive training famine. Hundreds of thousands of leaders are called by God to plant churches, but they just don't know what to do. Too often the church dies or the leader leaves the ministry. What a tragedy!

God gave birth to DCPI in 1995 to provide a solution to these problems. We are called by God to equip leaders to plant dynamic churches globally. The best way to reach people for Christ and disciple them is to establish a new church close to them. The best way to establish a new church is to train the leaders well. And that is what we do here at DCPI.

We must be filled with courage if we are to fulfill the *Five Million Church Vision* and complete the Great Commission! That is what this book is all about. It is a daily infusion of courage.

This book is written for church planters by church planters. Over 20 church planting leaders from the DCPI network all over the world have contributed. You are going to love this book. Most of the authors are dear friends of mine who have experienced discouragement from the Enemy and have found a Well of Unlimited Courage in their deep relationships with God. These authors are some of the very best people on the planet. They will fill you with wisdom, inspiration and courage.

Read a page every day every year and you will drink at a fountain of courage that will sustain you in your church planting journey throughout your life.

Until the whole world knows Jesus!

Dr. Paul Becker
Founder and President
Dynamic Church Planting International
Oceanside, California USA
www.dcpi.org

ACKNOWLEDGEMENTS

This book represents the love, hard work, and commitment of many people. I especially want to thank:

- Dionne Carpenter, my beloved wife. Without her heart for this project, this book would never have been completed. She suggested the overall design of the book around the DCPI Twelve Principles, spent countless hours editing every page, organized each month, and wrote many of the best devotionals.

- Dr. Mark Williams, a great friend for many years. His oversight kept us on track, and his wise counsel for church planters shows up throughout the book.

- Our authors. The men and women who wrote these devotionals are all busy with the greatest work under heaven – church planting. I am so grateful they somehow found time to contribute their encouragement and expertise to other church planters around the world.

- Tom & Debby Mauss and John & Marlys Hocker, friends and supporters from past church planting projects. Their generosity enabled DCPI to publish this book.

- Dr. Paul Becker, President and Founder of Dynamic Church Planting International. Paul's vision and tenacity have made DCPI a global force to equip and deploy church planters around the world.

- Melanie Gray, our graphic artist. Melanie's work is always exceptional, and being married to a church planter gives her a unique perspective that translates into the formatting and design of this book.

- Jeremy Jenson, an invaluable volunteer whose selfless effort gave us the boost we needed in the last laps before the finish line.

PREFACE

I began planting churches decades ago when, outside the New Testament, there was almost nothing written about church planting. I found church planting to be wonderfully rewarding.

Church planters see God's grace on display in ways that sometimes are not as obvious in more established churches. You feel like you're on the front-lines of spiritual warfare – because you are. The gospel is preached in its simplicity and power, sinners are saved, transformative disciple-making takes place, and churches are started in desperately needy places.

But I also discovered that church planting is a lonely business. Sometimes pastoral colleagues, if there are any, don't have much understanding of or sympathy for what we church planters are trying to do. The church planter's family regularly takes a beating and comes back for more. Often there isn't much of a support network for planters, let alone for spouses or children.

As a church planter, I learned early on that developing greater effectiveness was essential. But as important as skill development was, I needed encouragement even more urgently. Where would I find *courage*? And the people to *en*courage me?

Since my early days of church planting, God has blessed the Church with many, many resources to help improve the skills and enhance the vision of church planters. (DCPI offers wonderful training and many such resources at dcpi.org. You can read more about the vision and ministry of DCPI at the end of this book.) But though the technical information is far more abundant, church planters still need all the encouragement they can get.

Years ago God gave me a dream to produce a devotional book just for church planters, one that would give them a dose of courage and hope for every single day of the year.

And who better to write such a book than other church planters?

If you are involved in church planting, this book is for you. It was written by people who know by experience the church planting journey you're on. Our twenty-one authors are all veterans of the church planting life. They write from the trenches in India, Pakistan, Brazil, Colombia, Peru, Israel, Australia, South Africa, Mexico and the United States. (A brief biographical sketch of each author is included at the end of this book.)

I'm praying this book will truly encourage you. I'm convinced it will.

We loosely organized the twelve months of the year around Dynamic Church Planting International's *Twelve Principles of Church Planting*. (The DCPI Principles are listed on the next page.) Each month includes at least a few devotionals written to highlight that corresponding principle – devotionals designated by a special logo: ❧ But all the entries were penned to give courage, hope and inspiration.

Thank you, church planter, for your work of faith, labor of love, and steadfastness of hope! May God bless, keep, and use you and your family, and may this book encourage your heart.

Jim Carpenter
San Diego, California
August 2011

Twelve Principles
of Dynamic Church Planting

1. THE BOSS PRINCIPLE: Christ is Lord of church planting, and He has a vision for your new church.

2. THE POWER PRINCIPLE: Prayer is the indispensable source of God's power and wisdom in each phase of church planting.

3. THE NEHEMIAH PRINCIPLE: God's vision must lead to prayerful planning, the result of which should be a comprehensive TaskList set out upon a TimeLine.

4. THE BARNABAS PRINCIPLE: Every church planter needs a mentor. A mentor is someone who has been where you want to go and is willing to help you get there.

5. THE TEAM LEADER PRINCIPLE: The church planting pastor is most effective as part of a team on which he serves as the visionary leader.

6. THE MISSION PRINCIPLE: The central work of the new church will always be to help people put their trust in Christ and grow into maturity as His followers.

7. THE LEADERSHIP PRINCIPLE: Leadership development lies at the heart of the new church's mission, and the most important leadership quality to develop is spiritual maturity.

8. THE BRIDGE PRINCIPLE: Understanding (and communicating sensitively to) the hearts and minds of people in the target community is essential to reaching them effectively with the gospel.

9. THE MAGNET PRINCIPLE: When God plants a church there should be wide spread community awareness and interest.

10. THE BALANCE PRINCIPLE: The church planter's walk with God, family life, and ministry must be in biblical balance.

11. THE MULTIPLICATION PRINCIPLE: Healthy churches will reproduce, and daughter church planting should be envisioned and planned from the new church's beginning.

12. THE JOSEPH PRINCIPLE: Attending to organizational and administrative matters will protect and stabilize the new church and enable it to grow in a healthy way.

JANUARY

The Boss Principle

*Christ is the Lord of church planting,
and He has a vision for your new church.*

Why Plant?

*Let us not become weary in doing good, for at the proper time
we will reap a harvest if we do not give up.* ~ *Galatians 6:9*

READING: Galatians 6:7-10

If someone were to ask me, "Paul, why are you devoted to church planting?"
two answers top my list. First, I yearn to see precious people saved and growing
in Christ. At its best, a new church is a loving environment where unsaved
people can easily find Christ and grow in Him. Secondly, God called me to
church planting.

God has many wonderful and fulfilling ministries in his Kingdom. Church
planting is just one of them. During a personal prayer retreat in 1980, God called
me to plant a church. During many prayer retreats since, God has confirmed and
deepened that church planting call and guided me into the next steps on my
church planting mission.

When Jesus hung, dying, on the cross, he said, "It is finished." His work
was done. He had sacrificed himself for our sins. He had provided a way for us
to be saved.

'Crucial' means 'of the cross.' At DCPI, we often say that the crucial work
of church planting is the agony and the ecstasy every week. There is the agony
of seeing your dear friends leave and serve in another work and the agony of too
little money for the work. There is the agony of the church failing to grow the
way you hoped it would.

But ecstasy, too, seeing precious people become Christians through the
ministry of new churches all across the world. When we take up our cross and
follow Jesus in the ministry of church planting, it helps to know why we are
committed to the work so we don't give up.

---

*Great God, Strengthen your servants to finish your crucial church planting work. May
we serve you faithfully until we die or until Jesus comes! Amen.*

Paul Becker

Called of God

And he said to him, "Friend, how did you get in here without wedding clothes?" But he had nothing to say. ~ Matthew 22:12

READING: Matthew 22:1-14

Every Christian is at once called to salvation and to ministry. Christians minister because we are called of God. Sometimes a more specific calling is recognized to be on a person and that person is called out by his community to help equip other Christians to do better ministry. It is the responsibility of the church community to discern whether that calling should also include a transition from secular employment to paid full time ministry.

The Greek word for calling is *kaleo* which means "to call out loud or to invite." By definition, others must issue an invitation or a call. I cannot invite myself to someone else's wedding party. That is the prerogative of the host. God does the calling. A church community does the confirming.

Consider your own calling. Who's calling you? What are they calling you to do? The notion of calling gets tricky with church planting because the church community is yet to form and therefore yet to call. But, if we are indeed called, we answer to someone in some way. To whom are you accountable? As the apostle Paul says, no one can preach unless they are sent. Who is sending you?

Many church planters are rogue, isolated and unaccountable. They have invited themselves to a party without receiving any invitation. Jesus once told a sobering parable about a guest who was not invited and not properly dressed. He was promptly removed from the party lest the guest of honor, his son, be dishonored.

Are you called of God? Has your calling been confirmed by a community? Are you accountable?

Thank you, Father, for calling me and for using others to confirm it. Help me to walk worthy of my high calling with integrity and proper submission. Amen.

Peter Sung

Three Essentials of God's Call

*Paul, a servant of Christ Jesus, called to be an apostle
and set apart for the gospel of God… ~ Romans 1:1*

READING: Romans 1:1-6

Be optimistic, you are "called" by God!

Has the thought of your "calling" contributed optimism as you serve God? Indeed, our calling is an important matter to repeatedly recognize and realize in our ministry journey because it strengthens our commitment to the Mission of the Lord Jesus.

Paul realizes three distinct essentials in his "calling." The first essential is his *doulos* (δοῦλος) relationship with Christ Jesus. *Doulos* means a slave or a bondman. The root *deo* means "to tie, or to be bound or imprisoned, or put in chains." This signifies that Paul was chained up or bound with God and so moved wherever God was moving. He was subjected to the will, and wholly at the disposal, of the King of the universe and the Savior of the world.

The second essential is his authority that comes from the King, who is the pre-incarnated and post-resurrected Son. This realization made Paul confident of accomplishing his assignment. While God calls, He makes it clear by whom the 'called' ones are called.

The third essential is the unique purpose for which he is "called." He recognized that his "set-apart call" was to propagate the gospel of God, which includes the prophecies concerning the gospel, the descent of Jesus from David, His birth, ministry, death, and resurrection, the good news of the Kingdom to the Gentiles, and the spiritual blessings of Christians.

Is there any greater, more admirable purpose for a life? We are called to preach the Gospel that was promised beforehand, of His Son, and which is righteousness from God!

God, Thank you for your precious call. Help me to precisely obey and do my part to reach this unbelieving world under your shield of authority. Always keep me enthusiastic. Amen.

R. Jayakumar

My Father Promised This Land To Me

*I will give you every place where you set your foot,
as I promised Moses. ~ Joshua 1:3*

READING: Joshua 1:1-11, Matthew 28:16-20

The beautiful luxury buses were lined-up to leave for Karachi from Hyderabad (both within Pakistan), as Pastor Nasir and I climbed aboard to complete preparation for a large crusade in Karachi, having just finished our ministry in Hyderabad.

Is that God speaking to me? Or am I dreaming? As it was past midnight, I was exhausted, and this bus was cozy but noisy. Shaking hard, I questioned myself, while "THE GREAT COMMISSION" was bright and bold in my head. I heard, "I have called you for nations. Be loyal and obedient to me, and I will use you in the world."

In a split second I was on fire to win nations for Jesus Christ. The Holy Spirit focused my heart on Matthew 28:19, 20, to be the foundation for my just-born ministry. I asked Jesus, "Can I have a better scripture? This one seems to be too simple." I had no idea about the power and importance of my calling from Jesus Christ, that as a church planter He will take me to the ends of the world, and use me among the nations.

Although I come from a broken family (my parents divorced when I was one year), in fact, having no higher education, skills or even anything good in me, Jesus Christ has called me to serve Him in His great kingdom business of winning souls and planting churches. Now looking back, what a blessing it is, to have ten churches in Pakistan, having just started the eleventh, which is our first church in USA. It is now my goal to plant at least 500 churches around the world.

Heavenly Father, Thank you for calling me to serve you. I surrender and depend on your ability. Use me as you want. Amen.

Amir John Williams

What is Success?

No one serving as a soldier gets involved in civilian affairs –
he wants to please his commanding officer. ~ II Timothy 2:4

READING: II Timothy 2:1-14

The Apostle Paul, my hero, did not exactly "succeed" every time he attempted to plant a church. In fact, not only did he not "succeed," in some instances he was beaten, stoned, imprisoned and left for dead! It seemed like the soldier of Christ lost the battles.

Yet he was successful in each instance because of this: he pleased the Lord, his "commanding officer," in his efforts. He was successful because he sought and did the will of the Lord. He lost many battles, yet he won the war!

Paul repeatedly wrote about the success of pleasing Jesus. He proclaimed that "Our purpose is to please God, not people" (I Thes. 2:4b). In Galatians 1:10, he put it this way: "Am I now trying to win the approval of men, or of God? Or am I trying to please men? If I were still trying to please men, I would not be a servant of Christ."

Church planting leader, what is your measure of success? Is it numbers? Is it being liked? Is it growth? Is it progress, notoriety, comfort or admiration? None of these is the true biblical measure of success. All of them are good gifts if God gives them, but our ministry motivation should ultimately be one thing: to please our commanding officer, the Lord Jesus Christ.

All of us want "success." All of us will have it when we strive each day to please the Lord.

Lord, I want to be successful in church planting by pleasing You. Please help me keep that goal foremost in my life and ministry. Amen.

Mark Alan Williams

At the End of the Day

*Your word, O LORD, is eternal; it stands
firm in the heavens. ~ Psalm 119:89*

READING: Matthew 25:31-46

During college, as Jim and I pondered what to do with our lives, Jim heard an amazing comment by a missionary statesman, Ray Buker, Jr., who said that we know, of course, that God in heaven is eternal. But *on earth*, there are only two things that will last forever – God's word and the souls of people. Nothing else will survive. Nothing! However, everyone we pass on the street or glimpse in their hidden vulnerability, from the least to the greatest, will one day enter an eternal future either in heaven or in hell. Think about that!

His observation made a deep impression on us. What better way to make a lasting contribution than to devote ourselves to the only two things on earth that will last forever? We have never regretted that decision, and pass along Ray Buker's words to encourage you who have, like us, chosen to labor in the eternals.

Some days, I admit, when the work is frustrating and it seems like we're stuck in a backwater, it is easy to lose sight of that grand perspective and wonder if we made a mistake not to pursue a career doing something more tangible or more valued by society. Many things about church planting are fragile – temporary shelters at best. God doesn't promise that every church will last forever or every committee or every effort.

But the words of life will not return void. And the precious people who turned to Christ or became more receptive by seeds we planted and the watering we did, will last into eternity. The gallant kindness we extend and the message of the gospel we faithfully proclaim will resonate into eternity.

Dear Lord, Thank You for making our lives count for something. Help us to live with eternity in view. Amen.

Dionne Carpenter

Powerful Affirmation

*And he saw the Spirit of God descending like a dove and
lighting on him. And a voice from heaven said, "This is my Son,
whom I love: with him I am well pleased." ~ Matthew 3:16b, 17*

READING: Matthew 3:13-17

They say a little affirmation goes a long way. This was a powerful affirmation
for Jesus as He started His ministry. In that holy moment at the Jordan River,
God the Spirit and God the Father chose to be visually and audibly present in
a memorable confirmation for Jesus and His followers. With the three years of
tiring, tempting and often discouraging ministry ahead, this affirmation was
empowering and gave Jesus much needed encouragement for the days ahead.

What word of affirmation from the Lord do you most need today?

We also are engaged in ministry that is often tiring, tempting and
discouraging. Fortunately, as Christians we also have been given affirmation
from God's word that is highly empowering. For example, from God the Father
we receive affirmation of His love, adoption into His family and the provision of
grace for every need at every level. From the Son we have confirmation of His
continual intercession on our behalf, His promise to abide with us now and to
prepare a heavenly home for us. From the Holy Spirit we have verification that
He stands with us as our helper and advocate, that He provides all the gifts we
need to fulfill our call, and that He will give us courage for any situation.

That is powerful affirmation for today!

---

*Lord, Thank You for giving me such wonderful confirmation that I am Your child,
the affirmation that You minister to and through me and inspiration to go boldly,
courageously and confidently! With all I face today, I go in the strength of this powerful
affirmation! Let me not forget it. Amen.*

Ross Chenot

Lord of Church Planting #1
Selection

*While they were worshiping the Lord and fasting, the Holy
Spirit said, "Set apart for me Barnabas and Saul for the work to
which I have called them." Then after fasting and praying they laid
their hands on them and sent them off. ~ Acts 13:2, 3 (ESV)*

READING: Acts 13:1-3

Jesus is Lord of church planting. And that means Lord of *selection*. He is
the one who chooses the church planter. Jesus selects unlikely people. Sometimes
a leader someone else might ignore is the one Jesus chooses. This is to bring Him
glory and to leave no doubt that power and wisdom come from Him.

Years ago I met a young man who felt called to church planting. He went
through an extensive interview process with a well-known church planting
strategist, and in the end the "expert" told him he wasn't called to church
planting.

But the young man still believed Christ had called him, and others also
believed in him. The Lord led him to plant a great church which has now become
a church planting center in the region. Many daughter and granddaughter
churches have been planted, and many souls have been saved.

God is the one who selects the church planters! The new church at Antioch
waited upon the Lord in worship and fasting, and it was the Holy Spirit who
made known to them His call of Paul and Barnabas.

If you're called to church planting, it will be confirmed by others who will
catch your church planting vision and follow you in your mission. Submitting to
an assessment process is a good thing. But the "experts" are not infallible.

Ultimately, it is the Lord who says "set apart *for Me*."

---

*Thank You, Lord Jesus, for calling me to serve You in church planting. May You get all
the glory today! Amen.*

Jim Carpenter

Lord of Church Planting #2
Strategy

So, being sent out by the Holy Spirit, they went down to Seleucia, and from there they sailed to Cyprus. When they arrived at Salamis, they proclaimed the word of God in the synagogues of the Jews. And they had John to assist them. ~ Acts 13:4, 5 (ESV)

READING: Acts 13:4-12

Jesus is Lord of church planting. Not only does He select the right leaders, but He guides them into the right strategy.

I know a Filipino church planter who moved to a distant city with no contacts. God guided him to the marketplace where he waited till he saw other Filipinos. Then he simply introduced himself: "I'm starting a Filipino church. Would you help me?" He has led many people to Christ and planted a fine church.

Paul and Barnabas launched into unfamiliar territory, but God gave them the strategy: First go to the synagogues and preach to the Jews. So even in foreign cities, they found a ready audience among displaced Jews. The synagogue afforded a built-in opportunity to share the Scriptures. And part of their audience would be "God-fearers," Gentiles who were becoming converts to Judaism (see 13:43). Then if the Jews turned away, the larger Gentile community began to open up.

God led them; it was His strategy. Sometimes He used unpleasant circumstances to guide them (like the split between Paul and Barnabas in Acts 15:36 – 40). At other times He used supernatural means such as the Macedonian vision (Acts 16:9, 10).

God blesses certain strategies in some regions that He doesn't in others. This keeps us humble and prayerful, and compels us to seek the Lord of church planting for His strategy in our church plant.

Lord, This is Your church plant and I am Your servant. Please guide me to the strategy You want to bless in this particular church plant. Amen.

Jim Carpenter

Lord of Church Planting #3
Setbacks

*Now Paul and his companions set sail from Paphos
and came to Perga in Pamphylia. And John left them and
returned to Jerusalem... ~ Acts 13:13 (ESV)*

READING: II Corinthians 4:7-18

Jesus is Lord of church planting. He is Lord even when people and circumstances disappoint us. In one of my church plants I selected a young couple to handle our children's ministry. They were both teachers in a Christian school, had a good rapport with students, and seemed enthusiastic about the ministry. We planned and prepared for months.

The Sunday before our new church was to begin worship services, I glanced out my window in time to see my children's church leader depositing all his materials at my front door step. He quit a week before the church started.

Paul experienced setbacks of many kinds. John Mark, a young man whom he was mentoring, quit the church planting team, and his actions ultimately led to a split between Paul and Barnabas. But the Lord is still in control of us and of our church planting mission. He's never taken by surprise, and He rules and overrules to accomplish His will and display His glory.

God supplied other leaders for our children's ministry, and the young couple eventually came back to our new church.

The split with Barnabas meant that two church planting teams were mobilized. And in the end Mark was not only reconciled to Paul but God had worked to shape Mark into a useful teammate. (See II Tim. 4:11b.)

Setbacks may feel devastating, but God is still in control, and Jesus is still Lord of church planting!

Father, Thank You that You are in control of my life and of the church plant. Please continue to rule and overrule, to Your glory and the good of people throughout this community. Amen.

Jim Carpenter

Lord of Church Planting #4
Spiritual Warfare

*But the Jews incited the devout women of high standing and
the leading men of the city, stirred up persecution against Paul and
Barnabas, and drove them out of their district. But they shook off the dust
from their feet against them and went to Iconium. And the disciples were
filled with joy and with the Holy Spirit. ~ Acts 13:50-52 (ESV)*

READING: Acts 13:42-52

Jesus is Lord of church planting. But the church planting journey certainly includes its share of heartache and opposition. If the Bible were only a human book, the last verses of chapter 13 would never have been written. We would prefer to end the story with people being saved and the word of God spreading (vv. 48, 49).

But the Holy Spirit gave us the more realistic record. After great success, Paul and Barnabas were persecuted and driven out of the city. The gospel polarizes. Church planting infuriates Christ's enemies – human and demonic.

The Lord in His wisdom permits and uses this for His own purposes and glory. The murder of Stephen (Acts 7), and the persecution that followed, ignited the courage of ordinary Christians who left Jerusalem and told everyone everywhere about Jesus (8:1, 4).

My younger son served in the military. Just when he was completing his service term, he was unexpectedly called up to serve for over a year in a combat post overseas, a region of great violence and danger. Before he left home, his older brother encouraged him, "You are immortal until the Lord calls you home."

God's servants are immortal and invincible until the Lord calls us home. Jesus is Lord of church planting – even in the middle of spiritual warfare.

Lord Jesus, I acknowledge You as my Lord, and I plead Your blood and claim Your mighty name over my family and my church plant. To You alone be glory. Amen.

Jim Carpenter

Lord of Church Planting #5
Success

*And when the Gentiles heard this, they began rejoicing and
glorifying the word of the Lord, and as many as were appointed to
eternal life believed. And the word of the Lord was spreading
throughout the whole region. ~ Acts 13:48, 49 (ESV)*

READING: II Timothy 4:1-8

Jesus is Lord of church planting. He is the one who blesses and He is the one who defines "success." Sometimes He builds churches of multiple thousands and other times His church plants are of modest size. But in the end He accomplishes His purposes: to glorify Himself and to bring men and women to a saving knowledge of Him.

Paul's church planting throughout Acts 13 was anything but easy. By the world's standards, Paul often would not be considered a success. He taught in the synagogues (vv. 4, 14ff), rebuked evil men (v. 10), preached to city-wide audiences (v. 44), but then was driven out of town (v. 50). Later he was violently attacked and left for dead (14:19, 20).

But Paul's role was to be faithful and obedient, and he was. When the Gentiles first heard the gospel, the news was so wonderful they rejoiced and glorified God's word! Throughout Paul's journeys, the Scripture notes that all those people whom God, the Lord of church planting "had appointed to eternal life believed." So God's word continued to spread.

Paul was a successful church planter, not because He built huge congregations but because he faithfully preached the gospel in the face of opposition and disappointment. And the Lord of church planting used this faithful man to train leaders, preach the gospel, save lost people, and start churches throughout Asia and all the way into Europe!

Lord Jesus, Grant me success according to Your plan and will. May I be found faithful to preach the gospel and to persevere, knowing You are the Lord of all! Amen.

Jim Carpenter

Understanding a Difference between Men and Women

You husbands likewise, live with your wives in an understanding way, as with a weaker vessel, since she is a woman; and grant her honor as a fellow heir of the grace of life, so that your prayers may not be hindered. ~ *I Peter 3:7 (NASB)*

READING: I Peter 3:1-7

I'll never forget the night many years ago, when Jim and I sat in a living room, a thousand-mile journey from home and family, and I met the few people interested in our first church plant. The thought flashed through my mind, "Whatever was I thinking? How on earth can we feed our family by planting a new church?"

Now, years later, I better understand that moment of deeply feminine fear. It wasn't merely a lack of faith.

I've noticed that church planting *calls forth* all that is most deeply and nobly masculine within a man's heart – courage, hunting, overcoming obstacles, building something from nothing and conquering new territory. Church planting can reinforce a man's visceral sense of his own manhood.

We women, on the other hand, must *overcome* our most deeply felt feminine yearnings – for safety, security and stability – to follow our husbands into church planting. We must resist our female instinct for comfort and softness, summoning instead a more manly courage and pioneer spirit. That's why the same experience that might exhilarate you men may scare us just a bit – at least at first.

It calls for understanding, not condemnation; well worth the effort. A manly man who has learned how to be tender and considerate, partnered with a feminine woman who has risen to the challenge of living on the knife edge of courageous faith, together make a wonderfully well-balanced church planting team.

Dear Lord, Grant us today to serve you together as team mates, with mutual honor and kindness, that our prayers be answered. Amen.

Dionne Carpenter

Consistency in Purpose

Before I formed you in the womb I knew (chose) you,
before you were born I set you apart; I appointed you as a
prophet to the nations. ~ Jeremiah 1:4, 5

READING: Philippians 2:5-11

God sets a single exclusive purpose for each of us. For Moses it was to liberate the Hebrews; for Joshua it was conquest of the land; for David, to establish His Throne; forerunning was John's purpose; and exposing the mysteries of the Church was Paul's.

Asaph testified regarding David, "He chose David his servant and took him from the sheep pens; from tending the sheep he brought him to be the shepherd of his people Jacob, of Israel his inheritance" (Psalm 78:70). Ananias heard God saying this about Paul: "This man is my chosen instrument to carry my name before the Gentiles and their kings and before the people of Israel" (Acts 9:15).

The simple message illustrated by these examples is this: God chooses an exclusive design for His servants even in their mother's womb and wires them in such a way that they would become fruitful instruments of God as He intends.

Though the ultimate purpose of God cannot be thwarted, yet we have freedom to resist God's purpose for our lives. Some overturn their purpose like Demas who turned from God to the world (II Tim. 4:10). Others, like Jonah, have not departed from God yet disobey His direction (Jonah 1:10). Some are like David, scouting in places for their lust (II Sam. 11:2). Very few can stand along with Paul declaring their faithfulness toward God's purpose in their living (II Tim. 4:7).

Yielding to God's purpose demands a consistent close walk with God, and trustworthy mentors.

Lord, Keep me at the center of your purpose. I am fragile and easily yield to the patterns of this world. Give me a submissive spirit to listen and do as my mentors direct. Amen.

R. Jayakumar

God's Will for You

*...give thanks in all circumstances, for this is God's will
for you in Christ Jesus. ~ I Thessalonians 5:18*

READING: I Thessalonians 5:16-24

Although I may never have met you, I know God's will for you right now.
What is it? God's will is for you to always give thanks, no matter what happens.

If you receive encouragement today, God wants you to give thanks. Likewise,
if you receive discouragement, He wants you to give thanks. If you receive a big
offering or contribution, God wants you to give thanks. He wants you to thank
Him for a small offering as well. Every situation has a bit of blessing within it
if we look hard enough: If sick, we can thank God we are alive. If dying, we can
thank God we are going to heaven.

The Apostle Paul stated that he found the secret of being content in any
situation (Phil. 4:11). How did he do it? He gave thanks to God, no matter what
happened.

The opposite of contentment is complaining. Because I tend to keep things
to myself, sometimes I have been a "Quiet Complainer." But even though it is
not spoken, my discontent is still discontent.

To help combat this, I start my devotions each day by listing things I am
grateful for, including the trials I face. The old hymn "Great is Thy Faithfulness"
puts it this way: "Blessings all mine with ten thousand beside." My list of
blessings recently passed ten thousand.

God's will for you is the same – thanksgiving always. Let's live in an
attitude of gratitude and then watch our trials melt in comparison to God's
abundant blessings.

---

*Lord Jesus, You have blessed me in so many ways. My spiritual blessings alone are
unfathomable. Please help me to maintain a continual attitude of gratitude. Amen.*

Mark Alan Williams

Anointed for Service

Then the Lord said, "Rise and anoint him,
for he is the one." ~ I Samuel 16:12b

READING: I Samuel 16:1-13

Samuel had made the mistake once before with Saul. The Bible describes Saul as the most handsome man in Israel who stood one head taller than everybody else, and when Samuel first laid his eyes on Saul, Samuel was impressed, and anointed him as king. And now at Jesse's house, God had a lesson for Samuel to learn. With olive oil in hand, Samuel is ready and waiting to anoint, but God rejects each and every one of Jesse's sons. Finally God speaks: "God does not see as man sees, for man looks at the outward appearance of things but God looks at the heart" (16:7).

Jesse has one remaining son who is barely counted among his sons. This runt of the litter is out with the sheep, the lowliest of tasks. But God commands Samuel to anoint David as the king over all of Israel, and, when Samuel does, the Spirit of God rushes upon the young boy.

Have you learned this lesson? God does not anoint the strong or the wise. It is the way of God to choose the weak and foolish things of the world. We have been anointed for our task of church planting, not because we are great but because he is great and he does not want any case of mistaken praise.

David was anointed for service by God for reasons we are hardly able to see. We have been anointed for service for reasons only God is able to see. Our little church does not exist to showcase our strengths but to reveal God's grace. And his grace is sufficient for us.

Father, We repent for competing with you. Forgive us for thinking ourselves strong and wise enough to build your church. Amen.

Peter Sung

Does My Wife Need Her Own Call? #1

You are [Sarah's] daughters if you do what is
right and do not give way to fear. ~ I Peter 3:6

READING: I Peter 3:1-6

Church planting is so demanding you need to be called to it. But is it enough for just the husband to hear that call? Or must your wife hear her own call?

No, she doesn't. A married couple is one flesh and God honors that unity. God won't genuinely call one without implicitly calling the other. However, your wife's attitude is one of the most crucial benchmarks and hurdles that will prove whether or not your call is from God. If your call is genuine, she'll be able to wholeheartedly embrace your call as her own – maybe not immediately – but at least after a season of prayer and reflection. At some point, she may even hear God's call herself.

She's the most important team member you need to win over if you hope for long-term success.

Oftentimes, a man genuinely called to the pioneer work of church planting has married a shy, reserved wife. To her, the very thought of such a crazy life may seem quite daunting; never something she would have chosen on her own. Yet God is wise in uniting such men and women together in marriage. If you will allow your shy wife freedom to find her own ministry within the church planting endeavor, she will bring a much needed balance to your church plant. Quiet wives often spot things – overlooked people, overlooked details, and your own overlooked fatigue – and can bring blessed help behind the scenes. God will bless her willingness to step out in faith as Sarah's daughter.

Dear Father, Please bless our marriage and help us to honor and support one another as loving co-laborers. Amen.

Dionne Carpenter

Does My Wife Need Her Own Call? #2

Aquila and Priscilla greet you warmly in the Lord, and so does the church that meets at their house. ~ I Corinthians 16:19

READING: Romans 6:3, 4

Even if your wife has received a personalized call to church planting, how that translates into ministry may vary widely. Here's my story as example. I gave birth to our first child shortly before we launched our first church. I assumed I should follow Priscilla's example to take a very active role within our new church and be busier than our busiest volunteer.

It took me awhile to realize that although we usually needed more workers than we had, and even though, like Priscilla, I had plenty of ministry experience, my top priority needed to be to provide a stable home for Jim and our new baby. Many others could teach Sunday school or hand out flyers. But nobody else was in my unique position to support and love Jim, to give him a hot meal, a warm bed and a sympathetic ear.

In time I became comfortable with my unique support role, and evaluated every potential new commitment within the church in light of its impact on my ability to take good care of Jim and our children.

I also learned to periodically reassess my commitments in light of the changing needs of our growing family. When our sons were toddlers, they consumed most of my time, but after they went to school, it freed up time that I could in good conscience spend doing more overt ministry.

I still admire Priscilla, but now see that her biggest contribution was to provide a safe haven within which ministry could blossom.

Dear Father, Please make our home and our marriage an ongoing source of blessing. Amen.

Dionne Carpenter

Preach the Word

…I did not shrink from declaring to you the whole counsel of God. ~ Acts 20:27

READING: 1 Corinthians 1:18-26

Preaching is under assault, especially in church planting. Often church planting trainers, seminars, and tapes deemphasize preaching God's word. Instead they urge us to direct our time and efforts to the skills and techniques that will attract people to our new church. Preaching is often regarded as a hindrance.

This amounts to an undermining of our confidence that God's word is a supernatural book, and that it is God's word – not expensive media, sensitive marketing, or even Christian compassion – that changes lives, produces disciples and establishes churches that last.

Sure, the unbelieving world would vote against systematic study of the Bible. After all, "Jews demand signs and Greeks seek wisdom." Flashy "spiritual" experiences will attract a crowd. Practical advice for daily living feels like the right diet for post-moderns. But "we preach Christ crucified, a stumbling block to Jews and folly to Gentiles, but for those who are called…Christ the power of God and the wisdom of God."

In one of my church plants I tried to appeal mainly to "seekers" on Sunday morning. My heart was right, but I now believe my approach relied upon my very fallible understanding of people, instead of trusting the full counsel of God's infallible word. I gave them a shallow, tasty snack when what they really needed was the bread of life.

People are desperate for a word from the Lord. Self-improvement techniques with a thin veneer of out-of-context Bible phrases are no substitute for the timeless, soul-penetrating, spirit-lifting, character-transforming word of God.

Being boring is a sin. Using unfamiliar Bible words without defining them is arrogance. But not giving people the full counsel of God is a tragedy that will undermine their eternal foundation.

Preach the word!

Father, Show me how to teach your word accurately, sensitively, relevantly, systematically, and reverently. Amen.

Jim Carpenter

If You Had Been with Jesus

...and they took note that these men
had been with Jesus. ~ Acts 4:13b

READING: John 1:1-18

In Acts, people testified about Peter and John being with Jesus; they saw certain charisma in them. John's Gospel says that it was Jesus who came down to be with the disciples (John 1:14a). Who had been with whom? When Jesus dwelt among the disciples, they made use of His nearness and thus gained some positives, which led others to testify that they had been with Jesus.

Paul said, "... as I follow Christ, you follow me." He bore the marks of the cross of Christ. Although he was neither eloquent in his speech nor worldly wise, he was able to impact multitudes, build reproductive leaders and plant churches. People could see Christ when they looked at Paul.

If we have been with Christ, the community around us should endorse our being with Jesus by seeing our beings and doings. We are surrounded by core-leaders, seekers, young believers, mature leaders and unbelievers as we plant churches. Our intimacy with Christ is one of the essentials for impacting the communities around us. If we have been with Jesus, let us distribute His love, purity, humility, forgiveness, tolerance, compassion, forbearance, healing, courage and comfort to the communities around us. They are broken, wounded, immature, sinful, proud, wicked, violent and pagan.

There has been an increasingly heavy storm against the gospel propagation in almost every country. Verbal communication of the gospel of Christ may not be easily possible in the context of political and religious resistances. A demand for Christ-Incarnation is at hand.

We serve the King as His ambassadors. Let people see that we have been with Jesus.

Lord, Help me to remain the reflector of Christ Jesus. Help me to grow from maturity to maturity so Christ can be seen by others in and through me. Amen.

R. Jayakumar

How to Spot a Catalyst

I planted the seed, Apollos watered it, but
God made it grow. ~ I Corinthians 3:6

READING: I Corinthians 3:5-9

When Jim and I moved to Chino, California, to plant our first church, we both assumed he was a founding pastor and that we would retire in Chino after a long and enjoyable tenure. We loved that church and felt very much at home in that community.

After about seven years, Jim began to get antsy. His ears would perk up when someone talked about a new church planting project somewhere. He began day-dreaming about pioneer life in Alaska.

Mainly, he was bored to tears by the minutia of committee meetings and maintenance details inherent to running an established church. His passion was to win people to Christ, gather a cohesive core group and set up solid organizational structures so the church would thrive. When people began bickering over the color of the carpet in the sanctuary, he sort of lost interest.

It took awhile for him to sort out what it all meant. By the end of our second church plant we both understood his gifting better. He didn't have to apologize for his waning interest level once the church had the luxury to worry about such things as flower arranging and changing the light bulbs. It was a blessing to pass the baton to another pastor in an orderly fashion.

I must admit it was a nuisance to move on just when a church had stabilized enough to have a "real" church office or a sanctuary of its own, and we didn't have to cart in chairs each week.

All I can say is this: When I heard people start to talk about carpet color, I knew it was high time to pack!

Father, Thank You for letting us do what You've called us to do, and for showing us where we fit in Your vineyard. Amen.

Dionne Carpenter

Vision Despite Obstacles

So then, King Agrippa, I was not disobedient
to the vision from heaven. ~ Acts 26:19

READING: Acts 26:19-22

The vision Paul was referring to was the divine vision he saw on the road to Damascus, twenty-three years before, in which Jesus Himself gave him the mission of witnessing and spreading the gospel. Paul had been consistently and progressively obedient to the vision, even at great personal cost of being imprisoned and "about to be killed," which denotes laying down his whole life for the God-given vision. Painful episodes in his mission-vision journey and ministry challenges did not defeat his vision.

While working for an engineering company in India, I used to support many servants of God financially. I had the privilege of supporting a couple. He was a qualified printing engineer working for a huge printing press prior to his obedience to the vision of God, which led him to plant a church in a suburban area in Chennai, India. Obedience to God-given vision led him to extreme poverty. Experiencing poverty with a young wife and twin babies is not amiable. On one visit to his home I noticed his new-born babies were fed with the diluted form of the water used to cook rice. In India it used to be a hot beverage for extremely poverty-stricken adults.

The Indian Churches claim 7 to 10 percent of the nation's population as Christians. Perhaps the number is even higher. Beneath this glamorous figure there are many silent, sacrificial heroes of the faith of which Indian church history is not aware. Knowing your vision is "of God" will energize you to accomplish your vision. "Laying whole life" of a visionary makes him to be obedient to his God-given vision in all adverse days of his journey.

Lord, Strengthen me that I may continue to obey that vision consistently as I pass through my mission-journey. Amen.

R. Jayakumar

Never Despise Your Own Gift

I planted the seed, Apollos watered it,
but God made it grow... ~ I Corinthians 3:6

READING: Zechariah 4:4-10

Recently, I read an interview of the singer/song-writer Michael Card. He's not as famous or as flashy as other Christian musicians, but his songs have ministered deeply to my heart. His mentor gave him this sage advice: "Never despise your own gift and never covet another's."

Often, up to our hip boots in the work of church planting, we may be tempted to despise our own gift – that burning in our bones that steered us toward church planting instead of accepting what appeared to be the easier path serving in an established church with buildings, trained workers and full sanctuaries on Sunday morning. Or becoming a school teacher or plumber, for that matter!

We can despise the smallness of our church or feel guilty or inadequate that we've struggled for so long and have so little to show for it. We may preach great sermons and feel a bit wistful that so few heard.

To be at peace with our church planting gift is to realize that we are called precisely to the small work. We are called to midwife at the birth of a baby church, not necessarily to stay until the church grows up. We are called to plant seeds, to nurture tiny shoots of new growth, and to break new ground where future crops will grow. It may well be the task of others to manage the Lord's field when grain is tall and extends as far as the eye can see.

Meanwhile, one by one, we can bless precious souls, like Michael Card blessed me.

Dear Father, You who notice even the smallest sparrow, Be pleased to see and enjoy my small work today, and may I faithfully and gratefully exercise the gift You were pleased to give to me. Amen.

Dionne Carpenter

Faith and Works

*So keep up your courage, men, for I have faith in God
that it will happen just as he told me. ~ Acts 27:25*

READING: Acts 27:21-26

Why, when Paul had received a very specific promise from God that all lives would be saved, does Paul spring into action? Why does he say things like: "If these men escape, we're all going to die!"? Why does the promise of God make him active rather than passive? Why not just sit back and let God fulfill his promises?

We are creatures of faith, of hope, and of love. We have been designed by our creator to run on very specific fuel, that is, trust and hope in his love. Why did Paul act? Because he believed that it would happen just as God had promised.

The fact that God already knows my prayers before they form on my tongue causes me to pray more; the fact that the race has already been won causes me to run so as to win.

God's grace and promises are not conveyed through a vacuum but through our prayers and work. The dichotomy that exists between faith and works is a false one. It is not God *or* Paul but God *through* Paul.

Yes, God is the architect and builder of our church. It is his power, his vision, his timing, and it is for his glory. But God builds his church through us, by us, and for us. It is his will to use us and it is our privilege to be used.

Hear it and believe it for faith comes by hearing. Believe it and do it, for faith without works is dead. Work out your salvation with fear and trembling for it is God who works in you.

Jesus, Thank you. You love your church. You gave yourself for her, washing and cleansing her with your blood. Amen.

Peter Sung

God's Mysterious Guidance

*And they went through the region of Phrygia and
Galatia, having been forbidden by the Holy Spirit to
speak the word in Asia. ~ Acts 16:6 (ESV)*

READING: Acts 16:6-10

God will confirm His call to church planting, and sometimes He does so in unusual ways.

During seminary, I knew God was calling my wife and me to church planting. But we weren't sure about where. In my senior year we heard about an opportunity in another state. An association of churches wanted to recruit one couple from our school. The association's director flew to Denver to interview Dionne and me, and another couple, who were close friends of ours.

In our interview we expressed honest doubts about our fitness for the area, and serious concerns about that particular church planting environment. On the other hand, our friends had lived for several years in the state, loved it, and wanted very much to return.

In the end, Dionne and I were invited to come as church planters, and our friends were not. While we regarded it as God's guidance, it puzzled me why our friends were not chosen. Months later, after we moved to the state and began planting our first church, I asked the director why we were picked over the other couple.

He replied that they had expressed too many doubts, and didn't seem like they wanted to come. I was stunned – he had confused the two interviews!

Now many years later, it is clear that God used human error to accomplish His plan. We have had several decades of fruitful church planting, including writing and mentoring. The Lord led our friends in a different direction and has also blessed their ministry.

God's ways are always best – even if they seem mysterious at the time!

Father, Thank You for leading us. We trust Your character even when we don't understand Your ways. Amen.

Jim Carpenter

Without Complaining

*Do everything without complaining or arguing, so that you
may be innocent and pure as God's perfect children, who live in a
world of corrupt and sinful people. You must shine among them
like stars lighting up the sky. ~ Philippians 2:14, 15 (GNB)*

READING: Philippians 1:12-19

"Do everything without complaining…" (Phil. 2:14). When was the last time you complained? Perhaps it was not long ago. God tells us not to complain. I believe He gives us this command for three good reasons:

1. Complaining hurts us: it robs us of joy;
2. Complaining hurts others: we rob them of joy;
3. Complaining hurts God: it pains Him to see His children be ungrateful. Ephesians 4:30a says, "And do not grieve the Holy Spirit of God."

Church planting leaders can certainly find plenty of reasons to complain. Yet our problems are often trivial when compared to those of the Apostle Paul, who was used by God to give this command. He wrote the Epistle to the Philippians while sitting in jail just for telling people about Jesus; chained to guards twenty-four hours a day; awaiting trial; knowing that he could lose his life for the Gospel – which, of course, he did eventually.

What is the antidote? Our minds cannot run in a vacuum. The solution is thanksgiving – filling our minds with gratitude and praise to God for who He is and for all the blessings He has given us. Even if we have lost everything on earth, as Paul had, we can praise Him for our spiritual riches and for the glorious future that awaits us on the other side!

Lord, I confess my sins of complaining. I want to shine for you by being thankful. Please help me Lord. Amen.

Mark Alan Williams

Messing with Our Head

The devil said to him, "If you are the Son of God,
tell this stone to become bread." ~ Luke 4:3

READING: Luke 4:1-13

Tucked into the narrative of the temptation of Jesus, as a small aside to the main battlegrounds, there's an odd repetition in the devil's words which gives us a clue as to how he tempts us: "If you are the Son of God...."

Of course, Satan knew perfectly well that Jesus was, in fact, the Son of God. Yet he used that insinuating question to tempt Jesus to do something outlandish or extreme to prove his identity. *Turn these stones into bread... Throw yourself down from here.* He implied that Jesus needed to do something – anything – to prove what was actually innate.

He whispers the same sneer into our minds: "If you are a child of God, pray twice as long as you do." Or "If you are a church planter, then you will do such and so." Or "How can you call yourself a Christian, if you haven't done a forty-day fast?"

It's all rubbish!

If you are truly a child of God, it's because God did a sovereign work in your heart and you accepted Christ as your Savior. That's the criterion. You don't become *more* God's child by praying a lot.

If you heard God's call to church planting, as confirmed by the body of Christ, you *are* one, to God's glory, even on the days when you feel most frustrated.

No amount of fasting or toil, no flashy publicity stunt or miracle-working can make you something you already are. It's as counter-productive as trying to start a car engine that's already running.

So, be like Christ, secure in His identity, concerned only to please His Father.

Father, Help me to walk in simple obedience, and to laugh in Satan's face when he tries to mess with my head. Amen.

Dionne Carpenter

What Does Your New Church Need?

*…in whom are hidden all the treasures of
wisdom and knowledge. ~ Colossians 2:3*

READING: Colossians 1:13-2:5

Recently I took a short prayer retreat at a mountain cabin not far from a small lake. Every day I walked or jogged two miles around the lake while I prayed. One day I carried a sheet of paper in my pocket listing several issues that were heavy on my heart. I walked the entire way around the lake without feeling like I'd connected with the Lord.

I decided to sit and continue praying until I heard from God. I looked at my paper and one question stood out: "What does our church need?"

We church planters want the best for our new churches. Our wish list might include more trained leaders or a particular key staff member. We might request an upgraded computer system, a bigger building, expanded office space or a better sound system.

The bigger churches seem to have all these things, and when we want to accomplish great things for the Lord, we wish for the best: leaders, staff, facilities and resources. And sometimes we wonder; Is there a program we could use – or a special outreach focus – that would enable our church to reach more people for Christ in a more effective way?

So that's why I was asking the Lord, "What does our church need?" Finally I heard the Lord's answer: *Me. Keep preaching Christ.*

No, I didn't hear an audible voice, but the sense of His guidance was very clear. What the church needs more than anything is the Lord. Other organizations may have lots of leaders, large buildings and expensive equipment. But only the true church has Jesus. And He's the One who makes all the difference.

Lord, Thank You for the leaders, facilities, and equipment You send our way. But, mostly, thank You for Jesus. Help me to keep preaching Christ. Amen.

Jim Carpenter

Getting Your Vision Off the Runway #1
The Black Box

For you are my lamp, O LORD, and my God
lightens my darkness. ~ II Samuel 22:29 (ESV)

READING: II Samuel 22:21-51

I'm flying home after a long trip, hoping for a safe arrival along with my fellow passengers. Every time a plane crashes, locating the flight recorders is the single most important goal after rescuing the survivors. These boxes record the technical information from the plane as well as the conversations among those responsible for ensuring that the plane arrives safely at its destination. These boxes are necessary in order to piece together the answers to one simple question: "What happened?"

We have all seen ministry leaders attempt to get their vision off the runway and on its way to a wonderful destination. Some leaders excitedly lay out their vision to their friends and fellow-workers only to watch it struggle to gain altitude. Sometimes they do manage to get it into the air only to watch it crash suddenly. At other times, the plane barely leaves the jet way. Unfortunately, I've been that leader more than I want to admit. When these kinds of things occur, the question on every person's mind is the same as in a plane crash, "What happened?"

While there are many contributing factors in such failed starts and crashes, most of the factors can be divided into two broad categories, either faulty visioning or failed execution. Moving past the typical finger pointing and blame game, rarely do we examine the first category by pondering "Maybe we had the wrong vision in the first place," or "Perhaps our vision was cloudy." Sometimes a failed flight is the result of a vision that is out of sync with God's vision.

Dear Heavenly Father, Help us to gain insight and wisdom even from our well-intentioned mistakes so that our labor and passion are ever attuned with Your vision. Amen.

Sean Pierce

Getting Your Vision Off the Runway #2
The Runway Lights

For by you I can run against a troop, and by my God
I can leap over a wall. ~ II Samuel 22:30 (ESV)

READING: II Samuel 22:21-51

Uncertainty always marks the journey of effective leaders. It's the uncertainty of wondering, "How could we possibly do this?" or "I'm not sufficient for these things" or "I'm not really sure how to proceed right now." We can only imagine David's own struggle as he faced increasingly challenging assignments from the Lord. As church planting leaders, in many ways we walk the same path.

One test to determine if our vision is on target with God's is to ask, "Is the vision leading us into the unknown?" If we can accomplish it in our own strength and resourcing, then our vision is too small. If our vision doesn't stretch us past our comfort zone, it's too small. If it doesn't lead us to run against an army, or to attempt a leap over a formidable wall, then God isn't in our vision. It's something we created.

Conversely, just because a vision is big and would stretch us, doesn't mean it is automatically from God. If God isn't lighting our runway early on as we seek to get the vision into the air, then our vision is too big. Those little runway lights are the sequential "next steps" as we implement the initial plans in accomplishing the vision.

How does your vision for church planting and reaching unreached people line up with these two parameters? Does your vision lead you and your ministry into the darkness of the unknown? And is God providing runway lights in helping you actually accomplish it? Is it leading you into complete dependence upon Him?

Dear Heavenly Father, Show us Your true vision, and lead us to walk in obedience to it. Amen.

Sean Pierce

Handling Unbelief

Immediately the boy's father exclaimed, "I do believe;
help me overcome my unbelief!" ~ Mark 9:24

READING: Mark 9:14-27

An unnamed father had a son who was under the possession of an evil spirit which robbed his speech. He asked the disciples of the Lord to drive out the demon, but they could not. The teachers of the law began to argue with people in the gathered crowd.

Key subject matter in this passage is "unbelief." Unbelief gripped the teachers of the law, the crowd, disciples and the father. Unbelief begins to take control at the time of uncertainty. The boy was under possession from his childhood. None could do anything, including the disciples of the Lord. Unbelief generates strong scepticism. "If you can …" was an echo of the heart of a sceptic father. They were the words uttered with unbelief in his heart.

When loss and failures hit us, we are abandoned, our prayers are unheard, injustice defeats us, sickness deteriorates and unsolved problems accumulate. When we think our labor in the Lord is in vain – there unbelief creeps in.

In 1984, I endured a gulf of severe challenges. I could sense unbelief was gripping me. I knew I was becoming a sceptic. It even almost had led me to break my commitments, made before the Lord. I spent a sleepless night with great wrestling between my belief and my unbelief. God shook me up from the bed and led me to the passage of this day's meditation. All that I did in the middle of the night was – just cry before the Lord as this unnamed father cried. *Oh, Lord, I believe you but help me to get out of my unbelief.*

There was an instant answer. Yes, I felt the cloud of unbelief passing away from my boundary. There was a divine injecting of "belief" into me.

Help me, Lord, to believe you in all situations. Amen.

R. Jayakumar

FEBRUARY

The Power Principle

Prayer is the indispensible source
of God's power and wisdom in
each phase of church planting.

Paul's Prayer Life

I thank my God in all my remembrance of you,
always in every prayer of mine for you all making
my prayer with joy... ~ Philippians 1:3, 4 (ESV)

READING: Philippians 1:1-11

The person who has taught me the most about prayer is the Apostle Paul. His prayer life is so rich that some of his prayers are included in God's holy word. Most of these are prayers for the Christians in new congregations. (See Phil. 1:9 – 11; Eph. 1:16 – 23; 3:14 – 21; Col. 1:9 – 12; II Thes. 1:11, 12; Philemon 6).

Here are some of the lessons I've learned about praying for other people:

Pray for spiritual matters more than physical. While it's good to pray for people's ailments and finances, Paul's prayers are about becoming more loving (Phil. 1:9); knowing God more deeply (Eph. 1:17); walking worthy of Christ (Col. 1:10); and sharing the gospel effectively (Philemon 6).

Pray for eternal matters more than temporal. Of course Paul cared about what was going on in their lives *now*, but he constantly envisioned eternity. He prayed about "the day of Christ" (Phil. 1:10) and their glorious inheritance in heaven (Eph. 1:18; Col. 1:12).

Continue to point them to the glory of Christ. He prayed that their lives might be "to the glory and praise of God" (Phil. 1:11) and that Christ's name might be glorified in them (II Thes. 1:12).

Let them know you love them and are praying for them. "I do not cease to give thanks for you, remembering you in my prayers" (Eph. 1:16).

Church planters are usually people of action, but may God help us also to be people of prayer – like the Apostle Paul.

Father, Thank You for Paul's example as a prayer warrior. Teach me how to pray for the people You've given me. Amen.

Jim Carpenter

A Reminder to Pray

*But whenever you pray, go into your room and shut the
door and pray to your Father who is in secret; and your Father
who sees in secret will reward you. ~ Matthew 6:6*

READING: Matthew 6:5-13

And, of course, the reward is God himself. How often would you say
that your prayer times end with a sense that you have been in touch with God
himself?

As "professional" Christians, our prayers are often prayed for the hearing
and edification of, and judgment by, others. The moments are rare when our
audience is God alone. Scripture tells us that it is the glory of man to uncover
but the glory of God to conceal, to play hard to get, to be found only by those
who humble themselves, put in the time and pay a price. Having the ears to hear
is not easily accomplished.

One of the great losses of becoming a pastor is the business contract we
apparently sign when we answer the call. We loved to pray and now we get paid
to pray. But we can love to pray again. Find a quiet place to pray. A thousand
other thoughts will knock on your mind's door. Ignore their requests and they
will eventually go away. Realize that God is in secret, and not in plain sight. He
delights to reveal himself to those who create space for him in life and heart.

A reward is no reward if it is not rewarding. I have never connected with
God and regretted it. Each time is surprisingly rewarding, life-giving, and
illuminating. Sometimes I pray in words, sometimes in images, and sometimes
in emotions. Sometimes I am caught off guard by tears and sometimes I feel
nothing at all. Prayer is not magic but it works wonders for my soul. I invite you
to pray today.

Jesus, I pray with your first disciples: teach me to pray. Amen.

Peter Sung

Seeing with the Eyes of Faith

*Now Jericho was tightly shut up because of the Israelites.
No one went out and no one came in. Then the LORD said
to Joshua, "See, I have delivered Jericho into your hands, along
with its king and its fighting men." ~ Joshua 6:1, 2*

READING: Joshua 6

Joshua looks around. He sees the city stretched out before him, shut up tight. He hears what the Captain of the Host tells him to see about the city. And, sometimes, he glances at his sandals, discarded on the ground next to his bare feet, ground made holy because the Holy One Himself stands before Joshua.

The test of faith often comes down to what we choose to see. Will we see only the closed gates, the closed hearts and the high walls? Or will we take God at His word and see our city through the lens of God's promise?

When we planted a church in the desert community of Rosamond, Jim regularly climbed to the top of the rocky crag behind our house and, from that vantage point, prayed over the whole town spread out below. It helped him to reconnect with the Lord who had clearly directed us to that place, and helped him again and again to see the city through God's eyes.

God delights in people whose eyes have been opened to see by faith. We are so blessed as church planters to do something for a living that nurtures and strengthens this holy sight. Most precious of all, the eyes of faith enable us to see and hear our beloved Captain, standing beside us as we with bare feet survey our city.

Dear Lord, Sharpen my spiritual sight to see my city through Your eyes and use this church planting project to help me see all things through the eyes of faith. Amen.

Dionne Carpenter

On This Rock

...on this rock I will build my church, and the gates of
Hades will not overcome it. ~ Matthew 16:18

READING: Matthew 28:16 – 20

During the hot summer of 2000, Pastor Bashir Deewan and I prayed, planned and planted our first church in Francis Town, Karachi. How difficult it was to purchase this small piece of land in the slums of 8,000 homes. We hoped that this church would bring many to Jesus because this area was a common ground for drug trafficking. Sin was ruling in the streets.

Because of demonic strongholds, the opposition was very prominent. A time came when all the sin lovers got united against our church. This was the most difficult and challenging time for us. But we continued to pray fervently and the Holy Spirit gave us courage and power to stand against this big attack we were facing until we had the breakthrough.

My beloved co-worker, always keep this in your mind that, whenever we plant a church in an area which is under the heavy stronghold of the devil, unexpected challenges will arise. But the good news is this: The Holy Spirit is with us, giving us power to fight against the unseen.

Today our church in Francis Town is the strongest in that area, growing rapidly. Many of those who are possessed with demons are referred regularly to our Pastor, Bashir Deewan, and the Holy Spirit is giving them complete deliverance, healing and breakthrough.

If you have gone through or are now going through challenges like these, take courage. Jesus promised us in Matthew 16:18 that "upon this rock I will build my church and all the powers of hell will not conquer it." Keep planting churches!

Heavenly Father, Thank You for planting churches through me. I surrender and depend on Your ability; use me as You want. Amen.

Amir John Williams

Ask for Help

Do not get drunk on wine, which leads to debauchery.
Instead, be filled with the Spirit. ~ Ephesians 5:18

READING: John 16:7-14

Do you feel that ministry is too demanding – that you need help? You are right, you do need help. And the most important help you need is God's Holy Spirit filling you every day, empowering you for ministry. Without Him, you are handicapped.

Yet in many church traditions the Holy Spirit hardly receives mention. In the church where I grew up, due to controversies over spiritual gifts, He was almost shunned. These churches forgot God's command to "…be filled with the Spirit." This is not just a suggestion, it is a directive.

Ephesians 1:13 and Romans 8:9 are among several verses that indicate that the Holy Spirit enters our life at salvation. However, it is wrong to take His filling for granted. I Thessalonians 5:19 warns us to "quench not the Spirit" (KJV). Too often we quench His work in our lives through sin and disregard. We need regular refilling.

When D.L. Moody, the great evangelist of the nineteenth century, was asked why he said he needed to be filled continually with the Holy Spirit, he replied, "Because I leak!"

All of us leak the Holy Spirit. What is the solution? Jesus instructed, "If ye then, being evil, know how to give good gifts unto your children: how much more shall *your* heavenly Father give the Holy Spirit to them that ask him" (Luke 11:13 KJV)? Ask for help from the Helper! Take advantage of our great source of ministry power. If you want a powerful ministry, ask regularly for the power of the Holy Spirit.

Dear Lord, I confess my sins [name them] which have quenched your Holy Spirit. By faith I invite You to fill me again with Your Holy Spirit as You commanded me to be filled. Amen.

Mark Alan Williams

Time for a Prayer Retreat

But he would withdraw to desolate places and pray. ~ Luke 5:16

READING: Luke 6:12-16

If the holy and perfect Son of God needed regularly to go away and pray to His Heavenly Father, how could any of us survive as church planters without regular prayer retreats? Jesus regularly withdrew to pray. Despite the crushing need of the crowds and the short timetable to equip and train the Twelve, He took the time to separate Himself and pray.

For over 30 years I've been going away three or four times a year to pray. Long before I knew that anyone called it a "prayer retreat," I felt a great need to be alone with God.

All church planters need regular prayer retreats. Whether you're a veteran in ministry, or newly trained, you need regular prayer retreats. Whether you are energized by solitude or energized by being with people, you still need regular prayers retreats.

So what specifically would you pray about? Over the years I've gone away for a number of different kinds of prayer retreats.

Every January I take a prayer retreat *to intercede for my family* and for my own soul. This sets the tone for my personal intercession the rest of the year.

Prayer retreats *to receive a vision from God* or to inquire for His direction in ministry are crucial.

Sometimes we need *to pray to recover from intense spiritual exertion or to prepare for a spiritual battle ahead.*

Some retreats are taken *to help our staff or elders pray*, and to forge plans of ministry together.

You and I will always need the Lord, and we need to be with Him – to set aside the time to be alone with Him – through all the seasons of our life and ministry.

Father, Help me make plans today to take a prayer retreat. I'm looking forward to being alone with You. Amen.

Jim Carpenter

Only by Prayer

After Jesus had gone indoors, his disciples asked him
privately. "Why couldn't we drive it out?" He replied, "This
kind can come out only by prayer." ~ Mark 9:28, 29

READING: Mark 9:14-29

This is an encouraging passage for church planters. Read the entire story.
"Everything is possible for him who believes," Jesus says in verse 23. Then there
is the honesty of the father in verse 24: "I do believe; help me overcome my
unbelief!" We can all identify with those words.

In the process of facing this big challenge, the disciples made some
false assumptions. We're not sure if they underestimated the power of evil,
overestimated their own authority, presumed God would do their bidding
or were overconfident they had the faith formula down. In any case their
assumption and presumption were wrong.

Jesus said "this kind can come out only by prayer." Prayer is communion
with God. It is communication, conversation and hanging out with God. As
such, Jesus' statement would be about our seeking, petitioning, depending and
aligning ourselves with God's will and power. There is no room for presuming
upon God.

Church planting is the cutting edge of the kingdom. The full force of the
worldly culture, human nature and spiritual forces are united against us. Truly,
"this kind can come out only by prayer." God's servants plant great churches on
their knees.

Today, where can you carve out more time for prayer? While taking a walk?
Driving? Before you turn on your computer? Where can you find five or ten
additional minutes – or an hour or two – to align your will with God's to tap
into the power of the kingdom?

Lord, Like the disciples, I need to learn and relearn the power of prayer. Help me to
hear Your voice and experience Your presence working through me. Amen.

Ross Chenot

Grace and Prayer

Each man said to his mate, "Come, let us cast lots so we may learn on whose account this calamity has struck us." So they cast lots and the lot fell on Jonah. Then they said to him, "Tell us, now! On whose account has this calamity struck us? What is your occupation? And where do you come from? What is your country? From what people are you?" ~ Jonah 1:7, 8

READING: Jonah 1:1-10

The sailors asked: Who broke the rules? And what other rule can we keep that will balance breaking the other rule? These men lived in a world ruled by rules. Survival meant manipulating the rules.

Jonah broke a big rule by running instead of obeying. But instead of manipulating God he admitted his sin and threw himself into the sea of God's mercy or judgment. Belatedly, he said with Jesus, *I will drink this cup*; with Paul, *I don't care what happens to me, I will preach the gospel*; with Joshua, *you choose but I will serve the Lord*; with Esther, *if I perish, I perish*; with Peter, *you be the judge but I will keep speaking of Jesus as the Christ*; with David, *I will not give to my God what costs me nothing.*

Of the reading of church planting books, of attending conferences, of comparing and contrasting, of beating up the self every Sunday night and of keeping all the church planting rules, there is no end.

Asking for God's grace and mercy in time of trouble may seem simple enough but it takes a dying to self, a swallowing ego and a certain kind of boldness to approach God's throne. To do it repeatedly seems unfair for God.

Allow grace to become grace, perhaps for the first time, by praying for God's mercy. It is his glory and delight to be merciful to us.

Lord, Have mercy on me, a sinner. Amen.

Peter Sung

Grace and Worship

*Then the men feared the Lord greatly, and they offered
a sacrifice to the Lord and made vows. ~ Jonah 1:16*

READING: Jonah 1:11-17

The men rowed desperately to evade the storm. And when the storm subsided, their fear of the storm transformed into a fear and worship of God.

It's not that some are desperate and some are not. All are desperate, all are lost, and all are sick. But not all are aware. The storms on the great seas of life put us in touch with our desperate state. Storms humble us and help us to hit rock-bottom. Coming to the end of our own resources can be a wonderfully eye-opening gift in life and ministry.

Worship is the heart and life response of the desperate who have found mercy. Worship is worth-ship: the surprised and grateful attributing worth to the one who alone is truly worthy.

In I Corinthians 4:7, Paul asked: "What do you have that you have not received? And if you received it, why do you boast as though you did not?" Grace is the prelude to the worship of God just as works are the prelude to boasting of self (self-worship).

If the entire process of planting your church is to be an act of worship, every step of that process must be marked by encounters with God's grace, and not by your works. If you want your people to worship God, then Jesus must be the hero at every turn, and not you.

In reality, it truly is God who causes all things to grow healthy and fruitful. So in turn, God uses conflict, pain, and roadblocks to help us see life and ministry through his eyes of grace. Church planting will not, therefore, preclude redemptive pain.

In storm and in peace, I worship you, Jesus. You are worthy of my praise for you alone are the giver of all grace. Amen.

Peter Sung

Grace and God

Then the word of the Lord came to Jonah a second
time: "Go to the great city of Nineveh and proclaim
to it the message I give to you." ~ Jonah 3:1

READING: Jonah 3

We often ask of God, How much does he love me? But the relevant question is not how much God loves but when he loves. Romans 5:8 tells us that God loves us *while* we were helpless, ungodly, sinner, and enemies.

The word of the Lord came to his prophet long before the Ninevites had any thought of repenting. This is what infuriated Jonah, why he ran from God, and why he remained angry through to the end of the book. How could God reach out to such blatant sinners?

There is such a thing as resistance to grace. The counterintuitive truth is that grace, at its heart, is an indictment and proof of human depravity. I want to contribute; I *need* to contribute. If I cannot, what does that say about me? Grace is embarrassing because it is our last and only hope.

Grace is not only warm and fuzzy but it is also the terrifying and transformative power of God. We shun grace because grace, in the end, kills us.

Grace is also the persistent widow in our lives who is constantly knocking on life's door, asking to be invited in. And persistence beats resistance. God loved us then; he loves us now; and he will love us to the end.

Dear church planter, what is keeping you from humbling yourself under God's mighty hand? He wants to lift you up, vindicate you, and set you apart for his own pleasure and purpose. Go to God again and again, ask and receive, knock and invite Jesus into your daily grind of life and ministry.

God, I confess that it is very difficult for me to receive well and often. Please win me over. Amen.

Peter Sung

Grace and Repentance

*The Ninevites believed God. They declared a fast, and all of
them, from the greatest to the least, put on sackcloth.* ~ *Jonah 3:5*

READING: Jonah 3:5-10

Dr. Phil is a popular psychologist who teaches a technique called *Uncensored Talking*. In a group, he invites someone to come up and start talking, uncensored. He stands behind them and taps them on their shoulder if he hears them censoring their talk in any way with respect to impression management, others' feelings, or self-justification. As he taps away, the censored talking soon becomes honest, tearful confession. *I am ugly. I am a failure. I am to blame.*

Uncensored talking illustrates the essence of putting on sackcloth. Sackcloth is made of goat's hair and is the coarsest of fabrics. Only prisoners, the poor and mourners wore sackcloth. When the Ninevites put on sackcloth, they were praying to God and admitting to the world that they were spiritually poor and guilty as charged. This humiliating, naked declaration of insufficiency is the essence of prayer.

Kindness (grace) leads to repentance. When grace points out our sin, and we clearly see that our strength and goodness is not enough, there we stand, naked and vulnerable. That is where God-ward prayers are born – prayers of confession leading to prayers of dependence leading to prayers of hope. And hope does not disappoint because the Spirit in us cries out Abba! Father!

The church planter is often viewed as the gifted and strong one. But if the gifts and strengths are genuine, they come from the Spirit within. Charisma comes from the Greek word *karis* or *karismata*, meaning grace or gift. Your greatest strengths find sustenance only by admitting your greatest weaknesses.

---

*Lord, All day long, I justify, spin, manipulate, censor and lie. I am scared of being seen
for who I really am. Help me to come clean and hide behind nothing but the cross of
Jesus Christ. Amen.*

Peter Sung

Standing in the Gap #1

*I looked for a man among them who would build up the wall and
stand before me in the gap on behalf of the land... ~ Ezekiel 22:30a*

READING: Ezekiel 22:23-31

I'd never met the pastor's wife of the church in a neighboring town but when I heard she was facing back surgery in a few days, the Lord prompted me to go pray for her and, while there, to watch for a more urgent need than her spine.

Nervously, I called and asked if she'd be willing to have a complete stranger drop by to pray. She agreed. I drove out to their country church. As I parked, I noticed a low adobe wall encircling both the church and the parsonage where she lived.

After praying for her back, I drew her out in conversation. She shared that the parsonage often felt "creepy," as if someone lurked in the corners. The church ministry was struggling. Her children had suffered broken bones and other physical attacks in odd apparent coincidences.

I prayed for guidance and felt led to pray blessing for each family member. Suddenly, after the last blessing, I got a vivid impression in the Spirit, that their physical adobe wall reflected another spiritual one. I pictured evil spirits flowing freely back and forth through gaps in their wall.

Surprised but emboldened, in the name of Jesus I spoke closure to the breach and protection over this family. Instantly, I sensed I was done. We hugged and said farewell.

About a year later I ran into her again.

"Dionne, such good things happened after God sent you. He healed my back so I didn't need surgery. The house doesn't feel creepy any more. And best of all, the church has turned around and we're growing again!"

"Glory to God!"

---

*Father, Give us intercessors who will stand in the gap in their authority in Christ.
Amen.*

Dionne Carpenter

Standing in the Gap #2

...but the church was earnestly praying to God for him. ~ Acts 12:5b

READING: Acts 12:1-17

The best time to put a prayer team in place is before we need it. But how can we find reliable prayer warriors who know how to pray effectively for our church planting project?

Every circumstance is different. Sometimes our mother church or sending agency already has a well-established and well-seasoned team of intercessors. With a little wise networking we may be able to "hop aboard" and be blessed by what they're already doing. Likewise, relatives and family friends may be reliable prayer partners because of their long-term commitment to our success and well-being.

Financial supporters may be another good source of prayer supporters. Since they've already demonstrated their commitment to the project, it's a simple matter to encourage them to pray as well. And in this day and age of internet access, many church planters can also build a large "virtual community." This could be an ongoing project, adding more to our mailing list as we go along.

Years ago, when the church growth movement was starting up, they found that about 5% of the adults in a typical church was likely to have a recognized gift of intercession (regardless of denomination or country) – and about 80% of those recognized intercessors were women. If that's true, we might do well to consider gathering a "Grandma Brigade" of gifted intercessors since many of these women devote themselves to prayer after their children leave the nest.

At the very least, pay attention if a little old lady quietly volunteers the information that she is praying for you!

Church planting draws intense spiritual attack. A solid prayer shield of well-informed and effective intercessors is worth its weight in gold. We do well to make it a top priority.

Father, Help me find faithful prayer warriors who will stand in the gap. Amen.

Dionne Carpenter

Aged to Perfection

*And let endurance have its perfect result, so that you may be
perfect and complete, lacking in nothing. ~ James 1:4 (NASB)*

READING: Hebrews 6:1-16

Veteran missionary mentors told us we would need a pressure cooker for cooking meat in Colombia. But frightening memories of those hissing monsters that we saw in the kitchens of our mothers and grandmothers made us think anything would be better and safer than using a pressure cooker for cooking meat. One week after settling into our new home, we prepared our first piece of beef and placed it in the oven to roast. After two hours and several tests for doneness, the roasting fork bouncing off the unyielding texture of the meat gave us a new appreciation for aged beef!

Aging both physically and spiritually, life's process of maturing finds our physical bodies visibly deteriorating while being spiritually vibrant. Christian spiritual maturity becomes increasingly evident as we grow more intimate with God. It manifests through a humbleness that exhibits unhesitant responses to God's direction as it is revealed to us. Our heart, mind and spirit will remain hard and nonresponsive to the Holy Spirit if we do not let Him bring us through a process of aging that sometimes feels like we are hanging from a hook in what may seem like long periods of dry sub-freezing conditions! Willingness to respond without questioning God's wisdom shows we have aged to a tenderness of humbly stepping into places where He leads us. The mature Christian find the most joy in cheerfully yielding to the will of God when he calls us into passages of growth.

Father, Help me to yield to your direction for my life. As I present myself to you each day, make me into the person you need so that what you want will be accomplished in a manner pleasing to you. Amen.

Christine Cunningham

Open Doors and God's Will

So I say to you: Ask and it will be given to you; seek and
you will find; knock and the door will be opened to you. For
everyone who asks receives; he who seeks finds; and to him
who knocks, the door will be opened. ~ Luke 11:9, 10

READING: Acts 16:6-10

Most of us, in our pursuits of God and His will for our lives and ministry, seek open doors, which God opens. Finding open doors comes as a result of knocking and seeking and finding. The secret is to have a door that God opens, opened to you, and not one forced open by human effort. May God open His doors of opportunity to you that will bring Favor, Grace and Provision.

I trust that the following verse will be a *Rhema* word of God to you today! Revelation 3:8: "I know your deeds. See, I have placed before you an open door that no one can shut. I know that you have little strength, yet you have kept my word and have not denied my name."

The Apostle Paul operated only on the open doors God opened for him. He and his companions tested several possible options before Paul saw in a vision a man from Macedonia. They acted at once, "concluding God had called us to preach the gospel to them" (Acts 16:10).

May God help you and me to do God's work where He has led the way and where He has opened a door for the preaching of the gospel. Act on the open doors which God opens in your life.

Father, Bless each who read these words today. Encourage our hearts to continue to ask and seek and knock on doors, and by Your power, open the doors that will empower us to do Your will. Amen.

Hendrik Vorster

Open Doors and Opposition

*I know your deeds. See, I have placed before you an open door
that no one can shut. I know that you have little strength, yet you have
kept my word and have not denied my name. ~ Revelation 3:8*

READING: I Corinthians 16

Open doors are mostly greeted with excitement, appreciation, thankfulness, appreciation or even with amazement, surprise and amusement. Depending on whether you have been trusting God to open a door of opportunity for you, or whether an open door has taken you by surprise, open doors always relate something new and exciting to us.

Maybe you are trusting God for an open door today. It might be in your ministry, business, family or personal life. Regardless of the area or place or position you find yourself in, when you trust Him for this open door, keep His Word.

Notice what the Apostle Paul writes in I Corinthians 16:8, 9: "But I will stay on at Ephesus until Pentecost, because a great door for effective work has opened to me, and there are many who oppose me."

Sometimes open doors become confusing when they are accompanied by opposition. You might be in a place where you have pursued an open door and are suddenly faced with major opposition, and now doubt whether it was from God or not. Take encouragement from Paul. Sometimes open doors for effective work include a dimension of opposition.

Remember, when you are engaged in God's work you become a target of our enemy's assaults. Stand strong in God today! Be strong in the Lord!

Dear Father, I ask You to open many wonderful doors of opportunity for me and my family. Please give me the encouragement to faithfully pursue Your open doors, even when opposition arises. Please give me discernment about the open doors ahead! Amen.

Hendrik Vorster

He Will Guard You Against the Evil One

But the Lord is faithful. He will establish you and
guard you against the evil one. ~ II Thessalonians 3:3 (ESV)

READING: II Thessalonians 3:1-5

My wife and I were both instantly awake in the middle of the night. We sensed the presence of evil in our bedroom so strongly that, without exchanging a word, we dropped to our knees, and began to pray.

For months we had been in the middle of spiritual warfare. A couple within our new church was stirring dissension. They undermined my authority and criticized my leadership. I had never encountered such opposition before. Instead of focusing on winning people for Christ and building them up in the faith, my time and that of our elders was consumed by this crisis. The couple at the heart of the problem refused reconciliation, and continued to blame me.

That night my wife, Dionne, and I cried out to the Lord, pleading the blood of Jesus and claiming His mighty Name until the evil entity left our house. The prayer session in our bedroom seemed to be a turning point.

Ultimately our congregation took steps to remove the unrepentant members from the church. Church attendance, which had been declining, started to increase again.

God delivered us as we learned to fight on our knees! Attacks of the enemy are inevitable in church planting. Be humble, admit when you are wrong, build a solid base of support with your elders, and fight on your knees.

Claim the promise of our great God: He is faithful, and He will establish and guard you against the evil one!

Lord, Please build a hedge of protection around me and my family, and around our church. We trust You and stand on Your promises! Amen.

Jim Carpenter

Guidance

*Saul died because he was unfaithful to the LORD; he did not keep
the word of the LORD and even consulted a medium for guidance, and
did not inquire of the LORD. So the LORD put him to death and turned
the kingdom over to David son of Jesse. ~ I Chronicles 10:13, 14*

READING: I Samuel 23:1-5

One of the ways in which Saul was unfaithful to God was in the way
he asked for guidance. Rather than going directly to God, Saul consulted a
spiritual medium from Endor. Saul lost his leadership and his life as a result of
his unfaithfulness.

In contrast, David was a faithful man…a man after God's own heart. One
of his spiritual disciplines was to inquire directly of God for guidance. We see
this clearly in the story from I Samuel 23. We should always immerse ourselves
in the Word of God as our primary source of guidance.

David experienced success from the Lord because he asked God what to
do and then did it. One of the reasons that God loved David so much was
because David asked him for guidance so often. David was a man after God's
own heart. David expressed that heart for God by going directly to God for
guidance.

I love to take personal prayer retreats three or four times a year to inquire
of God. This has been one of my spiritual disciplines for many years. Most of the
major decisions in my life and ministry have emerged from these prayer retreats.

I encourage you to develop the habit of taking personal prayer retreats on
a regular basis. Prayer retreats help us to refocus on the Lord and to reorient
ourselves to walk in step with His will. They give us marching orders, greatly
enhancing our daily pursuit of his guidance.

Dear Father, Show me what to do and help me to follow where you lead. Amen.

Paul Becker

Transparent Prayer

Father, if you are willing, take this cup from me;
yet not my will, but yours be done. ~ *Luke 22:42*

READING: Luke 22:39-46

Jesus took His disciples to Prayer Mountain and then withdrew from them to pray. Luke says it was a usual act of Jesus, an ideal modeling from the Lord for "a habituated prayer retreating." Jesus taught His disciples to pray in order to escape from falling into temptation. It is not merely *that* we pray but *what* we pray that determines whether or not we fall.

When Jesus prayed about the Cup, He refers here to His role as the bearer of the sins of the world. Though, as God the Son, He knew His cup could not be removed, yet He prayed this transparent prayer because Jesus the man's agony was beyond His bearing. It was not a lip prayer; rather it was from His soul. As He prayed His sweat fell like blood drops, indicating the intensity of His emotions. Indeed, God the Father heard and responded by extending a special divine comfort.

How often have we cried "take this cup" as the result of intensified pressures and challenges in our journey? Our cup is painful but fashioned by the Sovereign Potter for a noble purpose. Church planters are very close to the architect of the Church (Matt. 16:18). So let us follow our Architect by praying a transparent prayer as He prayed.

Retreating helps us to speak to Him transparently. Things that we struggle with, areas where we struggle to please God, petitions that cannot be voiced when we pray with others, even our secret addictions and weaknesses can be spoken to Him as we retreat. How open are we before Him? To that degree we will be ministered to by God the Father.

Lord, Teach me to speak with no hidings with You. Make me a man of transparent prayer like Jesus. Amen.

R. Jayakumar

Obeying God's EXACT Instruction

*Does the LORD delight in burnt offerings and sacrifices as much
as in obeying the voice of the LORD? To obey is better than sacrifice,
and to heed is better than the fat of rams. ~ I Samuel 15:22*

READING: I Samuel 15:10-22

Because we're often trailblazers in uncharted territory, church planters typically are quite passionate about asking God for guidance and strategy. Hopefully, we wouldn't dream of willfully defying God's command the way Saul did, here in this story found in I Samuel 15. But we may inadvertently trip up if we aren't watchful.

It's vitally important, on those wonderful occasions when we hear God clearly, that we immediately and precisely record what we hear. Write it down. Note the pertinent Bible verse or passage.

Here's why.

God's voice, His promptings, His guidance (however we feel most comfortable to phrase it) is the voice of the Creator. And when we hear His voice, all of our own creative energy springs into action in response.

"Oh, I see it all now," we enthuse. "We could do this, and we could also do that, and we could do the other." On and on we go, brainstorming one idea after another. Before long, if we aren't careful, we may drift away from the exact thing we heard.

Beware of implementing your own conclusion, twice removed, instead of obeying God's simple command. Go back and check. What exactly did God communicate to you just now? Verify it all using the reliable standard of Scripture. God's exact word is our only firm ground.

It makes us happy and relieved when the plans and ideas begin to flow. But it delights the heart of God when we obey.

Dear Lord, Please guide me as I seek to plant this church. Help me to hear You clearly and obey You completely. Amen.

Dionne Carpenter

On the Altar

He said, "Take your son, your only son Isaac, whom you love and go
to the land of Moriah, and offer him there as a burnt offering on one
of the mountains of which I shall tell you." ~ Genesis 22:2 (ESV)

READING: Genesis 22

Starting our first church was very much the birth of a long-cherished dream, one I had been praying about for five years. The baby church was like my beloved child. It grew slowly but steadily, and many people became Christians. But when the church was five years old, trouble came. A divisive couple began to undermine my authority in an attempt to force my resignation.

Providentially I was preaching a series about Abraham. When I came to chapter 22, it became painfully alive to me. The Lord asked Abraham to sacrifice the one he had longed for and prayed for and dreamt about. Isaac was the fulfillment of God's promise and Abraham's guarantee of future blessing. To obey God meant the death of his dreams.

As Abraham bound his son and slowly raised the knife, I saw myself, ready to sacrifice the church I loved. God put me in a place where obedience meant helpless dependence upon Him. To face their criticism without guile or retaliation was to lay on the altar my past hopes and my future dreams. Like Abraham, I obeyed.

"...now I know that you fear God, seeing you have not withheld your son, your only son, from me," the Lord said (v. 12) as He provided a ram for the sacrifice.

The Lord saved our church, and me, but it took my laying down my dreams on the altar. I learned the church is never "my" church. It's always His. And He calls us to lay down everything in helpless dependence upon Him.

Father, Today I lay down my dreams and relinquish my hopes. My future is in Your hands, and I trust only in You. Amen.

Jim Carpenter

Interceding for Our People

*So I turned to the Lord God and pleaded with him in prayer
and petition, in fasting, and in sackcloth and ashes. ~ Daniel 9:3*

READING: Daniel 9:1-23

When we receive a calling from God to a particular group of people, God makes us responsible to Him for them. Many times we forget that He has a purpose for them and is looking to us to be their intercessor.

In Daniel 9 we can see that Daniel was concerned for God's people in captivity and sought to know what God would do with them. When he discovered in the Scriptures why his people were in captivity he began to intercede for them, confessing the sins of the nation and agreeing with God regarding them. Then he pleaded with God for mercy and deliverance for them. We can see in Daniel 9:23 and 10:12 that on the very first day Daniel began interceding, God sent a messenger who had been withstood for twenty-one days until there was finally a breakthrough.

God delivered His people in part because Daniel interceded for them. We need to hear from God for our people and intercede for God's will to be done for them. We need to insist in effective, fervent prayer until they have a breakthrough. God's hand is moved, His angels are sent and His provision is granted in response to our prayers.

Do you make time to get away and hear from God for your people and to intercede for them? There is nothing like time alone with God to hear what He wants for His people. Make it a part of your busy schedule to spend quality time away with God.

Heavenly Father, I confess that often I have not spent much quality time interceding for my assigned people. Please help me to pray diligently. I want to know and do your perfect will for them. Amen.

Ron Thiesen

Shepherding on Your Knees

*I do not cease to give thanks for you, remembering
you in my prayers… ~ Ephesians 1:16*

READING: Ephesians 1:14-23

"Pastor, your note arrived at a time when we were really hurting. I miscarried that week – nobody even knew we were pregnant – and it was such a comfort to know that you were praying for us."

That's what a young wife in my church said to me after my week of praying for her family. I had no idea she and her husband were going through a crisis, but God did. And my commitment to pray regularly for the families in my congregation was a source of encouragement and strength when they needed it.

As a church grows, how do you continue to "shepherd" them? You *will* need to share the pastoral care with others – home group leaders, pastoral staff, or elders.

But the senior pastor *can* continue to help shepherd his people – on his knees. I learned this from the Apostle Paul, who loved to pray for the Christians that were part of his church planting network. Often he included a summary of his prayers in the letters he wrote those churches. (See Philippians 1:9 – 11; Colossians 1:9 – 12; II Thessalonians 1:11, 12).

Each week I send personal notes to four church families, letting them know I'll be praying for them in the following week. I invite them to contact me with any requests they might have. My secretary makes sure I pray for all our people twice a year, and adds new families as they become regular attenders.

God has given me the privilege of systematically interceding for the people of my congregation. Knowing that I'm praying is a constant assurance that I love them and that their Heavenly Father loves them even more.

Father, Thank you for blessing me with the precious families in my church. Show me how to pray for them. Amen.

Jim Carpenter

Painting the Dragon Red #1

Be self-controlled and alert. Your enemy the devil prowls around
like a roaring lion looking for someone to devour. ~ *I Peter 5:8*

READING: I Peter 5:5-11

When Pastor Jim and Stephanie Boyd planted their first church in San Marcos, California, they enlisted a prayer team of thirty-one people who each promised to fast and pray for their church, one for each day of the month. So on the 11th of that month, my day, I pulled out their church prayer guide and began to intercede as usual.

Suddenly, God gave me supernatural insight regarding a demonic plot afoot to sneak a deceptive man into their church who, left unchecked, would cause their church great disruption. I asked God if I should call the Boyds immediately to warn them, but was prompted to pray until the burden lifted, which I did.

It appeared to me that Leann Payne's wonderful "Paint the Dragon Red" prayer would fit the purpose of the occasion. I prayed fervently, standing on Scripture as the Lord brought verses to mind, that God would supernaturally expose and thwart this pernicious plot.

Two weeks later, it happened that I went to their church. Stephanie took me aside and asked me to pray for them.

"Dionne, the weirdest thing happened. Recently a nice young man began attending our pre-launch Bible study. He seemed so knowledgeable – ideal leadership material. At our meeting last week he began spouting all kinds of bizarre heresy and gibberish. We were all shocked. Of course he can't be a leader here! In fact, he left in a huff. Please pray."

"Stephanie," I laughed, "I already did. And what you've just described actually means that God has answered our prayers in a big way." We rejoiced together when I told her what had happened, and praised God for protecting their church from harm.

Father, Help us to stay alert in prayer. Amen.

Dionne Carpenter

Painting the Dragon Red #2

And lead us not into temptation, but deliver us from the evil one. ~ Matthew 6:13

READING: I Peter 5:8

In her excellent book, *Listening Prayer*, gifted Christian psychologist Leann Payne tells the story of a time when she and her ministry team faced daunting and wide-spread spiritual attack. She suspected some degree of demonic warfare by the tell-tale confusion, deception and disorientation that rattled and divided her team, just when they needed to be most alert.

She began thinking about lions and other predators. Lions take advantage of their coloration, and sneak up on prey, camouflaged tan-against-tan in the tall grass. But what would happen if someone took a broad brush and painted the lion bright red? They'd stand out like a sore thumb!

She asked God if, in the Spirit, we could pray such a bold prayer – to paint the dragons red that crouch in the camouflage of messy interpersonal relationships. The prayer God helped her to craft has been mightily used by God and has four parts.

"Pray that:
1. The eyes of all who surround these people will be opened to see the situation as it really is;
2. Their associates will be given ways to speak truth and light into the situation (and be protected themselves);
3. Any demonic power within these people or situations manifest itself and that it be clearly discerned and seen by all;
4. What can be salvaged (in this situation and in the lives of your enemies) be saved, humbled and blessed by the Spirit of God."

Leann Payne cautions that if circumstances warrant this warfare prayer, that we pray in deep humility, simultaneously imploring God to "Have mercy on me, a sinner."

This prayer has amazing effect during times of spiritual attack to dispel confusion and give divine clarity to God's people.

Father, Make us bold and reliable intercessors as we stand in the victory of Christ. Amen.

Dionne Carpenter

Wait on the Lord

*But they that wait upon the LORD shall renew their strength;
they shall mount up with wings as eagles; they shall run, and not
be weary; and they shall walk, and not faint. ~ Isaiah 40:31*

READING: Isaiah 40:27-31

Many Old Testament passages tell us to "wait on the Lord." Perhaps the best known is this beautiful verse at the end of Isaiah 40.

Waiting in church planting is hard! We want to make progress rapidly and it usually is not quick enough! We want the people to mature quickly. We want God to move miraculously today. We want the church or ministry to grow remarkably NOW. We want abundant finances NOW! But the Lord wants us to wait on Him.

The Hebrew word translated "wait" (*kaw-vaw*) means "to bind together (perhaps by twisting), look, patiently, tarry, wait" (Strong's Hebrew and Greek Dictionaries). Why does God want us to wait? He desires to "bind" us together with Him and to cause us to "tarry" in fellowship with Him.

Here is a suggested definition: To "wait on the Lord" means to resist the urge to act impetuously and, instead, to clear away distractions and linger in fellowship with God, eagerly trusting Him to give perception, provision, protection, pleasure, perspective, power and perseverance for every life situation.

It would do your soul good to locate and study the passages on waiting on the Lord. You will find all these benefits. Do you want to soar like an eagle? Then spend time each day waiting on the Lord, enjoying His presence, His Word and His companionship.

Heavenly Father, Teach me to wait on you today. Show me how to linger in fellowship with You. Protect me from any action or delay that would depend upon my strength and not Yours. Grant me a clear vision of Your plan and a renewed trust to persevere in following You today. Amen.

Mark Alan Williams

Leaping Joy

*Praise be to the Lord, for he has heard my cry for
mercy. The Lord is my strength and my shield; my heart
trusts in him, and I am helped. My heart leaps for joy and
I will give thanks to him in song. ~ Psalm 28:6, 7*

READING: Psalm 28

David was facing a deadly peril. We are not sure what it was, but his enemies from within or from without were evil and did not have God's best in mind. So David prays for deliverance. In fact, he does not just shoot up a quick prayer. Rather, he pleads with God to hear him and save him.

Before the Lord even answers, David is exuberant with the confidence of just being heard! Read verses 6 and 7 again. The Lord has not yet actually delivered David and his people from the difficulty they face, but David is already leaping for joy because he knows beyond any shadow of doubt that God has heard his request and will intervene on his behalf.

When was the last time your prayer of request included a shout of joy and an exclamation of "Thank you, Lord!?" After you lift a burden to God for His deliverance do you ever jump to your feet and energetically – with lots of body language – give a shout of praise? "Praise God! Thank You for hearing me and acting on behalf of Your Kingdom!"

Lord, You know this concern and the anxiety I bring to You today. I need You to intervene and answer my prayer. My trust is in You! And, Lord, my dancing heart and dancing feet express my deep joy in knowing You have heard me and will only act with my best interest in mind! Hallelujah! Amen!

Ross Chenot

Beholding Your Beauty

One thing have I desired of the Lord, that will
I seek after; that I may dwell in the house of the Lord
all the days of my life, to behold the beauty of the Lord,
and to enquire in His temple. ~ Psalm 27:4 (KJV)

READING: Psalm 27

I caught sight of the bald eagle when she skimmed the surface of the lake and snatched a thrashing trout. In a flurry of strength she regained momentum and returned to her sprawling aerie hidden high in the Douglas fir. I stopped hiking, sat down and watched her for over an hour. My alert, observant focus was an "act of beholding," an unhurried savor of this serendipitous glimpse into her alien world.

I was almost fifty before I learned to behold the Lord. Church planters' prayers can be so need-oriented, so action packed. It's easy to inquire of God. It feels productive to pray through a list, to grapple over some problem and talk, talk, talk in the presence of God.

But we're worshippers first. We've been invited to tiptoe past that ancient veil into the Holy of Holies and simply behold our God. To *behold* is to fix our gaze upon Him in much the same way I watched that eagle, without agenda or ulterior motive. Beholding *in silence* creates a holy space for God to reveal whatever He wishes to disclose to our appreciative hearts.

I find it easiest to behold God by asking Him to give me a name to ponder. He has never failed to bring a name to mind. Then I silently focus on two things: (1) that God is here, as He promised, and (2) that He is that name. Sometimes He reveals treasures of insight or shares a delight. But often He restores my soul simply by letting me look at Him.

Dear Father, Give me stillness and grace to behold Your beauty. Amen.

Dionne Carpenter

MARCH

The Nehemiah Principle

*God's vision must lead to prayerful planning,
the result of which should be a comprehensive
TaskList set out upon a TimeLine.*

World of Numbers

*Some boast in chariots and some in horses, but we will
boast in the name of the LORD, our God. ~ Psalm 20:7*

READING: Psalm 20

How can we live *in* a world of numbers but not be *of* it, especially in the world of church planting? The measuring of things that are supposed to be growing seems unavoidable. When my baby was born I wanted to know her weight and length because I deeply cared about the health and vitality of my newborn. I did not know a better, clearer way to be reassured that she was doing okay.

Categories like attendance, offering intake, and number of conversions are real and often telling and therefore easy to trust and take comfort in. It's also easy to use these numbers to be critical or to boast.

The critical issue is not *whether* we take measurements but *why*. Human nature being what it is we tend to trust less in God and more in the human appearance of things. Numbers alone cannot be trusted. We can exceed benchmarks without making lasting kingdom impact. Activity is not the same as bearing fruit. Many leaders are busy, but really, there is only one thing that is truly important, and sometimes we have to choose. The Bible is filled with numbers but these numbers always tell the story of the glory of God.

On the great Last Day we will stand not before men but God alone. He is our judge, and we his servants. By his judgments alone we will stand or fall. And stand we will because he is able to make his servants to stand (Rom. 14:4).

Assess your church but assess also your heart for God does not see as man sees.

God, I want to do well in your eyes and in the eyes of man. Help me to stand. Help me to be in the world but not of it. Amen.

Peter Sung

Impossible Does Not Mean Unsolvable

*Here is a boy with five small barley loaves and two small
fish, but how far will they go among so many? ~ John 6:9*

READING: John 6:1-15

Insufficiency is not an uncommon word as we strive to plant churches around the globe. There are various kinds of insufficiency: insufficiency of funds, manpower, talents, skills, abilities, and physical strength, to name a few. How shall we handle insufficiencies and keep moving forward in our journey?

It was a challenging day for the twelve disciples, surrounded by five thousand men with unnumbered women and children, armed only with one little boy's lunch. By any human arithmetic calculation, it was a time of "insufficiency." They took the matter to the Lord. Praise God! Jesus was able to solve that math problem.

Jesus emphasized the challenge by asking them to seat the crowd in an order. He blessed the "insignificant and insufficient" lunch that was brought before Him. Then He instructed them to serve. By the end of the day they had a "surplus." Surplus is much more than sufficiency.

Insufficiency always ignites frustration. The alarm of "impossible" can echo louder till it panics us. Jesus demonstrated a beautiful lesson to the disciples on "insufficiency" that entirely changes our calculation.

Insufficiency is perhaps a threatening factor in your journey. Do what Jesus taught the disciples. Take stock of what you need. Conscious awareness of needs will make you more confident in God. Invest all that you have available, no matter how insignificant your resources may appear. Then seek for God's touch on it and obey His instructions with confidence.

GOD'S SUPERNATURAL MATH EQUATION: Conscious awareness of needs + My best investment + Seeking God's touch + Obedient action of faith = Meeting impossible needs + Surplus.

Lord, Help me to understand the supernatural equation you taught the disciples and apply it by faith whenever I face times of insufficiency. Amen.

R. Jayakumar

The Testimony of Planning #1

*Suppose one of you wants to build a tower. Will he not
first sit down and estimate the cost to see if he has enough money
to complete it? For if he lays the foundation and is not able to finish
it, everyone who sees it will ridicule him, saying, "This fellow
began to build and was not able to finish." ~ Luke 14:28*

READING: Luke 14:25-35

I was heartsick to learn about an enthusiastic would-be church planter who impulsively leased a store front to start public services right away. It sounded perfect to him – the previous tenant (also a church plant) had already built out the space to conduct services.

Our visionary (but unassessed) young man had no core group, no converts, no track record and no financial backing. He was too excited to heed the mentor his denomination tried to connect him with, who would have asked an obvious question: "If that property is all that perfect, then why exactly is it vacant?" Hint: The previous church didn't outgrow it.

There are wiser ways to plant a church.

But, admit it. It's dull and boring to fill out time lines, or think through the task list that DCPI recommends and methodically whittle through "To Do" lists. Like one humble brick on another, there's nothing flashy about demographic research, building core groups, gathering resources and filling out municipal paperwork. It just takes time to find receptive people in our community and discover, for instance, whether they'd prefer meeting in someone's home or in a ramshackle store front.

Those behind-the-scene tasks are the stuff of solid craftsmanship. Do them well. Do them to God's glory – because, eventually, poor planning and wise planning both tend to become obvious, even to the most casual observer.

Dear Lord, Give me wisdom to lay a solid foundation and holy craftsmanship to finish well. Amen.

Dionne Carpenter

The Testimony of Planning #2

I planted the seed, Apollos watered it, but God made it grow. ~ I Corinthians 3:6

READING: I Corinthians 1:18-31

OK, now let's look at this young man's story from a different point of view. While it appears obvious that he's making plenty of rookie mistakes, and while it would do him good to listen to wiser veterans, the exasperating fact of the matter is that all of us can probably think of at least one such improbable start that launched a fine, solid church.

The blessing of God is unpredictable. Our Lord enjoys showing mercy to the most unlikely folks and lavishes His favor in inscrutable acts of "random" kindness.

That young man's church plant may take off like a rocket for any number of intangible reasons. Maybe the previous church that met in that store front wasn't a good fit for its community and our young man is a perfect match who quickly leads multitudes to Christ. Maybe his funding will come from entirely unexpected sources. Maybe God will provide a core group, including an engineer-type guy who puts the DCPI task list on his laptop, effortlessly completes most of the tasks himself, and gives our visionary a weekly little memo of the few simple administrative items that require his involvement.

Maybe the very wackiness of the start shakes our church planter's former church out of their stuffy inertia and mobilizes enthusiasm and practical aid – in the same way that everyone rallies around to help a hapless woman who goes into labor in the backseat of a taxi cab miles away from the midwife.

There are wise ways and foolish ways to plant a church, but even an unorthodox birth may be dear to God's heart. Come to think of it, the baby born in that manger probably looked unplanned.

Lord, Help me to be wise myself but open-hearted when others do things differently. Amen.

Dionne Carpenter

Defeat Turned into Victory

Where, O death, is your victory? Where,
O death, is your sting? ~ I Corinthians 15:55

READING: I Corinthians 15:12-19

At the Battle of Waterloo, on June 18, 1815, the French army under Napoleon's command fought the allied forces of the British, Dutch and Germans under the command of Wellington. The English people in Great Britain depended on a system of signals to find out how the battle was going. One of these signals was on the tower of Winchester Cathedral.

Late in the day it flashed the words: "WELLINGTON DEFEATED." Just then a fog cloud rolled in, obscuring the tower. News of defeat quickly spread throughout the city. The whole countryside was sad and gloomy when they heard the news that their country had lost the war. Suddenly, the fog lifted from the tower revealing the rest of the message. The message had four words, not two: "WELLINGTON DEFEATED THE ENEMY!" It took only a few minutes for the good news to spread. Sorrow was turned into joy; defeat was turned into victory!

When Jesus was laid in the tomb, hope died in the hearts of Jesus' most loyal friends. After the frightful crucifixion, the fog of disappointment and misunderstanding had crept over the friends of Jesus. They had read only part of the message. "Christ defeated" was all they knew. But on the third day, the fog of disappointment and misunderstanding lifted, and the world received the complete message: "Christ defeated death!" Defeat was turned into victory; death was turned into life! This is the power of the gospel and the resurrection life.

Father, We thank you that the message we have to proclaim is that defeat has been turned into victory and death has been swallowed up by resurrection power. I ask that today and into the future more and more of your power will be made manifest in our ministry. Amen.

John Bond

Are You Ready to Plant This Church?

*For want of a skillful strategy an army is lost; victory
is the fruit of long planning. ~ Proverbs 11:14 (NEB)*

READING: Luke 14:27-33

It was quite an adventure to plant a church as a newlywed student. Far from my home in Brazil, I was going to Bible College in North Carolina at the time. Many of the fine local churches were reaching specific language groups such as the Spanish, Chinese and Vietnamese-speaking. But there weren't any local churches for Portuguese-speaking people, so I decided to plant a one.

My first strategy was to hold a service in Portuguese to attract the Brazilian community. I was impressed with the number of people that showed up at what we called "Christmas Celebration." We had another meeting at Easter. I was under the mistaken impression that being able to organize a special celebration for a few dozen people meant I was ready to plant a church.

As time passed, these people demanded more attention than I was able to give them. The new converts needed discipleship and I wasn't available for that. Some families requested pastoral care when I was either taking classes or working at my secular job. I thought everyone would be satisfied just to listen to a sermon in their mother language on Sunday. I would have been happy to delegate these vital tasks of discipleship, visiting and teaching if only I'd had a team to share the load.

Some lasting good came of my efforts and my heart was in the right place. But, in hindsight, I see that I planted that church prematurely. Perhaps this church would still be alive today had I waited for proper training and preparation before launching such a big project.

Father, I am sorry for taking more responsibility in ministry at times than I can handle. Show me how to honor you by doing everything with excellence. Amen.

David Godoy

The Stuff of Hope

*But by the grace of God I am what I am, and His grace
toward me did not prove vain; but I labored even more than all of them,
yet not I, but the grace of God with me. ~ I Corinthians 15:10*

READING: I Corinthians 15:1-11

Biblical hope is not wishful thinking but certainty of good and salvific things to come. We hope *after* we have done all that we can humanly do, not *instead of*. Hope is the farmer who looks forward to the coming harvest after he has worked hard from dawn to dusk. Hope is the preacher praying for his congregation after a full week of counseling, study and sermon preparation. Hope is the faith of the one whose works speak for themselves.

There is often a false dichotomy between planning and Spirit. "Spiritual" leaders often say something to the effect of: *Don't plan too much. Leave room for the Spirit to move.* In reality, the key to spontaneity is over-preparation, which allows me to go to the left or the right because I have been well-trained in both directions. Planning well, preparing diligently, and making every effort are the means through which God's grace is conveyed.

Professional athletes are most relaxed during critical moments of play. It is the amateur who grips the bat too tightly or misses game-changing free throws. The Spirit moves through those who are made ready through hard work.

So work hard. Plan well. Practice always. Do all of life diligently and wisely. And there you will find hope and Spirit. Work out your fears and conquer laziness. Fear and laziness are close friends and enemies of faith, hope, and love.

Jesus, I confess that I have been lazy and have often used my faith as an excuse to work less. I put my hands to the plow because I want to believe and experience your grace. Amen.

Peter Sung

What Makes a Nehemiah? #1
Compassion for Broken People

And they said to me, "The remnant there in the province who had survived the exile is in great trouble and shame. The wall of Jerusalem is broken down, and its gates are destroyed by fire." As soon as I heard these words I sat down and wept and mourned for days, and I continued fasting and praying before the God of heaven. ~ Nehemiah 1:3, 4 (ESV)

READING: Nehemiah 1:1-4

Nehemiah was one of the most remarkable leaders in Biblical history. God's judgment upon Israel sent His people into captivity in Babylon for seventy years. When the Babylonian Empire fell to Persia, the Jews were allowed to return to their homeland. Three different expeditions went back. Though the Temple was rebuilt, the city was still in disrepair and vulnerable to attack.

Nehemiah is the man whom God raised up to rebuild the city walls. His story is not unlike the story of church planters who are called to bring rescue to desperate people whose lives are broken and vulnerable to the enemy's attacks.

So what makes a Nehemiah?

Preeminently, he was a man of *compassion*. Though he had a comfortable job in the Persian palace, he cared about the people back in his homeland. Upon hearing that they were still "in great trouble and shame," his heart was broken. He wept and mourned for days.

A church planting vision is birthed in compassion for broken people who are on their way to hell apart from Christ. Our visions may include great plans for buildings, programs and influence. But more than anything, church planting starts with a heart of compassion for lost people.

Lord, Grant me a heart of compassion for people who so desperately need You. Remind me of Your grace in saving me. Amen.

Jim Carpenter

What Makes a Nehemiah? #2
A Man of Prayer

And I said, "O Lord God of heaven, the great and awesome
God who keeps covenant and steadfast love with those who love him
and keep his commandments, let your ear be attentive and your eyes open,
to hear the prayer of your servant that I now pray before you day and
night for the people of Israel your servants, confessing the sins of the
people of Israel, which we have sinned against you. Even I and
my father's house have sinned." ~ Nehemiah 1:5, 6 (ESV)

READING: Nehemiah 1:5-11

God used Nehemiah to rebuild the broken walls of Jerusalem. The Lord wants to use us to rebuild the broken lives of lost people through our new church.

So what does it take to be a Nehemiah?

Nehemiah was *a man of prayer*. At first we don't know much about his leadership ability, but we immediately know he was a prayer warrior. When he heard the news about Jerusalem's disrepair, he spent days in mourning, fasting, and prayer (v. 4). Then he lifted the Lord up in praise (v. 5); he confessed sin (vv. 6, 7); and he claimed God's promise (vv. 8 – 10). Finally, Nehemiah prayed for success in a very specific course of action – to speak to the king and to be granted permission to go to Jerusalem (v. 11).

Nehemiah's story is about leadership, mobilizing people, casting vision and accomplishing great things for God. But more than anything it is a story about the power of prayer.

May God grant you visionary leadership, great recruiting and equipping skills and effective soul-winning experience. These will help you succeed as a church planter. But more than anything, may you be preeminently a man of prayer.

Make me a prayer warrior, O Lord. Teach me how to fight on my knees. And give me a constant hunger to be in Your presence. Amen.

Jim Carpenter

What Makes a Nehemiah? #3
Patience

*The words of Nehemiah the son of Hacaliah. Now it happened in the
month of Chislev, in the twentieth year, as I was in Susa the capital... In the month
of Nisan, in the twentieth year of King Artaxerxes, when wine was before him, I
took up the wine and gave it to the king... ~ Nehemiah 1:1; 2:1 (ESV)*

READING: Nehemiah 2:1-5

We church planters are an impatient lot. In my third church plant I was
determined to begin public services for the new church in March, about a month
before Easter.

But my steering committee strongly advised me to wait till the fall. They
pointed out that I really didn't have enough leaders trained to start in March. So
I waited. But it was hard! Our launch date was moved forward to September.
God blessed the delay. We had a larger core group, more leaders, and afterwards,
I was glad for the lesson on patience.

At the end of chapter 1, Nehemiah is expecting to move forward quickly
to begin the rebuilding project. He prayed "give success to your servant *today*"
(1:11). Notice he asked this in the month Chislev, November/December in our
calendars.

But chapter 2 begins with the month Nisan. That's *April* – four or five
months later! Like many of us church planters, his attitude was, "Let's get going
– NOW!"

But God's timing is not our timing.

It's important for church planters to learn patience. Why? Because God
knows better than we do, and He is the Lord of church planting. Patience is
another name for *waiting*. And waiting upon God with an attitude of humility
is one of the prerequisites for church planting leadership.

---

*Father, I submit to Your plans and Your timing. May I move at the speed You choose,
to Your honor and glory. Amen.*

Jim Carpenter

What Makes a Nehemiah? #4
Planning

*And I said to the king, "If it pleases the king, and if your servant has
found favor in your sight, that you send me to Judah, to the city of my fathers'
graves, that I may rebuild it." And the king said to me… "How long will
you be gone, and when will you return?" So it pleased the king to send
me when I had given him a time. ~ Nehemiah 2:5, 6 (ESV)*

READING: Nehemiah 2:4-8

Some people seem to think planning is unspiritual. We church planters often have a tendency to move ahead without having a good plan. We can learn a lot from Nehemiah. Nehemiah had to wait for months before approaching the king about taking a "leave of absence" to travel to Jerusalem for the rebuilding project.

When he finally had the opportunity to speak to the king, the king asked him, "How long will you be gone, and when will you return?"

Some church planters might want to answer, "As long as it takes!" Or, "Until the Lord brings me back." But Nehemiah had a plan. He gave him a specific time, and this pleased the king and opened his heart to Nehemiah's proposal. Nehemiah revealed a comprehensive plan:

- He summarized the purpose and scope of the project (v. 5),
- The timetable (v. 6),
- Transportation challenges and solutions (v. 7),
- Necessary building materials (v. 8a),
- And what he would require for his own personal living accommodations (v. 8b).

One of the essential skills of church planting leadership is not only casting a vision but planning the steps necessary to reach that vision.

Father, Show me how to plan my work and work my plan and please raise up gifted administrators to help me. Amen.

Jim Carpenter

What Makes a Nehemiah? #5
Working Your Plan And Facing Opposition

Then I came to the governors of the province beyond the river and gave them the king's letters. Now the king had sent with me officers of the army and horsemen. But when Sanballat the Horonite and Tobiah, the Ammonite servant, heard this, it displeased them greatly that someone had come to seek the welfare of the people of Israel. ~ Nehemiah 2:9, 10 (ESV)

READING: Nehemiah 2:9, 10

Nehemiah wasn't a church planter, but he might as well have been. We can learn a lot from him about working to bring the transforming grace of God into a community rife with brokenness.

Nehemiah began with a compassionate vision. He prayed, and he put together a good plan. The steps he took next are instructive for any church planter entering a new community with a dream in his heart. Imagine if Nehemiah could give us advice.

First he might say, *work your plan.* As Nehemiah made his way from Persia to Palestine, he faced plenty of challenges. But he had done a thorough job of preparing ahead of time. His king had given him letters to permit travel and to requisition supplies.

Someone has said, "Plan your work, and work your plan." That's what Nehemiah did and that's what we must do, too.

Nehemiah might also say, *Expect opposition, but don't let it distract you.* Nehemiah had enemies from the day he arrived in Jerusalem. They were a thorn in his side throughout the project. But he didn't panic, and he didn't get diverted.

Church planting brings opposition. Don't be surprised, and don't be deterred. Keep praying, step out in faith, and trust the One who called you.

Lord, Please grant me holy perseverance to stay true to the plan You gave me. And deliver me from the evil one, to Your honor and glory. Amen.

Jim Carpenter

What Makes a Nehemiah? #6
Community Assessment

*So I went to Jerusalem and was there three days. Then I arose in the
night, I and a few men with me. And I told no one what my God had put
into my heart to do for Jerusalem. There was no animal with me but the one on
which I rode. I went out by night by the Valley Gate to the Dragon Spring and to
the Dung Gate, and I inspected the walls of Jerusalem that were broken down
and its gates that had been destroyed by fire. ~ Nehemiah 2:11-13 (ESV)*

READING: Nehemiah 2:11-16

"Every church planter needs a mentor. A mentor is someone who has been
where you want to go and is willing to help you get there." (From DCPI's *Twelve
Principles of Dynamic Church Planting*.) We all need mentors, but sometimes our
mentors come from the pages of Scripture. Nehemiah approached the task of
rebuilding Jerusalem's walls like a wise church planter plants a church. If he gave
us counsel, it would include: *Honestly assess the community.*

Some leaders might have roared into Jerusalem, shouting orders. Not
Nehemiah. He was there three days, and then he did a midnight tour of the
city. He wanted to make sure he knew for himself the exact condition of the city
walls and gates. He faced the challenges ahead with unflinching resolve. In v. 13,
the word "inspected" in Hebrew is a medical term for probing a wound to see
the extent of an injury.

Church planters need to assess their communities. What are the prevailing
sins, the biggest hurts and the greatest needs? Where does He want us to begin
rebuilding?

---

*Father, Grant me wisdom to assess the needs of this community, so my church may
rebuild the lives of broken people. Amen.*

Jim Carpenter

What Makes a Nehemiah? #7
Vision Casting & Teambuilding

*Then I said to them, "You see the trouble we are in, how Jerusalem
lies in ruins with its gates burned. Come, let us build the wall of Jerusalem,
that we may no longer suffer derision." And I told them of the hand of my God
that had been upon me for good, and also of the words that the king had spoken
to me. And they said, "Let us rise up and build." So they strengthened
their hands for the good work. ~ Nehemiah 2:17, 18 (ESV)*

READING: Nehemiah 2:17, 18

Nehemiah exemplified two of DCPI's *Twelve Principles of Dynamic Church Planting:*

1. THE BOSS PRINCIPLE – Christ is Lord of church planting, and He has a vision for your new church.

5. THE TEAM LEADER PRINCIPLE – The church planting pastor is most effective as part of a team on which he serves as the visionary leader.

Having assessed the community, Nehemiah cast the vision God had given to him back in Persia. He spoke of the great need ("Jerusalem lies in ruins") and painted a picture of a godly and glorious future ("that we may no longer suffer derision").

He spoke of how God had already guided him and blessed him: "I told them of the hand of my God that had been upon me for good."

God used Nehemiah to build a team of people ready to serve and sacrifice alongside him: "Let us rise up and build."

Nehemiah's task was different than ours, but his God is the same! We can trust Him to empower the vision He has given, and to raise up the teammates to fulfill it.

Lord, May Your vision so fill my life that it captures the hearts of those You bring into my life to help fulfill it. Amen.

Jim Carpenter

We've Never Done It That Way Before

*Neither do men pour new wine into old wineskins.
If they do, the skins will burst, the wine will run out and
the wineskins will be ruined. No, they pour new wine into
new wineskins, and both are preserved.* ~ *Matthew 9:17*

READING: Matthew 9:9-17

One of the major frustrations for many godly pastors serving in established churches comes when they suggest a promising new ministry strategy or urge a necessary course correction back to our prime directive. They run into the fierce resistance that somebody has dubbed "the seven last words of the church," namely: *"We've never done it that way before."* Many new churches have been planted simply because, as we say, it's easier to have babies than to raise the dead!

But every church, even our new church plant, has a relatively short "wet cement" stage when we can most easily shape the goals, the vision, the administrative mindset and our corporate identity. It's primarily during these pre-launch days of vision-casting and the early formative days after the launch when this vital work gets done. All too quickly we too may grow large enough to get sidetracked into meaningless committee meetings and flower arranging.

We must guard against any temptation to chase after the *avant garde* merely to "tickle men's ears" (II Tim. 4:3). Fortunately, many new churches represent courageous and holy experiments that attempt to bridge the shifting gap between God's changeless truths and the ever-changing culture around us. Many church plants bring a much needed refocus back to our core mission to fulfill the Great Commission.

So take heart! Jesus still reigns as head of the church. He is the stability beneath its ancient edifices and traditions, and the vitality within the new wine that renews the church in each new generation.

Dear Lord, Thank You for letting us enjoy "new wine" and help us fulfill our mission with joy. Amen.

Dionne Carpenter

The Pleasure of Planning

We should make plans . . . counting on
God to direct us. ~ Proverbs 16:9 (TLB)

READING: Exodus 25

We have a God who plans: He had a detailed plan for the Tabernacle (Exodus 25), He has a plan of salvation, a plan for eternity and a plan for your life. Clearly God enjoys planning and likes to see His plans come to fruition. He intends for us to have the same joy: the pleasure of planning. Yet sometimes we make planning more difficult than it has to be.

Here is a simple planning process to reach your goals:

1. Write down your goal;
2. Set a deadline for achievement;
3. List the obstacles you will need to overcome;
4. Identify groups and people you need to work with to achieve your goal;
5. List the necessary skills and knowledge you will need;
6. Develop strategies and list the tasks necessary to reach the goal;
7. List the benefits you will receive.

Doing a simple plan, based on these seven steps, can catapult you to achieving your dreams. It would not take long to sit down and complete these seven items as you consider one of your strategic goals. You could probably sketch out what you'd need for each of these steps within a half hour or so. You will likely refine the plan later, but that half hour will launch the process that could take you places you have only dreamed about before.

Do you have a plan to accomplish the vision God has for you? If not, have some fun planning today.

Lord, Thank you for the intelligence You have given me – the ability to make plans and then see them accomplished. Help me to be a planner like You are. Amen.

Mark Alan Williams

Why Do We Go
Through Storms in Life? #1

But he was in the stern, asleep on the cushion.
And they woke him and said to him, "Teacher, do you not
care that we are perishing?" ~ Mark 4:38 (ESV)

READING: Mark 4:35-41

It amazes me that the disciples went through a storm while Jesus was on the boat and while they obeyed a direct order from Jesus to go from point A to point B. When the Lord speaks, he commands; it's not an opinion or a suggestion.

Pastors, missionaries and church planters also go through storms occasionally. A "storm" might be a problem in the family, health, finances, church or your marriage. They can last a short or a long time. Whether you are in the church planting ministry or not, chances are you have already experienced one or will soon experience one.

But why does God allow his children to go through storms? Why do pastors have marital problems? Why do church planters' kids get addicted to drugs? Why are finances not enough? I believe the Lord allows us to go through storms for at least two reasons.

First, He wants us to go to Christ to ask for help (Mark 4:38). The disciples remembered Jesus was on the boat when things started to get rough. If you are going through a storm in your life right now, please remember that the boat where Jesus abides will not sink if we ask him for help.

Matthew 7:7, 8 reminds us: "Ask, and it will be given to you; seek, and you will find; knock, and it will be opened to you. For everyone who asks receives, and the one who seeks finds, and to the one who knocks it will be opened."

Heavenly Father, I know that nothing is impossible for you. You are the Captain of my life's boat and you'll never leave or forsake me. Amen.

David Godoy

Why Do We Go Through Storms in Life? #2

And he awoke and rebuked the wind and said
to the sea, "Peace! Be still!" And the wind ceased, and
there was a great calm. ~ Mark 4:39 (ESV)

READING: Daniel 3:17, 18

I believe the second reason why the Lord allows his children to go through storms is for us to see God manifest his power (Mark 4:39). God may choose to do a miracle through our circumstance to glorify his name. God turned water into wine, opened the Red Sea, raised people from the dead and multiplied bread and fish to feed multitudes. He can also help us solve our problem. Even if God chooses NOT to answer our prayers, HE IS STILL GOD.

I experienced extremes of joy and sorrow when my son Davi was born during a time I felt closest to the Lord. I was present in the surgery room when my wife Rebecca gave birth. I sang praise songs while my first child was born. Seeing his little face when he came out of his mother was one of the greatest joys I've ever known.

Immediately, however, the obstetrician handed him to the pediatrician in the room. I thought that was the normal procedure and continued praising the Lord! I didn't know that Davi had inhaled amniotic fluid during labor. He went straight to the Prenatal Intensive Care Unit. The doctor told my wife and me that as a result of this unexpected event Davi may have lacked oxygen in his brain. That meant he could have severe physical and cognitive impairments if he survived.

Our family, friends and church family mobilized to pray for Davi. Long story short, our son is perfectly healthy today. The Lord allowed us to go through this storm so we could watch Him manifest His power. What a miracle!

Lord, Manifest your power and glorify your name through whatever problem I face today. Amen.

David Godoy

What is Faith?

Blessed is she who has believed that what the Lord
has said to her will be accomplished! ~ Luke 1:45

READING: Genesis 15:1-6

Volumes have been written to parse the meaning of the word "faith." Here, let's look at one small aspect that particularly applies to us as church planters. Although divided by centuries, Abraham the Patriarch and Mary, the mother of Jesus, graphically illustrate the essence of faith, as understood by the Hebrew mind.

Webster's dictionary defines faith as "a confident belief in the truth or trustworthiness of a person, idea or thing." The Hebrew word for faith is *aman*, which means "to regard as true, to realize, to believe." Notice that both definitions talk about truth and belief.

The Hebrew word *aman* implies the idea of receiving a message from someone – a statement, a warning, a promise or a command. We "*aman*" by believing the message to be true. Abraham believed God's promise to give him a son. Mary believed the angel's message that she would conceive a child by the Holy Ghost.

Abraham and Mary each stood in that moment holding nothing but the message. Both of them could readily think of many logical and valid reasons to reject the truth of it out of hand. But in that fateful moment, they chose to believe, they chose faith.

If you are a church planter reading this book, you once stood in a similar place when the Holy Spirit spoke to your heart and called you to serve Him. In your mind's eye, you envisioned a new church where there was no church. You exercised faith. "Now faith is being sure of what we hope for and certain of what we do not see" (Heb. 11:1).

What you did, when you chose to believe, was a holy thing.

Father, Bless me abundantly because I choose to believe Your promise. Amen.

Dionne Carpenter
Adapted from *Trust Training* © 2008

The Act of Faith

*...faith, by itself, if it is not accompanied
by action, is dead. ~ James 2:17b*

READING: Genesis 6:9-22

The Hebrew concept of faith makes the practical assumption that if people truly believe a message (*aman*) they will act on it in some way. For instance, if I heard a news flash warning that a hurricane was headed my way, I would demonstrate that I believed the message by boarding up my windows and heading for higher ground.

In the Hebrew parlance, whatever people do simply because they believe the message becomes an *amunah* – an act of faith. When the Apostle James said that faith without works is dead, he was speaking from this thoroughly Hebrew mindset.

Noah's story illustrates this relationship between *aman* and *amunah*. Hebrews 11:7 states that, "By faith Noah, when warned about things not yet seen [that's *aman*], in holy fear built an ark to save his family [that's *amunah*]." Noah's "*amunahs*" included all the items on his "To Do" list: the carpentry tasks, work schedules, planning and design meetings, the collection of animals and food stuffs, as well as the sermons he preached to warn those who came to gawk.

Take heart, as you look at that long list of items on your "To Do" list, the TimeLine and TaskList as applicable to planting a church in your corner of the Lord's vineyard. Each one is a potential expression of faith. Each one has been infused with a deeper significance because it helps to bring your church planter's faith to life. Each seemingly trivial detail, when done in humble dependence on God, is counted by heaven's reckoning as an act of faith.

Father, Help me to do gladly, as an act of faith, all the little tasks necessary to turn the vision of this church plant into a reality. Amen.

Dionne Carpenter
Adapted from *Trust Training* ©2008

Quality vs. Quantity

For we must all appear before the judgment seat of Christ,
that each one may receive what is due him for the things done while
in the body, whether good or bad. ~ II Corinthians 5:10

READING: II Corinthians 5

Paul was an active itinerant who travelled throughout his life and accomplished things beyond any numbers. However, he did not boast about his quantity of work accomplished. He often talked about the quality of his accomplishments (I Thess. 1:2-10, Eph. 1:15-21, Phil. 1:9-11).

In like manner, he insists other servants of God be mindful of *what* they do rather than *how much* they have accomplished. Some of his illustrative exhortations in his last epistle reveal his emphasis on quality over quantity. He uses analogies like workmen approved by God, qualified reliable men, a soldier fighting the good fight, an athlete running according to the rules and a farmer of best harvest.

Every work we accomplish will be judged by Christ. If you are a visionary of church planting mission, you must have number targets. Make your number results to pass through a quality-indicating apparatus. Numbers can easily be attained without apparatus. Anyone can claim that "I had planted five churches" – but God must say the "Amen." People reasonably expect to see our quantity. However, God is concerned about quality. Quantity might make supporters give more; quality makes God give us Crowns. Quantity and quality are both important. Any quantity with no quality disappoints God.

Have you a strong and consistent commitment to planting healthy and reproductive churches? Are you investing your time in raising people in your church plant as Paul raised people in Thessalonica? How many Timothys have you fashioned? Are you an active God pleaser or a pleaser of supporters and onlookers? Would God accept your ministry reports?

Lord, May your Spirit drive me, not my numbers and timeline, though they are essential for my discipline. Amen.

R. Jayakumar

Dependence

*Elisha replied to her, "How can I help you? Tell me,
what do you have in your house?" "Your servant has nothing
there at all," she said, "except a little oil."* ~ II Kings 4:2

READING: II Kings 4:1-7

I love the comment in the Maxwell Study Bible regarding the story of this poor widow who came to Elisha for help: "There is something about 'nothing' that moves God's hand. He loves leading us to empty places where we can lean only upon His provision."

Typically, a new church begins with nothing but a God-given vision. There are no people. There is no money. There is no building. There is just the leader and the vision. The lack of resources forces the leader to become completely dependent upon God for everything. As a result, the miracles begin. The people are gathered. The money comes. The facility is provided. The church is born and grows.

Then, too often, like the widow who filled all her jars, the leader looks around and sees the resources and becomes dependent upon them. The miracles stop. The "dunamis," the dynamic power of God, is quenched.

God loves it when we are completely dependent upon Him for everything. Adopting this attitude prepares the way for miracles. Countless times, because of this dependence …this faith…this trust in God, I have seen Him perform miracles in my own life and the lives of many other leaders. No matter how many resources we have, we must be completely dependent upon GOD to provide.

What do you need? Are you completely dependent upon God to provide it? Have you told him in prayer? Are you continuing to pray in faith that He will provide it?

If you are…watch out…miracles are soon to follow!

Father, Help me to remember how miraculously You provide whenever I am totally dependent on You, and help me continually to rely on You alone. Amen.

Paul Becker

Dealing with Criticisms

*Moses listened to his father-in-law and
did everything he said.* ~ Exodus 18:24

READING: Exodus 18; Nehemiah 6:5-9

Critiques – do we like them? Of course, not many of us welcome criticism. But, in fact, critiquing is good for a servant of God. Both constructive and destructive critiques are to be treated as instrumental for our spiritual maturity. Most of us respond with resentment to criticisms. Perhaps, you are of this kind. If so, consider to follow the models of response by Moses, Nehemiah, Jesus and Paul when they were criticized.

Moses was more educated than Jethro, yet he listened to his critique and implemented his suggestions. When envious enemies, Sanballat and Tobiah, made destructive criticisms, Nehemiah did not become distracted by their provocations; instead, he made his petition to God. The criticisms of Pharisees, Sadducees, and the teachers of the law did not lead Jesus to resentment. When the apostolic authority of Paul was criticized by some of the Corinthian believers, he responded politely in his second epistle to them.

Moses' willingness to learn from inferior people, Nehemiah's godly response, Jesus' magnanimity, and Paul's politeness are ideal models for us when we are criticized.

We seldom want to listen to criticism made by critics we consider inferior to us. Since critical words hurt us deeply we may release our resentment either directly or indirectly, perhaps by ignoring or avoiding them. Any such reaction is an indicator of pride. Unwillingness to learn from criticism is a sign that arrogance resides within us. Treating critics as enemies signals the absence of Christ-likeness.

The humility of Moses, patience of Nehemiah, determination of Jesus and politeness of Paul should mark our response to the critics we encounter on our church planting journey.

Lord, Bring constructive critics into my life that I may hear them for corrections. Help me to respond appropriately to all my critics. Amen.

R. Jayakumar

In the Meantime #1

I am God Almighty; walk before Me and be blameless.
I will confirm My covenant between Me and you and will
greatly increase your numbers. ~ Genesis 17:1, 2

READING: Genesis 17:1-22

Abraham knew what it felt like to wait. He had been waiting for twenty-four years by the time God renewed His promises to him here in Genesis 17. "I will give you this land. Your descendants will outnumber the stars. Oh, and I'll give you a son by Sarah, your post-menopausal wife" [My paraphrase].

In the meantime, Abraham wandered around Canaan, tending his herds and expanding his entourage. We all live most of our Christian lives "in the meantime," in that limbo between hearing God's promises and seeing them come true. Many of us who labor for Christ by planting churches carry a godly but unfulfilled vision to see one church or ten or a hundred established and thriving.

What should we do while we wait?

Abraham never saw the complete fulfillment of God's promises. He lived to see only three descendants through Sarah, not a starry host. Isaac's twin sons were still teenagers by the time Abraham died seventy-five years later. When he died, the only bit of the Promised Land he owned was the cave near Hebron where he buried Sarah.

Yet Abraham shows what to do in the meantime. *He believed God for the long haul.* He believed God in spite of all the evidence to the contrary. He passed the promise on as a legacy to his son and his grandsons.

His descendants eventually conquered the Promised Land. And both spiritual and physical descendants are added in every generation – all because God always keeps His promise.

So, take heart, and, like Abraham, let us press on to believe God in the meantime.

Dear Lord, Give me Abraham's faith to believe You for my "child of promise." Amen.

Dionne Carpenter

In the Meantime #2

On that very day Abraham took…every male in his household,
and circumcised them, as God told him. ~ *Genesis 17:23*

READING: Genesis 17:23-27

Hip deep in the middle of planting a church it can feel as if God's promises will never come true. They may shimmer out there at the edge of our peripheral vision. And if we aren't careful, we may make the mistake of thinking all God's words to us are meant for some vague tomorrow.

I felt dejected the day I ran across Genesis 17 in morning devotions. In spirit I stood beside Abraham, hearing God reaffirm His promise. Abraham helped me refocus my energy "in the meantime" of my own smaller life story.

Abraham could have responded to God merely with a dreamy faith that lives in the fuzzy future. But he balanced his belief for the long haul with a practical and prompt obedience whenever God told him to do something.

In this chapter, God told him to circumcise every male in his household. He obeyed *that very day*. Back in Genesis 12 he packed up *immediately* and went to the Promised Land. In Genesis 21, although it broke his heart, he sent Ishmael and Hagar away *early the next morning*. Years later, when God asked him to sacrifice Isaac, he saddled his donkey *early the next day* (22:3).

Abraham steered me back to the small but pivotal daily obedience of returning phone calls, acting on His nudges and continuing to knock on doors. I love Abraham's courageous balance between the theoretical and the practical. He taught me to:

- Believe God for the long haul, and
- Obey God today.

Abraham helped me to relax and make peace with my limbo. Armed with faith that God's timing is best, I've learned to look for ways to obey God now – in the meantime.

Dear Lord, Please show me how to obey You today. Amen.

Dionne Carpenter

Never Give Up, Give In, or Give Out

So do not throw away your confidence;
it will be richly rewarded. ~ Hebrews 10:35

READING: Hebrews 10:35-39

Many times in our church planting careers we have a real need of patient endurance and to not cast away our confidence. We may have been working steadfastly to develop the right attitude in the hearts of our congregation and leadership when along comes someone else with more resources or a more flashy style. Unscrupulous ministers may blatantly make a higher offer of salary or benefits than we can pay, or some other attractive program to entice the people.

We are tempted to fall into their game and react in the flesh. But this is not the godly way to deal with these situations. Sometimes we can talk with our congregation and leadership about biblical principles we should follow. We can also talk with the ministers involved. However, usually we just have to trust God that what we have planted, God's eternal principles in His Word, will not return void but will accomplish within our people what God intends.

We must have patience and cast not away our confidence in God's Word. The word *patience* is normally translated *perseverance*. We must persevere in what is right and believe that God's Word will come true for our particular situation. It is often very hard to be patient and persevere.

We personally have had other ministries come into the villages where we were planting a church, split the church and plant unwanted seed in their hearts. Our long term experience has shown that if we have planted the right principles in their hearts and persevere in praying and doing our part faithfully, most of the time they will repent and return to godly principles they were taught.

Lord, Our confidence is in You. Help us to always trust Your Word to have done its work and continue faithful. Amen.

Ron Thiesen

Triumphs Through Trials

Consider it pure joy, my brothers, whenever
you face trials of many kinds... ~ James 1:2

READING: James 1:2-6

Trials are an integral part of our ministry journey. They can become a tossing wind against us or a blessing that strengthens our walk with God. It was a tossing wind for Elijah who said, "I have had enough, Lord" (I Kings 19:4). But trials were a blessing for Paul who responded, "... I am ready, not only to be bound, but also to die" (Acts 21:13). Two noteworthy responses from two strong men of God as they encountered times of trial!

The Book of James, considered the first written book in the New Testament, speaks first about life trials of believers. He advised us to "Regard trials in such a way that you have impeccable joy in them." Trials have biotic potential to generate faith, develop perseverance, mature character and generate sufficiency in God.

Paul, like James, testifies that his trials became blessings because they brought God's overflowing comfort, produced patience and endurance and taught him not to rely on himself but on God (II Cor. 1:9). This attitude motivated Paul and Silas to worship in gladness in the Philippian jail.

Christians are promised conquering grace for all our troubles, hardships, persecutions, famines, nakedness, dangers and swords through Jesus who loved us (Rom. 8:16, 17). This biblical interpretation of trials comes from God's wisdom. James urges us to ask God for wisdom (James 1:5, 6), in part, so we will interpret trials correctly.

Is it not for us as we face trials even today? Are we seeking for God's wisdom to interpret trials? Is it not a ladder for us to reach the peak of strength and maturity?

God, Help me to face trials like Paul. Give me wisdom as James exhorts. I know that I need to walk a long way. I need you and your strength. Amen.

R. Jayakumar

Be Content with What You Have

*For where envy and self-seeking exist, confusion
and every evil thing are there. ~ James 3:16 (NKJV)*

READING: James 3:13-18

It was wrong and I knew it, but I couldn't seem to stop envying a church planter in my area whose church seemed far more successful. In fact, every Sunday I had to drive past his church to get to my temporary facility and when I drove by, my thoughts were along the lines, "Why does he seem to have so much more success, Lord? It's not fair. He has a nice facility; I have a temporary facility. He has a big crowd; I have a little huddle."

It didn't occur to me that there were a lot of other factors involved. I knew virtually nothing about how his church started. I had no idea if they were leading people to Christ. I did not know about his walk with God. I did not consider God's sovereignty. I just knew I coveted what he had.

After a year or so of this sinful attitude, one night I attended an evening service at that church. Their District Superintendent was there. To my amazement, I had stumbled into a service where they were discussing what to do now that their pastor had been caught in adultery. His family was shattered, his ministry ruined, and his testimony to the community was stained.

God's warning in James is clear. "For where envy and self-seeking *exist,* confusion and every evil thing *are* there."

God's promise to us is also clear. "Keep your life free from love of money, and be content with what you have, for He has said, 'I will never leave you nor forsake you'" (Hebrews 13:5 ESV).

Lord, Please teach me contentment, no matter what. Thank you for all your good gifts to me. Amen.

Mark Alan Williams

Focus

*Sanballat and Nehemiah's other enemies sent a
message to distract him from completing the wall around
Jerusalem. The message read, "Come, let us meet together at
Chephirim in the plain of Ono." ~ Nehemiah 6:2a*

READING: Nehemiah 6

A few years ago, we felt convicted that we needed to write a book to equip churches to plant churches. But we passed deadline after deadline and still were no closer to completing the book. Finally, the problem became clear. We were not dedicating the needed time to the writing. In the midst of many other urgent ministry demands, we tried to "fit in" our writing. It just wasn't working.

We determined that we needed FOCUSED TIME to complete our book. So, we scheduled a Writing Retreat. The three of us went away for three days to write. As I remember, we completed five chapters in three days. Soon, the Handbook was completed. Since then, DCPI Leaders have been able to produce many workbooks and another new Handbook to help church planting leaders; all because we followed the principle of FOCUSED TIME.

It is easy for us as church planters to get distracted and to procrastinate about completing our big tasks. When distractions come, we should respond the way Nehemiah did: "I am doing a great work and I cannot come down. Why should the work stop while I leave it and come down to you?" (Nehemiah 6:2b-4).

God has given you a great work to do. Satan will place many hindrances and distractions in your path. Some of the distractions may even be good things. Let Nehemiah's words be your words when there are distractions that pull you away from your mission.

Dear Father, Help me to carve out FOCUSED TIME to tackle the projects crucial to the success of this mission. Amen.

Paul Becker

Preparing for a Blessing Today

He who sacrifices thank offerings honors
me, and he prepares the way so that I may show
him the salvation of God. ~ Psalm 50:23

READING: Psalm 50

Every day in our church planting ministry we hope that God will, in some tangible way, show up to touch a life, provide encouragement or answer a prayer request. Psalm 50 makes clear that the way we prepare for God's presence or intervention is by giving an offering of thanksgiving. Verses 14 and 15 restate this reality, "Sacrifice thank offerings to God, fulfill your vows to the Most High, and call upon me in the day of trouble; I will deliver you, and you will honor me."

Again, offering up thanks to God prepares for His active hand in my life and ministry. Acknowledging God in the good and beautiful, the everyday joys of life and health, the high purpose in ministry and service, and, yes, even the challenges – all can be offerings of thanksgiving. A thanks offering is high praise to our great God.

The act of giving thanks to God recognizes His sovereignty, Lordship, creation, provision, love and care. It bows the knee to God Most High and shifts the focus away from my efforts, pride and wants. Truly it prepares the way – sets the table – for God to continue His blessing ways in my life and in His church.

When we start our day by giving thanks, it becomes an act of faith as we bless God for His provision for the day, and for the ministry ahead.

Lord, Today, all day, as I eat, think of my family, walk, work and meet with people, I will do it as a thank offering, one that I lift up to You with joy. I ask that my sacrifice of thanksgiving be pleasing in Your sight. Amen.

Ross Chenot

Church Planting Conflicts

But when Peter came to Antioch, I opposed him in public,
because he was clearly wrong. The other Jewish believers also started
acting like cowards along with Peter; and even Barnabas was swept
along by their cowardly action. ~ Galatians 2:11, 13 (GNB)

READING: Galatians 2

Despite being with Jesus, despite their message being accompanied by miraculous signs and despite revelations that eventually became Scripture, the original church planting leaders experienced major conflicts from time to time.

Conflict in church planting ministry is unavoidable and sometimes opposition comes from those you least expect. Even Barnabas fell into the trap of legalistic behavior and the Encourager became a discourager when he opposed Paul.

As you and I face church planting conflicts, let's bear in mind these lessons from this passage:

1. It is normal to have conflict in ministry.
2. Always stand for the truth – refuse to compromise, even though conflict may result. Paul had to take on James, Peter, John and even Barnabas.
3. Remember that our goal is not to please people, no matter who they are, but always to please our Lord. In Galatians 1:10 (ESV) Paul wrote this powerful challenge: "For am I now seeking the approval of man, or of God? Or am I trying to please man? If I were still trying to please man, I would not be a servant of Christ."

True Christ-followers live only to please Christ. They endure any conflict, ridicule, criticism, rejection, ostracism, and even persecution when clear issues of faithfulness and integrity are at stake. Don't be a coward. Instead, stand for truth and endure any unavoidable church planting conflict for the sake of Christ.

Lord, Please help me to endure conflicts for Your sake and, when they involve issues of integrity for You, help me live only to please You. Amen.

Mark Alan Williams

APRIL

The Barnabas Principle

Every church planter needs a mentor.
A mentor is someone who has been where you
want to go and is willing to help you get there.

Been There, Done That #1

*[Apollos] had been instructed in the way of the Lord, and
he spoke with great fervor and taught about Jesus accurately,
though he knew only the baptism of John. ~ Acts 18:25*

READING: Acts 18:24-28

My wife and I and our six-month-old son had just arrived on the mission field. Our first task was to conduct a survey of the Ilocos region of northern Luzon in the Philippines and select the town where we would settle to learn the language and begin our ministry of planting churches. We chose the strategic town of Vigan. What a challenging time in our lives!

One of the biggest challenges I was wrestling with was the basic question of *how* to plant a church. Oh, I'd had a couple of classes in Bible college, and plenty of ideas were swirling around in my head; but I needed a focus, I needed "handles" that would give me something solid on which to grab.

Apollos was a highly-trained follower of Jesus who, independently of Paul, came preaching Christ in Ephesus. Priscilla and Aquila heard him speaking boldly in the synagogue. They recognized some defects in what he was teaching, but they did not condemn him as a false teacher or contend with him as a competitor. Rather, they invited him into their home and corrected him in the context of hospitality. Later the Christians in Ephesus encouraged him and provided him with letters of introduction, paving the way for Apollos to minister effectively in Achaia.

God answered my prayer for a mentor by sending a man named Charles.

Lord, I need help! I'm not sure I even know what I don't know! Please help me find the right person to 'be there for me' throughout the coming weeks and months. And prepare me with experiences and insights to share with others down the road. Bless me, Lord, and make me a blessing. Amen.

Chris McKinney

Been There, Done That #2

*When Priscilla and Aquila heard him, they
invited him to their home and explained to him the
way of God more adequately. ~ Acts 18:26b*

READING: Acts 18:24-28

Just as Apollos needed someone in Ephesus to correct his teaching, encourage him, and strengthen his credibility, back in Vigan what I needed was a mentor – someone who had already planted churches in the Philippines and could tell me exactly what to do. God knew my dilemma and provided me with a most excellent mentor. Charles was a veteran church planter with several decades of experience in the Philippines working with another denomination. Having already fulfilled his vision of planting clusters of churches in two other areas, he and his wife Dottie moved to Vigan the same month our family did, with plans to establish another cluster of new churches.

As the only Americans in town, our two families began spending time together. Although they could have seen us as competitors or even false teachers, Charles and Dottie drew in a confused missionary aspiring to plant churches. Charles began sharing church planting principles, methods, and a culturally-specific model with us. He made me confident that I had more than enough resources to plant a church successfully.

As I planted a new church for my very first time, I would often seek out Charles and Dottie to relate my experiences and observations, counting on affirmation and guidance. Charles and Dottie rejoiced with us, encouraged us, prayed with us, and somehow managed to focus, re-direct, and broaden our vision all at once.

Lord, Thank You so much for the mentors You have provided along the way. Help me to reach out to others with that same generosity of spirit. Amen.

Chris McKinney

I'm Too Busy!

*Moreover, look for able men from all the people,
men who fear God, who are trustworthy and hate a bribe,
and place such men over the people as chiefs of thousands, of
hundreds, of fifties, and of tens. ~ Exodus 18:21 (ESV)*

READING: Exodus 18

Recently one leader told me that he practiced juggling in school as part of his physical education class and now he knows why since he is juggling so many items in his ministry nowadays.

Sometimes we like the busyness because it makes us feel important, but it is our family who complains about this the most. If you read between the lines in Exodus 18, it sounds like Moses' wife, Zipporah, complained to her daddy, Jethro, that Moses was too busy caring for the children of Israel to care for his own two sons. Great things were happening (see v. 9) but it was coming at the expense of a happy family and proper balance in Moses' life.

Sound familiar? Don't sacrifice your family on the altar of church planting success. Besides, working yourself into ill health or death doesn't please Jesus.

Church planting leader, listen to Jethro's wise advice. Quit thinking you are the answer to everyone's problems! Stop thinking there is no way out. Instead, ask God for those you can place over groups and ministries. Raise up mentors and train leaders. Then set them free to minister. Remember, your job is "to equip the saints for the work of ministry" (Eph. 4:12).

Stop *doing* ministry and start *equipping* others for ministry. Your wife, children (and father-in-law) will thank you. More importantly, you will be doing what you were called by the Lord to do.

Lord, Help me to equip others and share ministry so everyone will be blessed, including my precious family. Amen.

Mark Alan Williams

Mentoring

*Praise be to the God and Father of our Lord Jesus Christ, the
Father of compassion and the God of all comfort, who comforts us
in all our troubles, so that we can comfort those in any trouble with the
comfort we ourselves have received from God. ~ II Corinthians 1:3, 4*

READING: John 1:35-42

Some years ago I took a life-changing trip to Africa. My favorite aspect of the adventure was befriending nine top national leaders of church planting movements in South Africa, Malawi, Kenya, Uganda and Ghana. Usually, when I met with these leaders they brought along their protégés. Top leaders mentor their protégés.

At DCPI we believe that every church planter should have a mentor. Our definition of a mentor is 'someone who has been where you want to go and will help you get there.' All of us need mentors. I have a mentor. I meet with him once a month and he helps me chart the course for DCPI.

You may need a mentor right now in your church planting mission. You may need a wise and compassionate leader who will listen to you and pray for you, an experienced leader who can help you avoid the landmines of church planting.

How do you find a mentor? Pray and ask God to bring you one. Look for a mentor in your relationships, your denomination or your geographical region. If you can't find a mentor close at hand, recruit a phone mentor. Be proactive. Ask the right leader to invest two hours in you each month.

Is God calling you to be a mentor? You are an equipper at heart. You know church planters are in trouble and under attack from the Enemy. You want to help other leaders and watch them grow. Through mentoring, you can increase your impact upon God's Kingdom by developing leaders for new churches.

Father, Raise up godly mentors among us. Amen.

Paul Becker

Watching Dad Pack the Trunk

*Now when they saw the boldness of Peter and John and
perceived that they were uneducated and untrained men, they marveled.
And they realized that they had been with Jesus. ~ Acts 4:13*

READING: Mark 3:13-19

Before one of our many car trips, I remember my dad packing the trunk. Suitcases and accoutrements adorned the driveway and he began methodically arranging them in the trunk. If he didn't like the way the bags fit in, he took them out and started over. His system was pretty simple: flat items first, then odd-shaped items to fill in corners.

I never decided to enjoy packing; it just seemed to flow from my father's veins into mine. Somehow the challenge of fitting a lot of stuff into a limited space turns me on. It's a good thing, since my wife is convinced that we have too much stuff for the size of our apartment.

What are we imparting to our spiritual sons and daughters? Even if we've established Bible colleges or leadership training centers, our students pay more attention to who we are than to what we say. My dad never said "Here, son, I'm going to teach you how to be a packer." He just did it and did it well. And I wanted to do it like he did.

There's no substitute for shared life. When we open our heart, our home, our schedule, our resources, our weaknesses, our strengths, our failures and our victories to our spiritual kids, they internalize who and what we are.

When Yeshua said to "Go, make disciples," He could have added "like I did." His was a "course for life" ministry leadership training experience they would never forget.

Father, As I invest myself in people who have a call on their lives to pioneer, help me to hold nothing back, but nurture and correct them and release them into their destiny in you. Amen.

Eitan Shishkoff

The Grace of Giving #1

*And you Philippians yourselves know that in the beginning of
the gospel, when I left Macedonia, no church entered into partnership
with me in giving and receiving, except you only. Even in Thessalonica you
sent me help for my needs once and again. Not that I seek the gift, but I seek
the fruit that increases to your credit. ~ Philippians 4:15-17 (ESV)*

READING: Philippians 4:14-20

We church planters know what it's like to trust God for finances. And nobody knew more about daily dependence upon the Lord than the Apostle Paul. He was in prison in Rome when he wrote to the Philippian church to thank them for two encouragements: the visit of Epaphroditus and monetary support. Paul's gratitude also gives great instruction about the grace of giving. He teaches us five lessons. We'll cover two today and three tomorrow.

First, *financial giving makes us partners in the gospel.* In v. 15, Paul says no other church entered into "partnership" with him. The Greek word is *fellowship*, literally, "common life." Financial giving means we stand together to share the gospel, to pray, to shoulder burdens. Together.

Second, *financial giving is an investment in eternity.* Paul tells them in v. 17 that he doesn't seek the gift but "the profit which increases to your account" (NASB). More than the money itself, Paul is thankful that their gifts do eternal good. It brings the gospel to save people from hell, it equips believers with God's eternal word, and it does a work of grace in the hearts of the givers.

Financial giving gives us the opportunity to connect with God's grace in partnering and investing for eternity.

Lord, Show me how to teach, and to model, the grace of giving. Amen.

Jim Carpenter

The Grace of Giving #2

*I have received full payment, and more. I am well
supplied, having received from Epaphroditus the gifts you sent,
a fragrant offering, a sacrifice acceptable and pleasing to God. And my
God will supply every need of yours according to his riches in glory
in Christ Jesus. To our God and Father be glory forever
and ever. Amen. ~ Philippians 4:18-20 (ESV)*

READING: Philippians 4:14-20

Many church planters find it difficult to teach about giving. They're afraid people will misunderstand, and falsely conclude their church is interested only in money. But the Apostle Paul had no such fear. He rejoiced in the grace of giving, gave thanks for his financial supporters, and in the process, taught us all a lot about this spiritual discipline.

Yesterday we looked at two great truths about giving. Here are three more: Third, *financial giving is an act of worship.* Paul calls their gift "a fragrant offering" and "an acceptable sacrifice" and says it is "pleasing" to God. He is comparing it to the Old Testament sacrifices. Giving is really a way of worshiping God. Done out of a heart of love, it is a statement of the worthiness, greatness and glory of our God.

Fourth, *financial giving brings a promise of God's provision.* Verse 19 is one of the most wonderful promises in the New Testament. Like many Bible promises, it is conditional: <u>because</u> the Philippians are giving sacrificially (v. 16) and are "filling Paul full" (v. 18), <u>as a consequence</u>, God will fill them full!

Finally, *financial giving is a commitment to God's glory.* Paul ends with a benediction: To our God be glory forever and ever! In the end, the discipline of giving means a life committed to God's glory above everything.

To God be the glory, great things He has done! Amen.

Jim Carpenter

Knowing What to Mentor

All Scripture is God-breathed and is useful for teaching, rebuking, correcting and training in righteousness, so that the man of God may be thoroughly equipped for every good work. ~ II Timothy 3:16, 17

READING: II Timothy 3:10-17

It is apparent in this passage that Paul had known Timothy for a long time and had mentored him from a young age. Timothy had developed a "track record" before Paul. You can never really know "who" a potential leader really is until the circumstances and pressures of life assail him. Then we see things that need to be changed. Though we are only agents of change, we must do our part from within a close relationship to that person.

As we read between the lines, it is clear that Paul mentored Timothy across a broad range of skills and topics, giving him generous doses of both more formal instruction in Scripture and practical experience gained as he traveled with Paul. We observe in Paul also a tender spirit of encouragement to speak to what might have been Timothy's personal susceptibility to timidity. On the one hand, Paul exhorts Timothy, saying bracingly: "God did not give us a spirit of timidity…" (II Tim. 1:7). But, on the other hand, Paul also gives kindly practical advice: "Stop drinking only water, and use a little wine because of your stomach and your frequent illnesses" (I Tim. 5:23).

Have you developed a relationship with someone in your team or church for whom you are willing to sacrifice your comforts, time, energies and finances to see them grow spiritually? What kind of a legacy will you leave behind you when you move on to another church plant?

Father, Show me who you would have me mentor. Help me to be willing to sacrifice my comforts, time and finances to see someone else succeed. Amen.

Ron Thiesen

From Pigs to the Pulpit

*...and what you have heard from me in the presence
of many witnesses entrust to faithful men who will be
able to teach others also.* ~ *II Timothy 2:2*

READING: II Timothy 2:1-3

He was a long-haired, seventeen year old runner who ran past my house with his dog. I stopped him one morning and introduced myself. His family had recently moved into our small Aztec town and he was a student of veterinary medicine in Mexico City. I invited him to visit some Aztec villages with me, and he readily accepted. At that time we were planting churches in about a dozen villages.

Our "Paul and Timothy" relationship lasted for two years. We traveled in my old yellow jeep to many Aztec villages to evangelize and disciple. My new friend was enamored with all the pigs which ran at will in the streets. As time passed, the young "Vet" operated on many of the pigs and thus earned the respect of the villagers.

Near the end of the second year of our journey together, he sensed God's call to ministry. Upon graduation from the University, he proudly donated his "Pig-skin Diploma" to his mother and stated, "This is what you have helped me through school to earn, but now I am going to serve the Lord."

He continues to operate on pigs when necessary but has been the pastor of the First Baptist Church in our city for twenty years. He has also trained 17 men to lead the new churches they have begun. II Timothy 2:2 is a work in progress in the life of my Pig-to-Pulpit friend. Hundreds of pigs have been helped, and thousands of men now know Christ because of him.

Dear Heavenly Father, Please open our eyes and hearts to see those around us who are longing for You. Teach us to teach others for the multiplication of Your Kingdom. Amen.

Buddy Johnson

You Can Mentor

Take the teachings that you heard me proclaim in the
presence of many witnesses, and entrust them to reliable people,
who will be able to teach others also. ~ II Timothy 2:2 (GNB)

READING: Mark 3:1-19

I was privileged to attend the Tokyo 2010 Missions Consultation with my wife, Carolyn. We arrived in Tokyo and on the first day we learned how to ride the subway, we found our hotel and we learned the Japanese words for "goodbye" and "thank you."

The next day, we met two guys who had just arrived for the consultation. They were so thankful that we could show them how to ride the subway, which train to take, where to get Japanese cash and how to get an umbrella. They assured me it was so much easier to have us as "guides." I couldn't help but chuckle at the novice mentoring role I was able to play. Here I was a 24-hour newcomer to Japan, yet I could mentor others who were newer than me.

We forget that mentoring is not about being the most accomplished expert. A mentor is simply, "someone who has been where you want to go and is willing to tell you how to get there."

Do you know someone who needs to learn what you know? Why not offer to mentor that person? You don't have to be the world's greatest. Just offer to share what you know.

Jesus, our Supreme Example, made mentoring a priority. He spent three years pouring Himself into the twelve. They changed the world. Likewise, those you mentor may also change the world.

Lord, I want to share what I know with others and raise up leaders like Jesus did. Please show me who to mentor now. Amen.

Mark Alan Williams

Mentoring the F.A.T.

*Whoever can be trusted with very little
can also be trusted with much. ~ Luke 16:10a*

READING: Luke 16:10-12

During college, I was mentored through our campus ministry program, with the goal in mind that I would mentor others. I was taught to look for people who were F.A.T. (Faithful, Available and Teachable). In general, that goofy little acrostic has been a handy guide. I have never had the time in any of our church plants to mentor all the women who needed mentoring. It's wise to devote energy on those with the most potential for fruit, and those most likely to become fellow mentors.

As I have looked for women to mentor, the F.A.T. guideline has helped me to spot young women who seem receptive to one-on-one discipleship or other kinds of leadership development. I've observed how they handle a small responsibility, whether they follow through on simple commitments like the promise to attend a meeting or bake cookies, and whether they're open to suggestion or godly instruction.

I confess that I've battled a carnal desire to invest most heavily in the women I personally like. It has been a good discipline to learn not to run after the candidates I'd prefer, but rather to prayerfully wait and allow potential "mentorees" to prove themselves by demonstrating their faithfulness and commitment.

I appreciate so much the faithful ones who poured themselves into my life back in college. How privileged we are to keep that holy chain reaction going by finding and investing in a new generation of believers.

Dear Father, Give me grace to focus my best attention on the people You want me to mentor. Amen.

Dionne Carpenter

Mentoring the Passing Parade

Freely you have received, freely give. ~ *Matthew 10:8b*

READING: I Corinthians 3:1-9

I'll never forget the comment that someone on the search committee made just before we moved out to California to plant our first church: "Pastoring a church in California is like preaching to a parade." Boy, he was right! Californians are truly a mobile bunch. It's not uncommon for people to move every three years, and that doesn't even count the mandated transfers for our Navy families here in San Diego.

This extreme mobility has been a mixed blessing for us as church planters. People in transition are generally more open to try out a new church plant, so newcomers usually made up the bigger percentage of our congregations. Their temporary receptivity led to their eternal salvation. Plus, they felt more motivated to immediately seize upon any offer of mentoring. On the other hand, it complicated the business of training up leadership or of allowing enough time for potential leaders to prove themselves.

It soon became apparent that we had to give up any expectation that we would necessarily enjoy the fruits of our labors. Time after time we have waved good bye to our best graduates. Occasionally we hear good reports back of someone's effective ministry within another church and of persevering faith in Christ. But typically we don't know what happened after they moved away.

Mentoring requires of us just such a generosity of spirit, a willingness to give our best, whether or not we see the results. Our particular mission field has been a parade of people, rootless, fatherless, hungry for stability, who wander within our range only briefly. It pleases God when we mentor well, even briefly, those who cross our path.

Dear Father, I miss the people who have moved away. Please bless them and keep them strong. I pray that they will give You pleasure wherever they go. Amen.

Dionne Carpenter

Mentoring the Broken

A bruised reed he will not break, and a smoldering wick he
will not snuff out, till he leads justice to victory. ~ *Matthew 12:20*

READING: Isaiah 42:1-10

My childhood home life concealed ghastly dysfunction. It took years before I found the courage to challenge the #1 rule in my childhood home: "Thou shalt not tell the secret." With my husband's kind support and unfailing encouragement, I began a long healing journey.

Today I am a wounded healer, walking in peace and much mind renewal. God restored to me the years that the locusts had eaten by giving me opportunities to counsel and mentor precious souls as broken as I once was.

"A bruised reed He will not break." I love the many names of God, but this description is one of my favorites. A reed is inherently fragile, and a bruised reed even more so. Our blessed Messiah balances the extremes of His character with perfect poise. He is, on the one hand, our mighty Creator, Judge and Victor. Yet, He is also this incredibly gentle healer, tenderly caring for the most fragile casualties of our sinful world.

People who have been deeply wounded may take a long time to heal. We mentor these wounded ones with steady faithfulness, a listening ear and a safe place to heal. We give people time. The best mentors for bruised reeds or smoldering wicks are often "reeds" Jesus has already restored to wholeness, and "wicks" Jesus has babied and protected until their sputtering flame begins to burn bright and strong again.

Oh, may our churches be safe places for wounded people to recover, and may we be the gentle hands of Jesus to these fragile ones so loved by God.

Dear Father, Thank You for being so amazingly patient with me, and thank You for continuing to heal my heart by letting me be a channel of Your grace to others. Amen.

Dionne Carpenter

God's Plans Are Good Plans

*"For I know the plans I have for you," declares
the LORD, "plans for welfare and not for evil, to give you a
future and a hope." ~ Jeremiah 29:11 (ESV)*

READING: Jeremiah 29:1-14

What promises from God's word do you hang onto as a church planter? When the challenges come, when you're tempted to quit, trust God's promises! Jeremiah 29:11 is a wonderful promise originally given to God's people after they had been carried into captivity in Babylon, assuring them that one day they would return to the Promised Land.

While Jeremiah 29:11 wasn't originally given to church planters, it *is* a great promise, a personal favorite that Dionne and I have claimed throughout our church planting journey. Here are four blessings:

First, *God knows – and rules – over everything about us.* The Lord begins by saying "I know." It's incredibly comforting that nothing about our circumstances escapes the wise control of our Heavenly Father.

Second, *God has a plan.* "Plans" in Hebrew could also be translated "thoughts." If God thinks about something, it's already a plan, isn't it? What He thinks, He does. He always carries out His intentions. God's plans are never spoiled or foiled. What He plans for you and your church plant *will happen.*

Third, *God's plans unfold in His timing, not ours.* When God originally spoke this promise, He told His people they must wait 70 years – but He would deliver them. Our church planting timetable sometimes runs ahead of God's. But He will deliver.

Finally, *His plan is for our blessing:* "plans for welfare and not for calamity…" "Welfare" is *shalom* – a Hebrew word often translated "peace." It means wholeness, fulfillment, harmony and well-being. The God who led you to plant churches intends *shalom* for you and for your church.

Father, Thank You for Your promises and for Your good plans. Give me patience and confidence to rest in Your perfect timing. Amen.

Jim Carpenter

Divine Appointments

*Many are the plans in a man's heart, but it is the
Lord's purpose that prevails. ~ Proverbs 19:21*

READING: Acts 8:26-40

A Kenyan leader, Dr. Francis Kamau, asked me to speak to about 100 church planters, pastors and spouses who are involved in a School of Ministers. We didn't discuss what he wanted me to teach. He just asked me to share my heart. I'd been praying about what the Lord wanted me to teach and felt led to share the Twelve Biblical Principles of Church Planting. The group of men and women were very attentive.

Then, I got to Principle #4: "Every Church Planter Needs a Mentor."

Francis laughed. Evangelist Teresa laughed. Everybody laughed but me. I knew something good had happened, but I didn't know what it was. The biblical foundation for developing leaders through mentoring was emphasized. I taught that our conviction at DCPI was that every church planter should have a mentor. How to find a mentor was covered. Being a mentor to others by sharing with them what you know was discussed. They asked excellent questions...the same questions that church planters in different countries of the world (including the United States) have asked.

My allotted time ended and I sat down. Francis Kamau stood up to close the meeting. He said, "This morning one of our primary prayer requests was: 'Lord, teach us about mentoring. Show us how to find mentors.' That prayer was answered this afternoon. Praise the Lord!"

Isn't that encouraging! Kenyan church planting leaders had a need for teaching on mentoring. The LORD purposed to meet that need by using an American who was almost halfway around the world from his home.

Dear Lord, Thank you for knowing our deepest needs for help in church planting and for arranging divine appointments when we need them most. We praise you and give you all the glory. Amen.

Paul Becker

Who Are You Mentoring?

*Paul left and took the followers with him to the lecture
hall of Tyrannus. He spoke there every day for two years,
until every Jew and Gentile in Asia had heard the
Lord's message. ~ Acts 19:9b–10 (CEV)*

READING: Acts 19:1-10

Paul had faithfully obeyed the Holy Spirit's call at Antioch, and at first he did this by becoming a church planter. But, by the time he reached Ephesus, he had expanded his focus to become a *trainer* of church planters. Every day for two years he taught leaders. As he equipped and sent out church planters, every "Jew and Gentile in Asia" heard the Gospel, multitudes were saved and many churches were established.

That should be our goal today! Like Paul, you and I cannot do it alone. What is the answer? The answer is to raise up and mentor others who will multiply ministry impact.

Paul never traveled alone on his short-term church planting missions trips. And when he stayed in Ephesus for two years, he trained and multiplied leaders.

Who are you mentoring into ministry? The small church I attended while I was growing up in Ohio was never very large at all. But the many "preacher boys" who came through that church are continuing to have amazing impact: pastors, college and seminary professors, missionaries. Several are authors.

That church experienced a devastating church split during my senior year in high school. The church was shattered, but their long-term ministry continues to thrive though those who were mentored there. You and I may breathe our last at any minute. Who will be our lasting ministry legacy? Who are you mentoring?

Lord, I want to raise up Timothys for ministry and become a trainer of church planters. Please multiply my impact for the kingdom through those I train and mentor. Amen.

Mark Alan Williams

The Gambler for Jesus

...for he nearly died for the work of Christ,
risking his life to complete what was lacking
in your service to me. ~ *Philippians 2:30*

READING: Philippians 2:25-30

Paul was under house arrest in Rome, facing possible execution. When the church in Philippi heard the news, they wanted to help and encourage their spiritual father. God had used Paul to start the church and lead them to the Lord. Now they wanted to support and comfort him. So they sent Epaphroditus. Though he's mentioned only in Philippians, you learn a lot about Epaphroditus in this short paragraph.

You could count on him to get the job done. Paul calls him *my brother, fellow worker,* and *fellow soldier.* He was the Philippians' *messenger* and *minister* to Paul's needs. Each description speaks of Epaphroditus' faithfulness. He faithfully carried monetary help to Paul (4:18). Paul entrusted him to carry his letter back to the church – the book of Philippians.

He was a loving friend. He cared so much for the church in Philippi that, when they heard he almost died, it overwhelmed him that they were so worried. That's why Paul sent him back to Philippi (v. 26).

And *Epaphroditus was a risk-taker*: "he nearly died for the work of Christ, risking his life..." (v. 30). "Risk" was a gambler's word; it meant rolling the dice. He traveled the 800 miles to Rome, a rigorous six-week journey, and nearly lost his life in the process.

In the early church a brotherhood of "gamblers" was formed to care for the sick and bury the dead when the plague ravaged a city. The Christians risked their lives, like Epaphroditus did, to show the love of Jesus.

Every church plant needs Epaphroditus; every church planter needs to be like Epaphroditus.

Father, Thank you for this hero of the faith. May I be like him and build a church of people like him! Amen.

Jim Carpenter

Lessons from a Mentor's Downfall #1

While Absalom was offering sacrifices, he also sent for Ahithophel
the Gilonite, David's counselor, to come from Giloh, his hometown.
And so the conspiracy gained strength... ~ II Samuel 15:12

READING: II Samuel 15:10-13

The little-known story of Ahithophel, King David's highly regarded counselor, vividly illustrates three insidious temptations that may particularly ensnare gifted mentors: 1) to foolishly squander our God-given wisdom in support of an unworthy cause; 2) to underestimate the degree to which those we counsel could undermine our integrity; and 3) to evaluate our worth and success by whether or not people take our advice.

Let's examine the first of these temptations.

David's rebellious son, Absalom, led a massive revolt that rocked the nation of Israel. Absalom almost succeeded, in part because he persuaded David's personal counselor to defect to his side. It was a major tactical and psychological triumph for Absalom because Ahithophel's advice was widely revered "like that of one who inquires of God" (II Sam. 16:23).

What lured Ahithophel away from serving David, the Lord's anointed? Why did such a smart man do such a dumb thing? Was he just naïve? Was he bored? Did he feel unappreciated? A mentor's wisdom is a sacred trust. It was a grievous sin for Ahithophel to bestow that precious gift on Absalom's poisonous rebellion.

Ahithophel's story is a cautionary tale for knowledgeable mentors in the church planting community to exercise discernment by vetting the many eager church planters who vie for our long-term help. Some church plants are nothing but divisive church splits, unworthy of our hard-won sage advice. Some church planters are rebels at heart, modern day Absaloms.

Expertise in church planting is a precious commodity. It should be used to support legitimate church planting efforts that glorify God.

Father, Help me not to be wise in my own eyes. Amen.

Dionne Carpenter

Lessons from a Mentor's Downfall #2

Ahithophel answered, "Lie with your father's concubines whom he left to take care of the palace." ~ II Samuel 16:21

READING: II Samuel 16:15-23

The God-given gift of wisdom can propel an astute and perceptive adviser into the heady inner circles of power and leadership. It feels incredibly gratifying to bring insight and direction to "movers and shakers" who are eager for clarity; to suggest a course of action and then watch those leaders mobilize people and resources to turn that whispered word of counsel into a reality.

The evil one reserves a few devious temptations that are especially designed to trip up a mentor – often the smartest man in the room. Ahithophel's odd story provides a valuable warning if we will humble ourselves and take it to heart.

Ahithophel relished his reputation as a highly respected counselor and yet he was unaware of the degree to which his advice was subtly influenced by the character of the leader to whom he gave advice. When he advised David, a godly man, his advice soared "like that of one who inquires of God."

Ahithophel didn't notice how much Absalom's low character soiled the advice he gave regarding the ten concubines (16:21). David would have been shocked by such advice! Absalom embraced his vile suggestion.

No matter how wise they may be, and how personally upright, mentors must be on guard as to who they allow themselves to mentor. And, whether in the trenches with rising stars or in the heady circles of denominational leadership, mentors must hang on tightly to personal integrity. Speak the truth, even the hard truth, and don't drift away from core principles.

Ahithophel lost the blessing of God because of the man he chose to support. Thank God for alerting us to this subtle danger.

Father, Help me to be truly wise as a serpent and innocent as a dove. Amen.

Dionne Carpenter

Lessons from a Mentor's Downfall #3

*When Ahithophel saw that his advice
had not been followed, he...put his house in order
and then hanged himself. ~ II Samuel 17:23*

READING: II Samuel 17:1-23

Recently I was asked to help shape curriculum for a lay counseling ministry and became quite frustrated and upset because the ministry leader wasn't taking my advice. The Lord used Ahithophel's bizarre story to help me sort out how to respond well in that situation. Reflecting on his extreme solution jolted me back to reality and revealed a path of peace for those of us in a position to mentor others.

Every spiritual gift has a natural upside and a built-in liability. They all need to be purified and redeemed; otherwise latent ability becomes an unyielded breeding ground for carnality and pride. Upon reflection, I confess I got upset because I wanted to control the outcome and because I fell into the trap of thinking somehow it made a statement about my personal worth if she took my advice.

Both parts were false. God used that experience to further purify the gift He gave me. I renounced my ungodly desire to control the outcome when people ask my advice. Ahithophel helped me to see the folly of judging my success by how others respond. That's a disastrous standard to set for ourselves. Scriptures are chock-full of stories about godly people whose good advice was spurned. Furthermore, we answer to Christ alone. He's the only Wise One (I Cor. 1:30).

Curiously, after I got my heart right and entrusted the outcome to God, that leader became more open to my suggestions. And it didn't matter. I felt at peace to brainstorm ideas and offer suggestions without any anxiety that it affected my worthiness in Christ.

All thanks to poor Ahithophel.

Father, Purify my heart so that my advice reflects the wisdom that comes from above. Amen.

Dionne Carpenter

The Value of Christ's Sacrifice

For by a single offering he has perfected for all time
those who are being sanctified. ~ Hebrews 10:14 (ESV)

READING: Hebrews 10:11-14

As a church planter I've had people confess terrible sins to me: murder of a child, the sexual abuse of a man's own children, adultery. What hope is there for such people?

Meditate on today's key verse. Think of those who are "being sanctified," the saved throughout history, from every tribe and language and people and nation. Try to imagine the massive volume and weight and height of their sins. Think of the stench of human wretchedness and rebellion, pride and debauchery, every commandment of God broken a myriad of times. Every imaginable form of human sin is represented over and over, a festering, oozing mass of misery and transgression.

What happened to pay this incalculably staggering debt to God's justice? How could God the Judge ever be just and still justify anyone? Yet Hebrews 10:14 says a single sacrifice did that – paid for it all. And not just a temporary reprieve, but "perfected for all time."

How could this be true? It is true only because of the infinite worth of the offering. The precious blood of Jesus is a million times purer, a hundred million times more righteous than the multiplied mass of human unrighteousness. That's why our gospel proclaims "the blood of Jesus cleanses from *all* sin" (I John 1:7).

Our gospel is not based on God's deciding to look the other way, to suspend His holiness to save sinners. It is based on the incredible worth of a Savior whose death and resurrection paid the debt and provided for the eternal life of all who believe on Him.

Oh, how blessed we are for such a Savior!

Lord Jesus, Thank You for saving me and for giving me a gospel to proclaim that is based on Your infinitely precious blood! Amen.

Jim Carpenter

The Mentor as Life Coach

Simon, Simon, Satan has asked to sift you like wheat. But I have prayed for you, Simon, that your faith may not fail. And when you have turned back, strengthen your brothers. ~ Luke 22:31, 32

READING: Matthew 28:19, 20

One of the things that is very close to the heart of God is the maturity in character that can only take place through discipleship, mentoring and encouraging. Through our long experience in church planting, I have come to realize how difficult it is to establish true discipling relationships in a church. It takes lots of time and is very demanding – time and energy that are in short supply – both in the mentor and in the disciple. The sacrifice that it requires is not easy to make.

One of the prime opportunities to mold character happens if the disciple should stumble. When his old sinful nature gets the disciple into trouble, if he is fortunate enough to have a godly mentor, that mentor who is close to him has a strategic moment in which to guide and encourage him, and insist that he take the right path to victory.

When Jesus spoke his poignant prediction to Simon Peter, he was acting the part of the godly mentor to Simon. He acknowledged that Simon would, in fact, stumble, but assured him of his prayerful intercession. He also showed Simon a glimpse of fruitful ministry beyond that failure.

God wants each one of us to be such a person in the life of others within our church. It is a costly commitment both for the disciple and for the mentor. It requires much time and emotional energy and, many times, financial cost. But it is worth it to see people develop a character that is stable and useful to the Kingdom of God.

Father, Help me to model your grace to those I mentor to mold their character into Christ-likeness. Amen.

Ron Thiesen

Courage

Have I not commanded you? Be strong and courageous.
Do not be afraid; do not be discouraged, for the LORD your God
will be with you wherever you go. ~ Joshua 1:9

READING: Judges 6

Are you ever afraid? Are you afraid of failing in your ministry or of the criticism of people? Are you afraid of persecution? One of the Enemy's most common attacks is "dis-courage-ment." He sucks the courage right out of us and replaces the void with fear. Fear causes paralysis. And, if we are not careful, the Enemy can win.

What we need is COURAGE to overcome our fears and move forward in our ministry. In Judges 6, God allowed the powerful Midianites to invade Israel. When the Israelites cried out to God for help, He responded by seeking out Gideon.

God told Gideon, "Go in the strength you have and save Israel out of Midian's hand. Am I not sending you?" (v. 14).

"Pardon me, my lord," Gideon replied, "but how can I save Israel? My clan is the weakest in Manasseh, and I am the least in my family" (v. 15). He was fearful because he had no power.

The LORD answered, "I will be with you, and you will strike down all the Midianites, leaving none alive" (v. 16).

It is a credit to Gideon that he did not just say, "No." Instead, he dialogued with God and confirmed His instruction by means of the fleece. Gideon became confident that God was with him and would save Israel by his hand. God's presence gave Gideon courage. He routed the vast Midianite army using just 300 men.

God's presence is also your courage and mine. When you are afraid, get closer to God through his Word and submit to the Holy Spirit's leading in your life.

The Lord is with you, too, wherever you go!

Father, Give me courage to go in the strength I have. Amen.

Paul Becker

The Prodigy Under Submission

*Then he [Jesus] went down to Nazareth
with them and was obedient to them.* ~ Luke 2:51

READING: Luke 2:41-52

Young seminary graduates or pastors are the ones most likely to become enthusiastic about planting a church. Their passion usually truly reflects a genuine call of God. But, an unacknowledged motivation within some gifted young adults may be an impatience and lack of respect for the old guard running their established churches and denominations. Our young pastors long to get out from under the thumb of old men doing church the same boring old way. They're eager to get out on their own and do church "their" way.

Even by age twelve, Jesus exemplifies the way of wisdom for such church planting prodigies. It must have been exhilarating for Christ as a self-aware deep thinker, fresh from His bar mitzvah, to finally converse with the religious intelligentsia of His day. He astonished them, one and all!

Jesus might have felt strongly tempted to start His public ministry right then and there, encouraged by their affirmation. Yet when His parents found Him, He meekly left the temple without a backward glance and returned to submissive obscurity for eighteen more years. Hebrews 5:8 tells us "He learned obedience from what He suffered."

Search your heart and repent if you find any hint of rebellion or scorn for the leaders God has placed over you. Yes, I'll even concede that your supervisors may be total idiots. Their hypocrisy or carnality may irritate you to no end.

On the other hand, with all their faults and foibles, these imperfect mentors may be God's chosen instruments, so that, like Jesus, you grow "in wisdom and stature, and in favor with God and men."

Dear Father, Give me a submissive attitude toward those You have placed in authority over me, even the ones who seem most imperfect. Amen.

Dionne Carpenter

It's All About God

*For the foolishness of God is wiser than
man's wisdom… ~ I Corinthians 1:25a*

READING: I Corinthians 3

I trained our launch team in how to go door-to-door calling. I taught them how to make a good first impression and ways to smoothly steer the conversation toward spiritual matters. After modeling our first contact for a block or so, everyone on the launch team got a turn. After each home I would make some comments to reinforce a key point and encourage the team member.

Then it was *her* turn. She was bold and enthusiastic but seemed too often to just not "get it." As we approached the next house, I repeated my instructions one last time. She knocked on the door, and I shut up and prayed. The door was opened by a young woman.

"Do you want to have a Bible study?"

I cringed inside. Yes, we were trying to set up Bible studies, but she had forgotten everything I said. I hoped God would not be too grieved that an actual family had such a poor invitation, that he would understand that part of our task was also to disciple people like her.

"Yes." With an equally direct answer, the young woman standing behind the door reminded me that Christ's efforts to build his church did not rely on my script or my smooth words. As Paul wrote the Corinthians, "Neither he who plants nor he who waters is anything, but only God, who makes things grow."

The Bible study in that home in the weeks that followed produced our new church's first worship leader, the husband of the young woman who had answered the door. And today, She-Who-I-Thought-Muffed-It is one of the most influential leaders at her home church.

---

*Father, Teach me to love and appreciate my brothers and sisters as you love them and
have uniquely prepared each of them. Amen.*

Chris McKinney

What's in a Name?

And he brought him to Jesus. Jesus looked at him
and said, "You are Simon son of John. You will be called
'Cephas' (which, when translated, is Peter)." ~ John 1:42

READING: John 1:35-42

What's in a name? Just ask Peter. He was impulsive and unstable. He was prone to make promises he couldn't keep and he even denied Jesus three times in one night. Peter was anything but the rock that Jesus dubbed him. Yet Jesus saw him as more than what he was at that moment. He saw what he could become.

When Jesus sees us, He sees more, more than we are right now. He sees us through a future lens that highlights our high potential, all we can be, our fullness as made in the image of God, the product of the Spirit's transforming presence. Jesus sees us with God's Kingdom eyes, and that means accepting us with love and a rich inheritance, and yet transforming us to be more than we presently are.

Jesus sees us through the lens of His transforming grace, His commitment to mold us into His image. There is "more than we are" in each of us – more love, more stability, more maturity, more holiness, more resilience and more joy. Just ask Him. He walks with us today, always bearing in His mind the image of what He will make of us.

What new name might Jesus be in the process of giving you? The stable one? Mr. Patient? Mr. Cheerful? Faithful? Warrior? The Servant Leader? Nothing is too hard for our God and no personality so fractured that He cannot heal and renew it.

Lord, You love me just as I am, but too much to leave me that way. You see me as so much more. Continue to remake me to be more than I am. Amen.

Ross Chenot

Saul or David?

*Day after day Saul searched for him, but God
did not give David into his hands. ~ I Samuel 23:14b*

READING: I Samuel 23

Saul and David both led "young bucks" but provide stark contrast between great and awful leadership styles. David consistently kept charging forward, courageously doing the jobs God assigned him to do. His own personal forward momentum of obediently following the Lord kept him from getting sidetracked into squashing his own people. He kept his focus on the enemies "out there" and welcomed the strength and skills of mighty men who joined him in his noble enterprise.

When Saul began to stall and sputter and dilly dally, he created a vacuum of leadership but deeply resented his young lieutenants who rose to the challenges he should have been first to face. He stopped focusing on Israel's true external enemies, and instead, became fixated on stamping out perceived rivals for his crown.

As church planters it is vital that we establish our leadership role within the church. Most fledgling churches attract a few prowling, carnal folks itching to become "a big fish in a little pond." We protect our congregation by dealing decisively with power grabs by these ungodly predators.

However – and this is a big however – keep your eyes on the main goal to build a thriving, healthy church body. If within a few years you have crushed every potential threat to your own leadership, you have also most likely driven off all the best go-getters who could help you accomplish truly great things as a church.

Conversely, if you encourage your young bucks, training and empowering them while *you* continually lead the charge to fulfill your own God-given mission, you will raise up an army of courageous, faith-filled leaders.

Dear Father, Give me holy boldness to do all You've called me to do and healthy discernment regarding the potential leaders in my church. Amen.

Dionne Carpenter

Crisis Management

The apostles and elders met to consider this question. ~ Acts 15:6

READING: Acts 15:1-21

Is your church plant undergoing a time of crisis? Attendance and offerings have fallen, members losing their interest and core leaders becoming cold? How would you handle it? Natural response at this juncture could either be "closing down" or "quitting."

When a doctrinal crisis shook the Church of Antioch, they sought for a panel of leaders in Jerusalem who knew Christ personally and had concern for His Church to arbitrate and give further direction.

Crisis desperation always should lead us to seek for arbitrators. Crisis will turn to a chaos if you do not find the right kind of men to solve the issues. In desperation, if you appoint an unqualified team of men, they will eventually tend to lay the blame on one or more of the following: the church planting pastor, certain officials, a cold congregation or a difficult neighborhood. Look for arbitrators who will build your plant, not blame people in it.

Your church may experience problems due to an all-out attack by Satan and/or demons. When you, as a Bible believing church planter, keep planting your church in accordance to the Word, and yet problems incarnate in various forms it must be from the Enemy of Christ. Men of Christ and His Word could easily discern Satan's hand in it. Call for a special prayer meeting of the saints and rebuke Satan.

Your pain could be by someone in the plant, like one who was a pain to the church in Corinth (II Cor. 2:5). The Church in Corinth punished him and then restored him at Paul's suggestion. People who know God and have concern for His Church will give solutions to build His Church.

God, Give me a godly band of men and women so I may receive insights from them as I face times of crisis in my plant. Amen.

R. Jayakumar

He Made Him to Be
Sin Who Knew No Sin

For our sake he made him to be sin who knew no sin,
so that in him we might become the righteousness of God.
~ II Corinthians 5:21 (ESV)

READING: II Corinthians 5:16-21

We church planters love Jesus. We admire Him more than anyone, we want to bring Him glory, and we want Him to be proud of us. We want to spend time with Him, obey Him, become like Him. We are church planters *because* we love Jesus and want to see others come to love Him, too.

We love Him because we remember what He did for us. We remember our sin. And we think back to the time when we heard the gospel. It was the best news we had ever heard, almost too good to be true.

We must never lose sight of the greatness of Christ's sacrifice for us. Paul kept reminding the churches he planted about Christ's atonement. When he wrote to the Corinthian church, he stressed two wonderful truths.

First, "for our sake he made him to be sin who knew no sin." The Father made Jesus, who was perfect and holy and sinless, to be so identified with our sins that He became sin in His sight. "He made him *to be* sin." Oh, how we love our Savior for willingly bearing the filth of our sins!

But that's not all. The second truth follows: "so that in him we might become the righteousness of God."

God has "reckoned" Christ's record of obedience and perfection as ours! Though we are *not* righteous, He has declared us to be righteous because of Christ!

Thank You so much, Lord Jesus, for bearing my sin upon Your own sinless life, and for letting Your righteousness be reckoned unto me. I love You, Jesus. Amen.

Jim Carpenter

Communion

After he said this, he took some bread and
gave thanks to God in front of them all. Then he
broke it and began to eat. ~ Acts 27:35

READING: Acts 27:33-36

Paul and his captors are about to die. By boat, they are en route to Rome when they find themselves caught in a fierce storm for days on end. But earlier, Paul received a promise from God that all would be safe. Nevertheless, the storm is tearing the boat apart and the sailors are starving themselves in hopes of appeasing their gods. And it is in the midst of this storm that the apostle Paul takes bread, breaks it and gives thanks to God.

If this were a movie, this moment would be the climax of the script. It is at this point that Paul finally convinces the men that death has met its match. Communion in the midst of the storm normalizes the storm and all can see and taste and feel that God is in control, that death has lost its sting and that God keeps his promises.

As we navigate through the storm of church planting, a survival mentality can cause us to fear, react and panic. But the raging waves, the pouring rain, the thunder and winds are all normal and natural aspects of church planting. It is the storm that gives us an opportunity to trust God, in our hearts and in our actions.

The Lord Jesus, on the night he was betrayed, took bread, and breaking it, he said, "This is my body, broken for you. Take and eat. And when you do, remember me" (I Cor. 11:24).

Jesus trusted his Father in the midst of his storm and he beckons us to trust him in the midst of ours.

Jesus, You are the Lord of the storm. Please come and be my Prince of Peace. Amen.

Peter Sung

MAY

The Team Leader Principle

*The church planting pastor is most
effective as part of a team on which
he serves as the visionary leader.*

Missional Leadership
Is Not a Solo Effort

So after they had fasted and prayed, they placed
their hands on them and sent them off. ~ Acts 13:3

READING: Acts 13:1-5

Ministry was never a solo journey! This is clearly revealed from the earliest days of Christian ministry as modeled by Christ and the Apostles. Jesus sent the disciples out on their first forays into ministry two by two!

The Antioch church had been greatly blessed when the capable team of Barnabas and Saul came to minister in their midst. The church loved them both. When the Holy Spirit directed the church of Antioch to set apart these two men and send them out, they obeyed, sending off not one, but two, of their finest teachers so others might hear. The Christians at Antioch continued to support the ministry of Paul and Barnabas as they received reports of how God was blessing others through them.

A closer look at the text shows that John also went along as their helper. Right from the beginning, church planting ministry was done by teams. A minimum of two, but teams up to six, are mentioned in Scripture. As churches were planted, a plurality of leaders was appointed to minister in the local congregations (see I Timothy 3 & Titus 1).

The isolation and loneliness of a solitary leader is one of the greatest weapons of destruction in church planting ministry. If this is your struggle, ask the Lord for a team to stand with you. Although working with others may be challenging for pioneering leaders, team ministry has always been God's pattern. As you read the Book of Acts and the rest of the epistles you find this principle reinforced again and again.

Father, Help me to be a team player, a team member and a true team leader. Please give me the team you desire so we accomplish your purposes together for your glory. Amen.

John Bond

Christian Fellowship

*For Peter and all who were with him were astonished at the
catch of fish that they had taken, and so were James and John,
Zebedee's sons, who were Simon's business partners.* ~ Luke 5:9, 10

READING: Luke 5:1-11

The Greek word for the oft-used Christian word, "fellowship" is *koinonia*.
Christians use the word to describe non-activity or non-purpose, e.g., "just
fellowshipping." In reality, *koinonia* means the exact opposite: business
partnership, that is, purpose-driven friendship. Luke 5 tells us that James and
John were in the fishing fellowship with Peter. JRR Tolkien picks up on this
true meaning by titling his novel *The Fellowship of the Ring*. It tells the story of
characters who were natural enemies but become the best of friends through
their common purpose to destroy the Ring of Power.

Indeed, purpose and friendship come together quite perfectly. The blessing
of friendship without purpose often degenerates into a curse that is off balance
and unhealthy while purpose-oriented friendships strike a balance that keeps
them proportionate and appropriate. Business partnerships without friendship
become self-centered, abusive, and corrupt. Friendships without purpose become
insular and idolatrous and eventually disappoint. Move together towards a
common goal and invariably you will move closer to each other; only move
closer to each other and collision and implosion of sorts is inevitable.

God has designed every human being for fellowship because the very
essence of our triune God is a fellowship. What are the implications of this
deep reality for the Christian church? Common are previously outward-looking
churches that have devolved into naval-gazing cliques. Trendy are church
plants that overemphasize mission to the neglect of community and intimate
friendships. Do both well, and you will begin to taste of the raw emotion and
satisfaction of a joy that is made complete.

*God, You created me for love and for mission. May every friendship be guided by
purpose and driven by love. Amen.*

Peter Sung

The Good Shepherd

It was he who gave some to be apostles, some to be prophets,
some to be evangelists, and some to be pastors and teachers, to
prepare God's people for works of service… ~ Ephesians 4:11, 12a

READING: Ephesians 4:1-17

It is very important that we plan out the different stages of a church plant and make sure we have the God-ordained gifts in place or in training. According to these verses in Ephesians, God has given us, within our body of believers, special ministry gifts to train up the saints: apostles or "sent out ones" who establish churches; prophets who receive special messages from the Lord for the congregation; evangelists; pastors and teachers. Each of these giftings has a specially prepared part to play in God's plan for planting churches.

While we are all called to do the work of an evangelist, the drive that a person with this special mantle for evangelism has, can make the initial stages of a church plant most effective. Sometimes, the team leader may not have a pastor's heart for the sheep. Although an evangelist may be totally sincere in his desire to plant the church, the sheep often react against the drive and push that an evangelist often possesses.

We need to be sure that there is a pastor-gifted person to care for the sheep from the beginning. These new believers need the mercy and love and patience that God imparts to the pastor's heart.

Have you identified your ministry gifting? Does your church planting team include both leaders with an evangelistic drive and leaders with a pastor's heart? Your church needs both.

Dear Lord Jesus, You have gifted people for your church in all areas. Please show me those with the evangelistic gifting and pastors to be a part of our church planting team. Please give me good ideas to help people discover their gifts in the body of Christ. Amen.

Ron Thiesen

Recruiting

*Jesus went through all the towns and villages, teaching
in their synagogues, preaching the good news of the kingdom
and healing every disease and sickness. When he saw the crowds, he
had compassion on them, because they were harassed and helpless, like
sheep without a shepherd. Then he said to his disciples, "The harvest
is plentiful but the workers are few." ~ Matthew 9:35–37*

READING: Matthew 9:27-37

"I need to recruit more leaders for my ministry!"

If you are a church planting leader this is a thought you have had and a need you have experienced. It is so helpful to see how Jesus handled this problem when He encountered it in His earthly ministry.

When we see the 'crowds' of people who need all that Christ has to offer, we, too, feel compassion for them. They are harassed and helpless, like sheep without a shepherd. Like Jesus, we know that we must find more leaders to join us in our mission. It is only as we expand our leadership base that we can reach more people for Christ. But how do we find these leaders? What is the first step to take?

Jesus gave us a command that empowers us to recruit more workers. He said, "Ask the Lord of the harvest, therefore, to send out workers into his harvest field" (verse 38).

Recruitment begins with *Asking Prayer*. Ask the Lord of the harvest to send the right leaders to join your 'harvest team.' Pray for these leaders by ministry position in your private daily prayers. Circulate a prayer request to your prayer partners, asking them to pray for God to fill these ministry positions with just the right leaders. After all, your harvest field is a part of God's great harvest field throughout the world.

Lord of the Harvest, Please provide the workers we need to reap the great and precious harvest we see before us now. Amen.

Paul Becker

Fruits of Repentance

*Therefore, he is able to save completely those
who come to God through him, because he always
lives to intercede for them. ~ Hebrews 7:25*

READING: Luke 3:8-14

John the Baptist told the crowds to bear fruits of repentance. They asked, "What shall we do?" He told rich people to give to the naked and the hungry. He told tax collectors not to extort. He told soldiers not to steal or accuse people falsely, and to be content with their wages.

People coming to new faith in Christ have two initial transactions. First, they receive from God a measure of the gift of grace enabling them to believe in the Lord Jesus Christ. This produces faith and the ability to repent, turning their old existence into new life. The process of salvation then operates to produce fruit in two separate areas: faith and action. Sadly, many people are taught that belief in Jesus is only a "decision," one that doesn't require repentance.

The Greek present participle for the word 'come' in Hebrews 7:25 emphasizes a 'continually coming activity.' Yes, faith in Jesus Christ is the only condition God requires for salvation. But true faith doesn't stay there. It produces a change of heart that must grow and be strengthened (John 1:12). True saving faith is an activity that people do. It is not a static belief in the redeeming work of Jesus; rather a loving, self-abandoning commitment that constantly draws us near to him as Lord and Savior.

New believers must understand the depth of this experience. Confession of faith means asking, 'What now shall we do?' then stepping beyond baptismal waters to produce fruits of repentance. Fruit bears seed. Seed bears trees. Trees bear fruit.

O Lord! Let me not forsake the responsibility of helping new believers understand the depth of the commitment they have made. Help me to impart true faith and not a counterfeit faith. Amen.

Christine Cunningham

The Apostolic Leadership Model

It was he who gave some to be apostles, some to be prophets, some to be evangelists, and some to be pastors and teachers... ~ Ephesians 4:11

READING: Ephesians 2:19-22; 4:11-16

It has always been the Lord's desire to use apostolic teams for the building up of the foundation of the church. With today's reading in mind, let me suggest a model that we have used with great success to utilize Christian leaders with these specific spiritual gifts in our association of churches and how we have tried to follow the pattern of Ephesians 4:11.

QUALIFICATIONS:
Leadership team members must demonstrate obedient submission to the authority and power of God. They must show humility and an entering into the fellowship of the sufferings of Jesus. See Philippians 2:1-11; 3:7-11.

FUNCTIONAL DEFINITIONS:
- Apostolic – These leaders function locally and trans-locally in establishing new Christ-centered missional churches and ministries while overseeing their development and the team.
- Prophetic – These leaders discern the mind of Christ in a given situation, and declare that in a Christ-like way to further his mission.
- Evangelistic – These leaders communicate the gospel of Christ in such a way that people respond in faith and discipleship.
- Pastoral – These leaders embody the love of Christ, discipling people to health, wholeness and mission.
- Teaching – These leaders communicate the revealed wisdom of God so that people grow in Christ, becoming mature disciples who are able to lead others to Christ.

How is your team shaped? Do you have a balance of these types of leaders? Are there some you need to add to your team?

Father, Thank you that I don't have to do it all! As I am involved in church planting, I am to do this in the context of an apostolic team. Thank you for your plan to provide strength to the church and to us as leaders. Amen.

John Bond

Woulda, Coulda, Shoulda

*But one thing I do: forgetting what lies behind
and straining forward to what lies ahead, I press on
toward the goal for the prize of the upward call of God
in Christ Jesus. ~ Philippians 3:13b, 14 (ESV)*

READING: I Timothy 1:12-20

One of the blessings of church planting is that you don't have to live with the mistakes of others – you get to make your own! This can lead to deep regret about missed opportunities, bad decisions, wasted time, words we wish we could take back and so on.

Someone shared with me his terrible regret over past sins. He said, "I don't deserve to live." I asked my remorseful friend if he had ever killed someone – he hadn't. The Apostle Paul, however, assisted in the murder of Saint Stephen. If he had allowed it, remorse over that incident alone could have destroyed his ministry. But Paul, the self-confessed "chief of sinners" (I Tim. 1:15) did not allow himself to focus on past errors. He pressed on.

We all make many mistakes, big and small. Of the twenty or so church planting landmines we teach, I have hit virtually every one! Many could have been avoided if I were smarter, more mature, better organized. If I dwell on my missteps, I can become discouraged quickly.

But like Paul, I have one thing to do: press on toward the goal.

Whatever mistakes you have made, in ministry or in your personal life, follow Paul's example: forget the past and press on. Don't drag chains of regret through life and ministry. Confess to Jesus whatever you did that was a sin, and not just a misstep. Make amends if appropriate. But then leave it all at the cross. Learn from your mistakes and press on to victory in Jesus!

Lord, Thank you for your abundant forgiveness. Help me to forget the past and press on for you. Amen.

Mark Alan Williams

Are You an Asset to the Team?

…then make my joy complete by being
like-minded, having the same love, being one
in spirit and purpose. ~ Philippians 2:2

READING: Philippians 2:1-11

How many of us have our favorite team, maybe soccer team or American football team? Teams that are united and understand each other play well together and win. It's fun to watch how each team member does his part, making the team a well oiled machine to win the game.

Oh that it would be so with our church planting teams or church leadership teams! The reality is often that we are a bunch of talented people with personal ambitions and character faults that clash and never really mesh together. Our past unresolved issues drive our present actions in self defense and ambition. It's an established fact in mission circles that interpersonal relationship problems are the number one reason teams fail or people leave the team. So we must learn to get along.

Are you an asset to your team or a liability? Does your input contribute toward the corporate goal or does it further your personal ambition for more leadership recognition or position? Paul urges us to be of like mind with Christ and his goals for the church plant.

Our minds should be on the lives of the people that we are there to reach for Him. We should be of one accord, one mind, having the same love for souls. We should strive to be a useful part of the team, doing our part for the greater good of the team, not for our own vain glory, but rather esteeming others as better than ourselves. Jesus humbled himself and became obedient.

Are you a humble obedient servant on your team, toward your mentor and toward those you wish to win for Christ?

Heavenly Father, Show me any attitudes that hinder my team's efforts and mold me into a useful team member. Amen.

Ron Thiesen

Defensive Trust Battles

*And we know that in all things God works
for the good of those who love him, who have been
called according to his purpose. ~ Romans 8:28*

READING: Job 1

For most of my Christian life I found it easier to exercise faith in God than to trust Him. Hoping to learn more about how to trust God, I noticed that God often used actual Israelite battles to teach His people lessons of trust. Frustrated by the fuzziness of well-wishers who gave me one-size-fits-all advice to simply "Trust God" – no matter what – it has clarified my task enormously to differentiate between offensive trust battles and defensive trust battles.

Defensive trust battles are troubles and hard times that we would never willingly choose. Job's troubles, the disciples terrified by the storm at sea, and Jehoshaphat hearing about three armies headed his way vividly illustrate defensive battles. As church planters, we often face defensive battles such as financial reversals, long waiting seasons while bureaucrats or denominational leaders dither, physical illness or the loss of a crucial core family.

In a defensive trust battle we come face to face with our own inability to control everything. The trust battle focuses mainly on our *reaction* to circumstances we didn't initiate. *The biggest trust issue in most defensive trust battles is whether to accept that God could love us and still allow it to happen.*

Our goal when facing defensive trust battles is to come to the conclusion, as quickly as possible, that even though we may not know why something happened, we will trust that God allowed it to happen to us for reasons that reflect His character and His perfect love for us.

Father, In these hard times that I would never have chosen, help me to trust You by resting in Your love for me and by relying on Your sustaining grace. Amen.

Dionne Carpenter
Adapted from *Trust Training* © 2008

Offensive Trust Battles

*...the Son can do nothing by himself; he can
only do what he sees his Father doing... ~ John 5:19*

READING: Numbers 13:26-14:45

Unlike defensive trust battles that hit us without our permission, we hold the power to choose what to do in an offensive trust battle. In Bible times, believers saw a problem or an opportunity of some kind and had to decide what to do. The critical trust battle was fought on the brink of the action while they debated what to do. They could choose to do nothing, to do something in their own strength, or to do something that obeyed God and relied on God's strength. If they chose to obey God, then their entire endeavor became an offensive trust battle.

The Israelites at Kadesh illustrate this perfectly. When the twelve spies gave their report, the Israelites would have trusted God by obeying His command to commence the conquest of Canaan. (Later, they conversely displayed their lack of trust in God when they launched an attack right after God forbade it.) Jesus fought offensive trust battles in the Garden of Gethsemane, and when He tarried two days after getting Mary and Martha's message regarding Lazarus.

Church planters routinely encounter offensive trust battles as we consider whether or not to follow the call to plant churches, choose where to plant the next one or debate the myriad intermediate action steps.

While defensive trust battles focus on our reactions, offensive trust battles focus on *godly action. The key trust issue in offensive battles is to figure out what it means to obey God.* Are we willing to obey God even if it means taking a risk? And if we launch out by taking a step of obedience, will we stick it out even when the going gets tough?

Father, Help me to trust You by obeying You implicitly and courageously. Amen.

Dionne Carpenter
Adapted from *Trust Training* © 2008

Following Jesus #1
Sacrifice

As they were going along the road, someone said to him, "I will follow you wherever you go." And Jesus said to him, "Foxes have holes, and birds of the air have nests, but the Son of Man has nowhere to lay his head" ~ Luke 9:57, 58 (ESV)

READING: Luke 9:57-62

The late A.W. Tozer is reputed to have criticized "easy-believism" by characterizing it this way: "I want some of your blood for the forgiveness of my sins, but I don't have any intention of following you or obeying you, and now if you'll excuse me I'd like to get on with my life."

Church planters have to fight against the desire to "make decisions" rather than make disciples. We must never compromise the message because of our compassion for the audience.

Jesus' dialogue with this man who promised to follow Him is instructive. If Jesus had been a modern evangelist, He might have congratulated the man for his "decision." Instead Jesus told him he hadn't counted the cost. Essentially He said, "You think you're willing to follow Me wherever I go? You don't have any idea where I'm going. The Son of Man doesn't even have a place to lay His head."

Following Christ takes us out of our "comfort zone." It requires sacrifices of many kinds. Sometimes the sacrifices are financial. Sometimes following Christ requires that we sacrifice some friendship or family ties. Every true disciple of Christ must sacrifice his or her own will and plan for Christ's.

In truth, following Jesus costs us everything. And He is worth it.

Father, Thank You for calling me to follow Jesus. Help me to proclaim the truth to others without compromise. And thank You that any sacrifice is worth knowing Christ! Amen.

Jim Carpenter

Following Jesus #2
Loyalty

To another he [Jesus] said, "Follow me." But he said, "Lord, let me first go and bury my father." And Jesus said to him, "Leave the dead to bury their own dead. But as for you, go and proclaim the kingdom of God" ~ Luke 9:59, 60 (ESV)

READING: Luke 9:57-62

When I was a young Christian I tried to persuade all my friends to become Christians, too. I told them, "All you have to do is pray this prayer...." My heart was right, but I didn't really understand the cost of discipleship.

Jesus challenged this man to follow Him, and at first glance the man seemed to accept the invitation. But he made what seemed like a reasonable request: "Let me first go and bury my father."

The Lord's reply might seem harsh: "Leave the dead to bury their own dead." But the truth is that this man's father was most likely still living. This potential disciple was really saying that he wanted to wait. His priority was to delay – perhaps for years – until his father died, so he could receive his inheritance.

Jesus was calling this man to *undivided loyalty*. Following Christ means putting Jesus first. Christ's words remind us of another hard saying: "If anyone comes to me and does not hate his own father and mother and wife and children and brothers and sisters, yes, and even his own life, he cannot be my disciple" (Luke 14:26). Jesus wasn't contradicting the commandment to "Honor your father and mother," or "love your wife." He was simply demanding undivided loyalty.

Jesus is not just the Gentle Shepherd. He is the King of all Kings. He demands and deserves to have first place in our lives.

Lord Jesus, Teach me to give You the loyalty You deserve, and to lovingly call others to put You first in their lives, too. Amen.

Jim Carpenter

Following Jesus #3
Urgency

*Yet another said, "I will follow you, Lord, but let me
first say farewell to those at my home." Jesus said to him, "No
one who puts his hand to the plow and looks back is fit for
the kingdom of God." ~ Luke 9:61, 62 (ESV)*

READING: Luke 9:57-62

When I was in college I made a trip back to my hometown. An old friend and I spent hours talking in the city park. I shared the gospel and urged him to become a Christian that night. He told me he wasn't ready, but that he was happy to know we could talk again on the subject.

Sadly, many years have passed and I have never had opportunity to speak to him again. While it's true that we can't force people into decisions for Christ, following Jesus is a matter of urgency.

In today's text, a man volunteered to follow Jesus, but he first wanted to say farewell to his family. Jesus replied by emphasizing that the question of becoming His disciple was an eternally urgent matter. Earthly things will always demand our attention and distract us from eternal matters. Jesus said, "You can't put your hand to the plow and look back." Looking back when plowing will only produce a crooked furrow!

He meant that the matter at hand must have your immediate and undistracted attention. Plowing and looking back are incompatible.

Our ministry as church planters compels us to share the gospel. We must never manipulate people into making "decisions" they don't understand, but we must always stress the urgency of settling things with Christ *now*. "Now is the day of salvation" (II Cor. 6:2).

Father, Show me how to present the gospel with urgency. Please bring precious people to a saving knowledge of Jesus. Amen.

Jim Carpenter

Weeping

Jesus wept. ~ John 11:35

READING: John 11:17-44

Years ago, I was in a small gathering of church planters. A young and very successful church planter told the story of his leaders coming to him a few years after the church was begun. They told him: "We feel like you just used us. You didn't love us."

In our presence, this young man confessed, "I knew they were right." He began to sob uncontrollably. He was so successful in the eyes of the church world and yet he was wracked by guilt for using his friends.

As church planters, we rely on God to bring people into our lives who will help us start a new church. Many people find their place and serve sacrificially to see any church get established. We lead them. We tell them what to do. They take our direction. But do we really serve them, like Jesus did? Or do we just expect them to serve us?

JESUS WEPT. It is the shortest verse in the Bible and it has great meaning for me. Jesus was weeping for his friend, Lazarus. When the Jews observed Jesus, they concluded, "See how he loved him!" Jesus loved his friends. He met their needs. He taught them and challenged them and discipled them and gave them a ministry and a mission.

How can we love the ones we lead? We can listen more and talk less. We can encourage and affirm them. We can value them for who they are as individuals. We can find places of ministry and mission for them that truly reflect who God made them to be. We can pray regularly for them and their families. We can endeavor to love the ones we lead in a 'love language' they can receive. What will you do?

Lord, Help those I lead to know without a doubt that I love them. Amen.

Paul Becker

Barnabas
Introduction

Joseph, a Levite from Cyprus, whom the apostles called
Barnabas (which means Son of Encouragement)... ~ Acts 4:36

READING: I Thessalonians 5:11-15

Over the next five days I would like to focus on five practices, based on the life of Barnabas, which will assist you in finding more leaders. One of my favorite Bible characters has long been Barnabas. The poor guy doesn't get much attention in Sunday school classes or sermons. At first glance he is remarkably second fiddle – a mere role-player in a cast of superstars. And even then, he is not in the storyline for long, exiting halfway through the Book of Acts after a testy exchange with the Apostle Paul over staffing priorities for an upcoming mission's trip.

But when it comes to finding and empowering people for ministry in the New Testament church, Barnabas had no equal. I can make the argument (at least from the human perspective) that without his significant contribution and nose for finding, training and developing leaders, there would have been no Apostle Paul, no Book of Romans or any other of Paul's other New Testament letters, no Gentile Christians, and no Gospel of Mark. That's quite a legacy for someone who gets so little attention from theological pundits and preachers.

I've come to the conclusion that those who are most successful at building teams inevitably share with Barnabas the five traits that make up what I call *The Barnabas Factor*. At the same time, those who habitually bemoan a lack of volunteers, low morale and a chronically high turnover rate tend to lack these same five traits.

So what are these powerful traits that made Barnabas so different? And what can we do to build them into our own life and ministry?

Father, Help me to encourage others as Barnabas did. Help us all to become Sons of Encouragement to your glory and for the blessing of the church. Amen.

John Bond

The Barnabas Factor #1
Financial Generosity

*...[Barnabas] sold a field he owned and brought
the money and put it at the apostles' feet. ~ Acts 4:37*

READING: Acts 4:32-37

The first thing we learn when Barnabas bursts onto the scene in Acts 4 is that he had recently sold a field and given the money away to help others. Apparently, this wasn't an isolated act. You see, Barnabas wasn't his real name. It was a nickname that meant *Son of Encouragement.* His given name was Joseph. But when you start selling your stuff to help out others, word gets around.

It's no accident that Barnabas is introduced by a story highlighting his generosity. It's an important window into his character and heart. It's also a key trait found among those who excel at finding and empowering others.

Stingy people tend to be threatened people. They protect and hoard. And not just possessions – they also clutch prestige, power and preferences and view them all as a zero-sum game. If someone else gains, they lose. So they won't let anyone else "win."

Stinginess of heart sabotages healthy growth. It causes us to reject anyone who might crowd into our space or fly higher than we've flown. It creates a hostile ministry environment, particularly targeting our best people, the ones with the strongest leadership potential. It's no wonder they bail out at the first opportunity.

Frankly, if I'm unwilling to share my temporal riches with those in need, that stingy attitude will undermine my efforts to share my true riches with the lost.

That's why I tell church planters that the first step to building a great team is not found in developing better people skills (as important as this is); it's found in developing a heart of generosity. Once that's in place, everything else flows much easier.

Father, Help me be a generous giver in life, resources and ministry. Amen.

John Bond

The Barnabas Factor #2
Quickness to Forgive

*Then Barnabas went to Tarsus to look for Saul, and
when he found him, he brought him to Antioch. ~ Acts 11:25*

READING: Acts 11:19-26

The second thing that strikes us about Barnabas is his readiness to forgive. The next time he shows up in the Book of Acts, he's sponsoring and supporting the ministry of a former arch enemy. It's no stretch to assume that Paul (Saul) had previously jailed and persecuted some of Barnabas' close friends. Saul clearly collaborated in the death of Stephen. That's a lot to get over. Yet Barnabas was willing to look past what Paul had done to see what God was doing. It allowed him to see potential where everyone else saw only past sins. What God forgave, Barnabas forgave – quickly.

Ironically, years later, after John Mark deserted the team, Paul was unwilling to give him the same kind of second chance that Barnabas had offered to Paul. Paul said, "No way," and parted ways from Barnabas. Barnabas forgave John Mark and together they set sail for Cypress (Acts 15:35 – 41).

Yet, on this point, time seems to have vindicated Barnabas, not Paul. Paul eventually commended John Mark for his usefulness for ministry (II Tim. 4:11). And far more importantly, God chose to use John Mark to write the Gospel of Mark – a pretty prestigious assignment. Looks like Barnabas made the right choice to quickly give him a second chance.

Being quick to forgive doesn't mean ignoring sin. It doesn't mean someone gets a platform in the immediate backwash of sin and repentance. But it does mean seeing people through the lens of what God is doing in their life now, rather than through the lens of whatever they may have done in the past.

Father, Help me to reflect your love and forgiveness to others and not to hold a person's past sins against them. Amen.

John Bond

The Barnabas Factor #3
Focus on Anointing – Not Pedigree

So for a whole year Barnabas and Saul met with the
church and taught great numbers of people. ~ Acts 11:26b

READING: Acts 11:19-30

Along with a willingness to forgive whatever God had forgiven, Barnabas also showed remarkable insight into what actually qualifies someone for effective ministry. I'm sure a pulpit committee or ministry assessment team would have quickly pointed out that Paul lacked the prerequisites and pedigree necessary for ministry. Not only did he lack the early church credentials of having walked with Jesus, he also possessed a sordid past, a public record of bad theology and blood on his hands.

Yet, somehow, Barnabas was able to see past all that to dial in on the amazing things God had done and was doing in Paul's life – and the spiritual fruit that backed it up.

Over the years, I've found that many of the most effective volunteers, lay leaders, and staff members of my church are people who likewise don't fit the ministry mold! Whether it's a past sin or failure, a lack of formal education in their specific area of ministry, or simply never having taken the time to jump through all the normally prescribed hoops, these are folks who have been literally cast aside or passed over by other ministries that considered pedigree or education more important than anointing. So we picked up the pieces, and they have blessed us beyond measure.

Nothing clamps a lid over volunteers and leadership development like a rigid insistence that everyone must first pass through some man-made, artificial gauntlet of training or experiences before being allowed to unleash the gifts God has given to them.

Father, Help me to see the potential in people. Help me to be discerning about how and where people can minister. Help me to build teams that make a difference for you. Amen.

John Bond

The Barnabas Factor #4
Defending the Right to be Different

*Some men came down from Judea to Antioch and were teaching
the brothers: Unless you are circumcised, according to the custom taught
by Moses, you cannot be saved. This brought Paul and Barnabas
into sharp dispute and debate with them. ~ Acts 15:1, 2*

READING: Acts 15:1-29

A fourth trait that set Barnabas apart was his willingness to defend those who did things differently – really differently. Twice he stepped forward to aggressively defend ministry to Gentiles. Frankly, I can't imagine that Barnabas was all that comfortable with it. It must have struck him as strange that a large group of people wanted to follow the Jewish Messiah, yet were unwilling to become full-on Jews. It must have been disconcerting to attend an Antioch potluck filled with uncircumcised Christians eating pork sandwiches!

Yes, Jesus said new wine needs new wineskins, but how many of us really believe it – or realize how quickly our new wineskins become old wineskins? Looking back over the years, I'm saddened to realize how often I've seen a fledgling young leader marginalized simply because something about the way they looked, dressed, or approached ministry was uncomfortable to the pastors and leaders in charge. More to the point, it's amazing how often God used that rejection as the impetus to launch a new ministry (sometimes literally down the street) that quickly sucked all the youth, vitality, and future out of the very church that once so dismissively wrote off their new way of doing ministry as inappropriate or "unspiritual."

We'll never find and develop leaders for the future if we insist on judging what God likes by what we like. Barnabas knew better. He judged what God approved by what God blessed, not by his own personal comfort zone.

Father, Help me to be a leader who assesses situations by what you approve and bless regardless of my personal feelings. Amen

John Bond

The Barnabas Factor #5
Willingness to Step Aside And Take Second Place

The proconsul, an intelligent man, sent for Barnabas and Saul...
As Paul and Barnabas were leaving the synagogue... ~ Acts 13:7, 42

READING: Acts 13

Perhaps the most amazing thing about Barnabas was his willingness to step aside and take second place. From the beginning it was always Barnabas and Paul – the mentor and the mentored. Then suddenly, in Acts 13 and 14, everything changes. Paul pulls off a powerful miracle and then delivers an anointed and convicting message. From that point on, Paul was the recognized leader of their mission team, expressed in Acts by referring to them as Paul and Barnabas.

Not many people can go graciously from the top-billing to second place. But, apparently, Barnabas had no problem with it. He must have realized that Jesus wasn't kidding when he said the path to greatness is found in serving others. He must have known that the mission is far more important than our status. But more than just knowing those truths (after all, most pastors and Christian leaders I've known would agree in principle), he was willing to live them out.

Barnabas was obviously more concerned about exalting Jesus than himself. He didn't fight to protect his turf or power, as if it was really his in the first place. He had a passion for expanding God's kingdom whatever the cost, which explains why God was able to use him to find, train and empower some of the greatest leaders in church history – the kind of leaders the fledgling New Testament church so desperately needed, and the same kind of leaders we still so desperately need today.

Father, Help me focus on you and what is best for your work. Help me to remember ministry is not about me, but what is going to be best for the kingdom. Help me to know when to step aside. Amen.

John Bond

A Church Planter Must Look Fear in the Eye and Rebuke It!

*Fear not, for I have redeemed you; I have
summoned you by name; you are mine.* ~ Isaiah 43:1

READING: I Peter 3:12-17

Every church planter must learn to look fear in the eye and rebuke it. The Apostle Paul, the great church planter, reminded Timothy, the young lead pastor: "For God hath not given us the spirit of fear; but of power, and of love, and of a sound mind" (II Tim. 1:7). When an older group of well-intentioned core group leaders calls a meeting to "discuss the direction of the new church," the church planter must look fear in the eye, cling to his call, and not flinch. Being the "keeper of the vision" for a new church plant is sometimes a difficult task. It is amazing how many people have hidden agendas or have a wonderful plan for your new church.

When a "big giver" threatens to leave and take his offerings with him if he doesn't get his way…don't flinch or bat an eye. When a certain worship style is demanded…don't blink! When a stubborn lady threatens to leave the church if her eight-year-old child cannot work in the nursery with her, against leadership policy, hold the back door open for her with a smile! When an off-key soloist wants to be the lead singer or else…choose the "or else." Raising the bar high and striving for excellence is not easy!

In all of this "be gentle, respectful, and not malicious," displaying the love of our Lord Jesus Christ who knew how to rebuke in love, yet died on the cross for sinners.

Loving Father, Help me to never compromise the vision you have given me for my church plant. In my firmness, demeanor, language and attitude, help me to always show the love of Christ without wavering. Amen.

Sam Douglass

Networking with Sister Churches

*...they urgently pleaded with us for the privilege of
sharing in this service to the saints. ~ II Corinthians 8:4*

READING: Acts 15:36

In my years living in Peru as a son of missionary linguists, Wes and Eva
Thiesen, and the years of experience as a church planter along the rivers, I
have noticed one very important principle. A church must be connected in a
living, real way to an organization of churches that will commit to visiting and
encouraging each church and leader on a regular basis. I don't believe there is a
single church that can last if it is isolated from fellowship with others.

In our travels we have often found villages and towns that once had a
church, but, because they lacked a committed network, they got discouraged and
eventually disbanded.

It is one of my highest priorities to establish a network of sister churches
that functions well with a vision for the long term. We teach our leaders the
value of visiting and encouraging sister churches close by, and even encourage
them to visit the ones that are harder to reach.

In our network, the key for me is to invest my life in the individuals that
God has sent to work with us. Jorge has a strong calling and love for the people
out there on the rivers. He in turn is training, discipling and mentoring a dozen
men that each represent a smaller geographical area. In these men and their
wives we hope to cultivate that internal, God-given motivation to plant and
build in the lives of the church leadership in each of the villages around them.

How related are you to other sister churches? How willing are you to be an
encourager to the leadership of other churches?

---

*Father, Please help me to remember that I am part of a larger body of believers who
need encouragement and a friendly visit. Amen.*

Ron Thiesen

When Dream Teams Become Nightmares

When a man's ways please the LORD, he makes even
his enemies to be at peace with him. ~ Proverbs 16:7 (ESV)

READING: Philippians 2:3-13

Serving Jesus with believers is usually a wonderful blessing. But not always. When conflict disrupts a ministry team, it can be discouraging. We expect more. Dream teams can become nightmares.

Jack Walker, a seasoned Christian leader, counseled me about conflict in the ministry workplace. "Keep your expectations low and your hopes high," he said. Part of the problem is that we have the unrealistic expectation that we won't ever encounter conflict. We need to remember that the Apostle Paul, Barnabas and John Mark had conflict and an unhappy separation early in their first missionary church planting journey. Conflict is normal; how we handle it is the key.

He also counseled that the problem is usually not aptitude but attitude – particularly pride and an unwillingness to humble ourselves. Scripture has much to say about humility and serving others, such as, "Do nothing from rivalry or conceit, but in humility count others more significant than yourselves" (Phil. 2:3). "But whoever would be great among you must be your servant, and whoever would be first among you must be slave of all" (Mark 10:43b, 44). Walker emphasized that it is most important for the team to agree together to "speak the truth in love" (Eph. 4:15).

Finally, he told an inspiring story about the well-known reference book, *The Preacher's Outline and Sermon Bible*. Although over a million copies are in print, the author insists on being anonymous. The author also refused an offer of a million dollars royalty for his work, believing God would have him serve with minimal compensation.

I wonder if there would be a lot less ministry conflict if all of us were that selfless and humble.

Lord Jesus, Please help me to humble myself and be the slave of all! Amen.

Mark Alan Williams

The Nearness of God

The LORD is close to the brokenhearted and
saves those who are crushed in spirit. ~ Psalm 34:18

READING: Psalm 34

The Lord is near to those who are brokenhearted and he delivers those who are discouraged. There is such a thing as something I would call a theology of "more-ness." When we feel most alone and abandoned, God is, at that precise moment, most close to us. Grace abounds when sin abounds. Jesus forsakes the ninety-nine to find the one that is lost. Pure and undefiled religion before God the Father is epitomized by ministry to the widows and the orphans.

In a world of fast preaching preachers and fast growing churches, our little struggling church plant can look *less than*. But the opposite is true. God has never been a respecter of persons. It is quite impossible to impress Him. The weaker we are the closer God draws. The fact is, we may be further away from God after we preach a home-run sermon than when after we have had "one of those Sundays."

The kingdom of God is not built on the successes and victories of man but through the power of God which flows through the weak, the foolish and the downcast.

Many Sundays will come and go, as will events, programs and personalities. In a sea of churches and sermons, preachers and choirs, there stands Jesus, the Faithful One, building his church, and the gates of hell will not overcome it. His strength is perfect when our strength is gone. In fact, he never needed it in the first place.

Why so downcast, O my soul? Put your hope in God!

Dear Lord, I confess my discouragement and feelings of failure and inferiority. I rest today under the shadow of your wings. Amen.

Peter Sung

Lord of the Harvest #1
Compassion

*When he saw the crowds, he had compassion for
them, because they were harassed and helpless, like sheep
without a shepherd. ~ Matthew 9:36 (ESV)*

READING: Matthew 9:35-38

Carl (not his real name) had a loving family and a good job, but he also had a secret life. He was addicted to alcohol and he was gambling away huge amounts of money. If he had continued on this self-destructive path he would have lost his family, his livelihood and his health. Ultimately, he would have lost his soul for eternity.

He was no different than the crowds who flocked to Jesus as He preached and taught throughout Galilee. They were "harassed and helpless, like sheep without a shepherd." "Harassed" means mangled, like skin that has been flayed and stripped. These poor sinners were like sheep that had been skinned alive. And they were "helpless" – wounded, cast down and left for dead. Lost people are so lost. They are so desperate and so hopeless. They need a shepherd, but not just any shepherd. They need the one true shepherd – Jesus.

Jesus reacted to these people with compassion. The Greek word implies deep emotion. Sometimes we speak of feeling something "in your gut." He was moved by the sight of these pitiful, hopeless people.

New churches start for many reasons, but the most basic comes from the heart of our Savior – compassion for shepherdless people like Carl.

Carl's wife, Terri, was a baby Christian in our new church, and she started telling her husband about Jesus. I remember being on the phone with Terri late one night, coaching her as she shared the gospel with Carl. The next morning he gave his heart to Christ.

Lord Jesus, Please give me Your heart of compassion for lost people, and may many of them find the Great Shepherd in our new church. Amen.

Jim Carpenter

Lord of the Harvest #2
Urgency

*...therefore pray earnestly to the Lord of the harvest to
send out laborers into his harvest. ~ Matthew 9:38 (ESV)*

READING: Acts 8:1-4

My friend, Bob, a new Christian, was estranged from his dad, who had been a terrible father. But then his father became hospitalized with only a few days to live. Bob had tried to forgive his father, but couldn't. One night he left the hospital thinking it was the last time he would ever see the abusive man who had been a father in name only.

Later that same night Bob felt an urgency to go back. Although his father could no longer speak, Bob took his hand and began to share the gospel. *Dad, squeeze my hand if you want to say yes.*

Dad, you're a sinner, and deserve to go to hell. Squeeze.

Jesus died in your place and paid for all your sins. Squeeze.

Do you want to accept Christ as your Lord and Savior? Squeeze.

Bob led his dad in the sinner's prayer. *Dad, did you pray that prayer?* Squeeze. And with that last squeeze, the man died.

Jesus commanded us to "pray earnestly" because – though the harvest is plentiful – the laborers are few. So beseech the Lord of the harvest to "send out" laborers. "Send out" means to "throw out." The words "ball" and "ballistic" are from this Greek verb.

Bob was "thrown out" to share the gospel. In spite of childhood pain, the Lord of the Harvest thrust him into his father's life at the last moment, and he reaped a harvest.

We must pray that the Lord of the Harvest will "throw out" people from the church into the harvest field. We must teach our people to pray this way. When they do, He may throw them.

Lord, Show me how to teach people to pray this way. And, please, send out workers into Your harvest. Amen.

Jim Carpenter

Lord of the Harvest #3
Sovereignty

...pray earnestly to the Lord of the harvest... Matthew 9:38 (ESV)
I planted, Apollos watered, but God gave the growth. I Corinthians 3:6 (ESV)

READING: Acts 16:6-10

John planted a great church in California. Starting with no core group, he was tireless in prayer and personal evangelism, and within a few years the new congregation was close to 1,000 in attendance. Many hundreds of people came to faith in Christ through the efforts of John's new church.

He stayed and pastored that church for 15 years. Then he sensed God's call to start another church. He moved to a nearby city to establish another congregation. His second plant was also a fine church, but its attendance never exceeded 200. Though people were saved, the number was noticeably smaller than in his first church.

What made the difference? John worked and prayed just as hard in both places. The communities were very similar, and John was a good fit as a leader in both. If anything, John might have expected to plant a larger church because he was a wiser and more experienced church planter the second time.

The truth is that the harvest is up to the Lord. That's why Jesus called him "Lord of the harvest." As Paul said, we labor, but it is God who gives the growth. That's why the Holy Spirit forbade Paul's church planting team to speak the word in one region, and they weren't allowed to go to another. Instead, the Sovereign Lord of the Harvest sent a call to a brand-new region through the Macedonian vision.

Bigger doesn't necessarily mean God's blessing. Church planting demands prayer, hard work and careful assessment of leaders and community. But in the end the harvest is the Lord's.

Lord of the Harvest, Grant me persistence and effectiveness. I trust You to give the growth as You see fit. Amen.

Jim Carpenter

The Reluctant Leader

*Who am I that I should go to Pharaoh and bring the
people of Israel out of Egypt? ~ Exodus 3:11 (GW)*

READING: Exodus 3:1-4:17

Not all great Bible leaders led because they had volunteered. In fact, some definitely fought the call. God called Moses by name in a burning bush. He promised a land flowing with milk and honey and clearly commissioned him in Exodus 3:10.

What was Moses response? "Who am I that I should go to Pharaoh and bring the people of Israel out of Egypt?" God asserted His authority and identity by saying, "I AM that I AM" (3:14). But Moses wasn't satisfied. When God validated His message to Moses by miracles, Moses thought up another excuse: "Please, Lord, I'm not a good speaker. I speak slowly, and I become tongue-tied easily" (4:10 GW). Wow!

Gideon was another reluctant leader. When the Lord told him that he would rescue Israel, he replied, "Excuse me, sir! How can I rescue Israel? Look at my whole family. It's the weakest one in Manasseh. And me? I'm the least important member of my family" (Judges 6:15 GW). Then he demanded a sign, which the Lord graciously granted. Later he again asked for a sign: a wet then a dry fleece test.

The Apostle Paul was not the team leader at first when he and Barnabas left Antioch, witnessed by Barnabas' name being first. It took time for his leadership to manifest (see Acts 13). By contrast, the Apostle John mentioned someone overly eager to lead, named Diotrephes "who loves to be in charge" and was causing problems (III John 9, 10).

Are you a reluctant church planting leader? You're in great company! Don't be discouraged, keep leading anyway. God loves to turn the meek into the mighty.

Lord, I, too, am sometimes reluctant to lead. Help me to lead anyway when you ask it of me. Amen.

Mark Alan Williams

Good and Bad Starts

*They went out from us, but they did not really
belong to us. For if they had belonged to us they would
have remained with us... ~ I John 2:19a*

READING: I John 2:18-27

I don't know the statistics, but I suspect that many churches have started as a result of a church split or someone leaving and going to start their own church. Sometimes, the leadership team will attempt to "save the day" by belatedly bestowing their blessings on people or groups that were leaving anyway. However, the circumstances surrounding the plant's origin suggest a lack of understanding of the principles of submission and authority.

Sometimes, a person who was not converted in your church may bring baggage from another church and eventually they may move on again. We have had these experiences and, in every case, the one who left to start their own church was someone who started out in another vision. Church plants produced from that sort of division or rebellion encounter much difficulty. They have issues that have to be dealt with later and likely reap what they have sown.

As we develop a church planting team, we need to take pains to know the team members, their motivations, and their history in order to avoid serious problems. Here are some good questions to bear in mind:

- Are they native sons from your own church? Do they have the same heart for the church plant and your methodology?

- Have they been taught the principles of submission and authority? Do they have a proven track record in the local church of walking by these principles?

- Are they doing this for monetary gain as hirelings or are they truly called?

Dear Heavenly Father, Please give me patience to discern the people that you want to work with me on this church plant. Help me not to get in too much of a hurry. Amen.

Ron Thiesen

Receiving the Lord's Command #1

*At the Lord's command they encamped, and at the
Lord's command they set out. ~ Numbers 9:23a*

READING: Numbers 9:15-23

Pastor Ralph (not his real name) served as assistant pastor at the church where Jim did his seminary internship. We both respected Pastor Ralph a great deal, admiring his good work ethic and his commitment to Christ.

One morning during his quiet time, Ralph thought he received a powerful word from the Lord illuminating a devotional by Oswald Chambers. He thought God was moving him on to a senior pastor position. Within hours Ralph tendered his letter of resignation, before so much as informing his wife, and then began sending out resumes and feelers. Needless to say, his family suffered through many unnecessarily austere months before he found his next job.

While Ralph's instant obedience was commendable, it was short-sighted. Based on the six times that Jim and I have found ourselves in Ralph's position of hearing God's word to move on, here's a bit of wisdom we've gleaned. In hindsight, we noticed that God usually gave us a clear hint when our tenure at each church plant or ministry position was winding to a close, often a year or more before we actually left.

The wise response was to immediately and seriously wait upon the Lord for further instructions: When? Where? How? We watched for open doors and perked our ears for unfolding revelation. God's gracious hint hit us differently depending on whether we loved our current ministry or suffered in a painful place. That interval, whether long or short, gave us time to send out feelers and resumes, opportunity to wrap up loose ends and space to make our peace with His will.

We're grateful that He gave us ample time to pack our tents before leading us to our new campsite.

Lord, I trust You to lead me. Help me to walk at Your pace. Amen.

Dionne Carpenter

Receiving the Lord's Command #2

*Now an angel of the Lord said to Philip, "Go south to the road –
the desert road – that goes down from Jerusalem to Gaza." ~ Acts 8:26*

READING: Acts 8:4-8; 26-40

OK, now let's look at this topic from another perspective. Yes, normally it's much wiser to wait patiently on God as He gradually unfolds His will about moving on to our next ministry position. But, of course, we can all think of times when God moved someone suddenly and without any hint of warning. Those sudden moves may be just as God-ordained.

It reminds me of our experience in Iowa. When denominational upheaval shut down our church planting project in California, we transitioned using just such an unfolding timetable as I've described. God unmistakably led us to Iowa, as we supposed, to set up a state-wide church-planting program and to plant the first of several churches in the Des Moines area.

But Jim hit one road block after another completely beyond his control. Within a year, flexible to God's Plan B, Jim joined the staff of a thriving young church with a like-minded pastor who shared Jim's vision for regional church planting. Suddenly, that pastor had a moral failure. Because God had just placed Jim on that church staff, God used him to lead that shell-shocked church through their difficult ordeal. Jim seamlessly served as their stabilizing interim pastor until they found a permanent pastor.

Our experience gave us greater empathy for the sense of whiplash Philip must have felt when God plucked him out of his thriving ministry in Samaria, dropped him into a strategic encounter with one man and then whisked him away afterwards.

Take comfort if God moves you suddenly, whether by illness, family or political crisis, or career change. Nothing happens to the yielded servant of God by accident.

Father, Help me to trust Your unseen sovereignty even over abrupt changes. Amen.

Dionne Carpenter

JUNE

The Mission Principle

*The central work of the new church will
always be to help people put their trust in Christ
and grow into maturity as His followers.*

Keep the Main Thing... the Main Thing

...do the work of an evangelist... ~ II Timothy 4:5

READING: II Timothy 4:1-5

A few months ago a young church planter called me and cried, "HELP! I don't know what I am doing wrong. Can you fly out and sit down with me to assess my situation?" I could not imagine what was happening. He had a strong mother church that had paid his salary for a year, rented him a state of the art facility, given him six strong families as a launch team, bought his sound system and his computerized video equipment, paid for huge mailers and a cutting edge website with all of the bells and whistles.

Upon arriving at the airport, I quickly found the root problem when I asked him the BIG QUESTION: "In the last fifteen months since you launched your church how many families do you have in your core group?" He had "grown" the church to ONE remaining family. I was shocked, and followed up with the obvious second question: "How many people have you led to Christ in the past fifteen months?" Answer: ZERO.

A person recently asked me "What is the ONE THING a church planter must do?" Above all else, he must do "the work of an evangelist." One can have the best web site, marketing strategy, facility and location, but the lead pastor must lead by example and do "the work of an evangelist." The celebration of transformed lives is essential to building momentum within a church plant.

Just as Paul reminded Timothy, the young church pastor of Ephesus, to "do the work of an evangelist," even though Timothy probably didn't have the "gift of evangelism," the church planter MUST do the work of an evangelist.

Lord Jesus, Do your work in and through me to make it hard for people to go to hell from my church field. Amen.

Sam Douglass

Christ the Power and Wisdom of God

For Jews demand signs and Greeks seek wisdom, but we
preach Christ crucified, a stumbling block to Jews and folly to Gentiles,
but to those who are called, both Jews and Greeks, Christ the power of
God and the wisdom of God. ~ I Corinthians 1:22-24 (ESV)

READING: I Corinthians 1:18-25

I was sharing the gospel with a young couple who came to me, asking to be married. More than marriage and more than one another, they needed Christ, I told them. Though both had religious backgrounds, it seemed neither was a Christian. Neither seemed ready to repent and believe in Christ.

"Suppose after you leave my office, would you know what to do if you feel God calling you to become a Christian? How would you respond? What would you do?" I asked.

The young woman said, "I guess I'd say I was sorry for my sins. But everyone is a sinner." And her boyfriend responded, "I guess I would just give my life to Christ."

They spoke some of the right words, but there was no real spark of understanding.

When we share Jesus with others, sometimes it doesn't make sense to them. Paul said that some people want to see miraculous signs, and others are seeking wisdom. For them, the simple message that Jesus died in the place of sinners is offensive or foolish.

Our job as church planters is to share this message faithfully, counting on God to work a miracle in people's hearts. Because when God is at work, the foolishness of our preaching is transformed, and Jesus is revealed as God's power and wisdom!

Lord, Thank You for the privilege of proclaiming Christ. Please work Your miracles in the hearts of people, and call them to Yourself. Amen.

Jim Carpenter

Saving Faith

*If you confess with your mouth, "Jesus is Lord,"
and believe in your heart that God raised him from
the dead, you will be saved. ~ Romans 10:9*

READING: Romans 10:5-13

Faith in faith does not save us. Faith in God does not save us. What Christians believe is very specific. There is a lot of generic and even Godward faith all around us but the Bible is clear: If we confess with our mouths that Jesus is Lord and believe in our hearts that God raised him from the dead, we will be saved.

General graduation prayers abound. There are an abundance of godly sermons preached on Sundays. Weekdays are filled with spirituality. But we preach Christ and him crucified because we are not ashamed of the Gospel for it is the power of God for salvation for all who believe. We believe that if we lift up Jesus, he will draw men, women and children unto himself.

But for many, Jesus is a stumbling block, or at least he makes things inconvenient or socially awkward. In some situations, saying the name "Jesus" is politically unhelpful or at least conversation ending. There is something to be said about being wise and relationally savvy.

The reality is that God has given us the glorious knowledge of God in the face of Christ, and unless we lift him up and make him known, God the Father and his love will remain unknown and obscured. Jesus is the way, the truth and the life. No one comes to the Father but by him.

Preachers, if you must preach, preach Christ.

Jesus, You humbled yourself and became a servant. You submitted to death, even death on a cross. Therefore, God has exalted you above all else, and I do, too. Amen.

Peter Sung

God Is Not Willing That Any Should Perish. Are You?

*The Lord is not slow in keeping his promise, as some
understand slowness. He is patient with you, not wanting anyone
to perish, but everyone to come to repentance. ~ II Peter 3:9*

READING: II Peter 3

Church planting is founded upon, its reason for being, and its overriding purpose is to see people repent and believe on the Lord Jesus Christ. In II Peter 3:9, Peter reminds us that God's heart is that none should perish. We should make it our goal to motivate and train another vital group of evangelists within our church to reach the masses and individuals that have yet to make a commitment to Christ.

When we were first called to plant churches in the Amazon River region, I made a trip to the area to evaluate the situation and hear God's heart. I was astounded that after many decades of *the church* being nearby in Iquitos, the outlying communities were mostly still unreached with the gospel. As we made evangelistic trips to reach a few villages it became urgent to me to get to as many of the villages as possible to tell them about Jesus.

With help from evangelistic groups that come in the summer months we began evangelizing in the villages, offering evangelism meetings in the evenings and a new believer's class and children's ministry the following mornings.

God put a strategy on our hearts to come back every three months to train spiritual leaders for each village. As a result, there have now been, by the grace of God, over fifty churches planted with leadership from their own villages.

God is not willing that any should perish. What is your commitment to seeing that everyone has a chance to know Christ?

Lord, Please give me your heart for the lost, your passion to see the unreached come to know you, and show me the way. Amen.

Ron Thiesen

The Blessing of Babies

Blessed is the man whose quiver
is full of them… ~ Psalm 127:4a

READING: Psalm 127

We have three grandchildren between the ages of two and four. There is nothing quite as wonderful as seeing the world fresh through their eyes – to watch them experience a dainty lady bug tickling their arm for the first time. Or see their eyes get wide as saucers the first time they see the ocean. Or hear them sing "Amazing Grace" for the first time. We treasure their first words or first wobbly steps.

As adults, it's so easy to get all caught up in the rat race and the minutia of things that seem important – so terribly urgent. We can get tied up in knots over the most esoteric things, as if straightening out the error on our bank statement was all that matters in life.

And then along comes a toddler who asks us to tie her shoelace or read her a book. Suddenly, our priorities shuffle back into the true verities and we become young at heart.

It's the same way with baby Christians. We old-timers can get pretty stuffy and jaded, arguing about how many angels can dance on the head of a pin, or thinking that Christianity is mainly about being on the right church committee.

Then along comes a baby Christian, wide-eyed at his first answer to prayer or astonished by the wonderful story of Jesus or full of questions about how to witness to his non-Christian friends. With a lump in our throat we recall the joy when we first saw the light in our Savior's smile.

Hanging out with baby Christians and helping them grow keeps us in touch with the essentials of our faith. And all's right with the world, because these messy, inquisitive babies are the future.

Father, Thank You for the blessing of babies. May our churches be full of them. Amen.

Dionne Carpenter

Life in Christ

Jesus said, "For the Son of Man came to seek
and to save what was lost." ~ Luke 19:10

READING: Luke 19:1-10

Bishop Yindi, a prolific and gifted church planter in Tanzania, was taking me to visit a new Maasai church plant near Kilimanjaro. As we were driving there, we came upon a terrible accident. At a bridge, two mini-vans had collided.

As we approached, I saw a dead man on the bridge. His face was pressed against the pavement. There was blood on his head. His limbs were contorted. He was utterly lifeless.

We offered our help but there was nothing we could do. We drove on to the Maasai church, off the paved road onto a dirt road and through the savannah to a small structure with concrete walls and a tin roof held up by some thick wooden branches. The sound of singing and great rejoicing came from the church. There were Maasai men and women and children standing and singing and praising God. It was heaven on earth in Africa!

Our driver, a young Muslim named Abdullah, walked through the church door and began to join in the celebration. When it came time for me to preach, I told these precious people that God loved them and that I loved them. I told them about the dead man on the bridge. I said, "If he was a Christian, he graduated to heaven today. If he wasn't a Christian, he finds himself separated from God for all eternity. He is in hell. His opportunity to make a decision for Christ is over. We must saturate Tanzania and the world with churches to reach precious people for Christ like that man on the bridge."

Church planting is the best way to save the most people around the world for Christ.

Father, Help us to share your good news to rescue the lost. Amen.

Paul Becker

Unlikely Target

He told her, "Go, call your husband and come back." ~ John 4:16

READING: John 4:1-26

The original *Sent One* is Jesus, sent by his Father, and so he sends us. Who did Jesus target? Filled with love and sense of mission, Jesus made it a point to stop by Samaria and engage in dialogue with a rejected and confused Samaritan woman. Her history was filled with pain and brokenness, but Jesus refused to judge her as others had done (and as his own disciples would soon do upon their return). Why not? Because he knew her full story of shame and rejection.

On top of being a Samaritan and a woman, by the time Jesus found her, she had been abandoned five times by five husbands. Love had evaded her all her life. The living water she needed most was Love. But where would she find such water? Nowhere. It had to find her. Jesus saw the whole person and loved the whole person.

The world says that love is blind. Jesus shows us that love does not see less but more. And acceptance is the door through which transformation begins.

A primary purpose of church planting is to target and reach those that are often and easily missed by other more established churches. Evangelism is a lifeline for church plants in many respects. Beyond those who can give back to the church, do you see as Jesus sees? Do you see through Jesus' eyes of love, through fearless, condition-free acceptance of the least, the last and the lost? Jesus still goes out of his way to target the Samaritan woman, the widow and the orphan – through you and your church. Love must find them. You must find them.

Jesus, I confess my fearful and calloused heart. You are the Lord of church planting. May you be the Lord of my church plant. Help me to see as you see. Amen.

Peter Sung

Why God Has No Grandchildren #1

Truly, truly, I say to you, unless one is born
again he cannot see the kingdom of God. ~ John 3:3 (ESV)

READING: John 3:1-8

This is probably a familiar saying: God has no grandchildren. *Physical* life is passed on when we have children; they grow up, marry, and have children – our grandchildren. But *spiritual* life from God doesn't work that way. Spiritual life isn't automatically passed on when God's spiritual children have physical babies. You can be born again, but your children may not be.

Jesus revealed to Nicodemus why God has no grandchildren. If they are ever to see heaven, all people need an inner change that is *impossible* for them to make: "you *cannot* see the kingdom of God (v. 3)." "You *cannot* enter the kingdom of God (v. 5)."

Maybe you have heard preachers describe "three steps to being born again." But no one can engineer their own birth. And even more impossible, people don't produce their own spiritual life. New birth is not within their control.

It is right to command that sinners repent and believe, but wrong to think that becoming a Christian is just about praying a prayer or making a decision, as if it was all a matter within the sinner's control.

As Paul said: "But a natural man does not accept the things of the Spirit of God, for they are foolishness to him; and he cannot understand them, because they are spiritually appraised" (I Cor. 2:14).

How can any "natural man" repent and believe in Christ? Answer: he cannot, on his own. Cannot. Every converted soul is a miracle of God. The Spirit of God must do a work within each one to make that person a new child of God. Not a grandchild.

Thank You, Father, for the miracle of the new birth. Please work this miracle in great abundance in this community. Amen.

Jim Carpenter

Why God Has No Grandchildren #2

*The wind blows where it wishes and you
hear the sound of it, but do not know where it comes
from and where it is going; so is everyone who
is born of the Spirit. ~ John 3:8 (ESV)*

READING: John 3:1-8

God has no grandchildren, because each person needs a radical internal transformation (new birth) that must come directly from the Lord Himself. It is not passed on derivatively by human parents.

The beauty and wonder of the new birth is easy to miss in the day-to-day efforts we make at evangelism. Reaching people does require hard work, knocking on doors, and patiently sharing the gospel. But God's miracle-work is what Jesus stressed in His discourse here with Nicodemus.

Why did He speak of "wind?" Because the word "wind" in Greek is the same as the word "spirit." Jesus used the wind to illustrate three miraculous truths about being born again. First, *sovereignty.* "The wind blows where it wishes." We owe our new birth to God, plain and simple.

Second, *impact.* "You hear the sound of it." We can't measure the Spirit's work with an MRI machine or by an X-ray. But when someone is born again, there is an impact. You can't see it with your physical eyes, but you can see the unmistakable impact of God's Spirit.

And third, *mystery.* We "do not know where it comes from and where it is going." The new birth is mysterious. It is not controllable by human beings – either by lost sinners or by determined church planters. It takes a sovereign work of God's grace. And when new life happens, it is a miracle!

God has no grandchildren – only gloriously, miraculously born again children.

Father, Thank You for the new birth. May our new church never take for granted the new birth! Amen.

Jim Carpenter

The Biotic Potential for Churches to Grow

I planted the seed, Apollos watered it, but
God made it grow. ~ I Corinthians 3:6

READING: Mark 4:26-29

Biotic potential is the inherent capacity of an organism or species to reproduce and survive. Since God is the Lord of our vision for new church plants, our churches must bear results, grow, reproduce and survive. However, challenges and obstacles, as well as some of our practices, may tend to blind church planters from seeing this inherent potential for growth and reproduction.

The church plant is constituted by God's people coming together for God's purpose. God has vested spiritual gifts and authority on every believer for the purpose of fulfilling His mission. His Word has life, His gifts are given for the common good, His people are commissioned, His presence is guaranteed, His Spirit is convicting the world, and His coming for the finality of His Church is irrevocable. Biotic potential must make every church plant grow.

Then what is our role in this endeavor? Our role is not to be the seed of our plants; but rather to release the God-given biotic potential within the church plant. Paul, who had this insight, said "*God* makes it to grow."

Do we desire to build a community of God in our church plants? How much pre-eminence do we give to God's word as we disciple clueless people into Christ-like disciples? Are we contented to attract crowds or do we fashion disciples of the Lord Jesus? Are we utilizing the God-vested spiritual gifts within His people to grow His Church or do we permit Christians to remain merely spectators of attractive church-gymnastics? Do we merely preach on the Great Commission or do we execute it by reaping a harvest of reproducing disciples?

Lord, Help me to see Your inbuilt growth potential in all my church plants and to do nothing detrimental as I plant this church. Amen.

R. Jayakumar

The Revelation of God's Love

...and to know this love that surpasses
knowledge – that you may be filled to the measure
of all the fullness of God. ~ Ephesians 3:19

READING: Romans 8:9-15

God's love is so wide, so high, so deep, and so long, that Ephesians tells us it surpasses knowledge. We cannot come to know it on our own. Books, other people, experience – nothing of this world can cause us to learn of the love of God. If it is unlearnable, how can we come to understand it?

God's love is alien; it is out of this world. God the Father had to break into our world and reveal it to us. The love of God in Christ is nothing less than revelation. In Romans 8, Paul tells us that this love is so other (holy) that God must put his Spirit in us and cause us to cry out, "Abba Father."

The love of God the Father – demonstrated on the cross and made alive to our hearts by the Holy Spirit – these are potent truths that we preachers are called to proclaim.

There is no preaching good enough, no argument savvy enough, and no personality charming enough. The application of God's love to the human heart is a divine work that only the Holy Spirit can do. Cleverness of speech was insufficient for the apostle Paul and it is insufficient for us. We who are dead in our transgressions are made alive to God by the power of God, and on this work of God we are wholly dependent.

Prepare your sermons diligently and faithfully. But pray and trust even harder knowing that the most important work is done by the Holy Spirit. Has not God made foolish the wisdom of this world lest the cross of Christ be emptied of its power?

God, Awaken me to your love by the power of your Holy Spirit. Amen.

Peter Sung

"I Have Many People in this City"

*One night the Lord spoke to Paul in a vision: "Do
not be afraid; keep on speaking, do not be silent. For I am
with you, and no one is going to attack and harm you, because
I have many people in this city." ~ Acts 18:9, 10 (ESV)*

READING: Acts 18:1-11

Church planting can be a fearful thing.

We are often called to plant churches far from home. We may have little money and few contacts in the community, and we may feel the pressure of not only starting the church, but also providing for our families.

Sometimes we start churches where there is outright hostility to the gospel. Church planting places us on the "front lines" of spiritual warfare. The devil hates Christ, His gospel and His church.

Thank God we have the witness of church planters who have gone before us, like the Apostle Paul. He knew the personal price of starting churches in enemy territory. He was hated, slandered, beaten and left for dead.

But through it all he knew God was in control. In the Greek city of Corinth, Paul faced a society where many cultures and religions mingled. Pagan immorality and idolatry were rampant as well as a prideful trust in the human intellect.

But the Lord reassured him: "Do not be afraid; keep on speaking, do not be silent. For I am with you, and no one is going to attack and harm you, because *I have many people in this city.*"

God has a plan for your church plant! When God calls us even to hostile territory, we're under His protection. And the Lord of the harvest knows the ones He is calling to Himself: "I have many people in this city!"

Thank You, Lord, that this church is Your project. Please show me the people You are calling to Yourself. Amen.

Jim Carpenter

Messages in the Wilderness

... in the high priesthood of Annas and Caiaphas,
the word of God came to John, the son of Zacharias,
in the wilderness. ~ Luke 3:2 (NASB)

READING: Luke 23:32-43

Bill lives in a building guarded by electric doors and surrounded by razor wire topped walls. Rolls of razor wire coil on the ground between the wall and building. He lives in a high security prison serving several life sentences. He will never again be on the outside of the razor wall. He is a serial killer. He cannot even remember how many he murdered.

Bill is also a Christian. God has so changed his life that he works as prison steward and librarian. Bill beams when he shares the love of Jesus with fellow prisoners. He graciously accepts his prison condition believing it is God's sovereign plan for his life, enabling him to speak God's word to some of the roughest criminals in the prison system.

John the Baptist was the son of a priest who cleared the way for the Lord in the wilderness. God's word was not lost in John's wilderness, and it is not bound in the confines of a prison. God's word came to Ezekiel among the captives by the river of Chebar and to the apostle John on the isle of Patmos. It came to Bill in his prison cell.

Wherever we are, when we speak the word of the Lord to others, history will be impacted through changed lives. Epic history may not change, but when the destiny of one life is impacted by God's word, we are history changers.

When we feel the word you have given us is not changing lives, Father, remind us of the lives of those who have spoken your words and changed the course of life and history. Help us to speak the word you give us so we can be world changers. Amen.

Christine Cunningham

Such Were Some of You

*And such were some of you. But you were
washed, you were sanctified, you were justified in the
name of the Lord Jesus Christ and by the Spirit
of our God. ~ I Corinthians 6:11 (ESV)*

READING: I Corinthians 6:9-11

One day during the planting of my first church, I met a young woman named Mary (not her real name) and asked her if she would be interested in our new church. In reply she asked me a question: "What would you think if prostitutes and homosexuals and drunks started coming to your church?"

"I think that would be great," I said. "We're starting a church for people just like that."

Mary then explained that she worked as a bartender in a topless bar. She and her husband were friends with the kind of rough people she had mentioned. Within a few weeks I started a Bible study with Mary, her husband Bob, and two of their close friends. All of them turned from their sins and trusted Christ to save them! Our young church welcomed Mary and Bob, loved them, and helped them to grow spiritually. Mary quit her job in the bar and eventually became my secretary.

In I Corinthians 6, Paul lists a whole series of sinful lifestyles that are incompatible with the kingdom of God. But then he gives praise to God's saving grace by saying: "And such were some of you. But you were washed, you were sanctified, you were justified in the name of the Lord Jesus Christ and by the Spirit of our God."

We start new churches to reach people who desperately need the Savior. And those are the people Jesus saves!

Father, Thank You for Your amazing grace! Please help our church to reach the lost, the forgotten and the desperate, to Your glory. Amen.

Jim Carpenter

Power in Persecution

If they persecuted me, they will persecute you also. ~ John 15:20a

READING: John 15:18-21

Countries like India face increasing persecution. This wave will eventually reach every nation. Christian persecution started with Jesus himself. *Christian Martyrs of the World* lists thousands of brutal killings throughout the history of the Church. Christian persecution didn't slow the growth of the Christian faith during the first few centuries after Christ. Even as its early leaders died horrible deaths, Christianity flourished throughout the Roman Empire.

Persecution is the result of the non-compromising and non-conforming stand of the adherents of the Truth toward the pattern of the world. Wherever persecution becomes severe it is an indicator that Truth is actively penetrating that region.

Our fellowship with Christ cannot be thwarted by any degree of persecution (Rom. 8:35 – 39). Persecution is a light to be dawned on His people to prove to the world that Christians are the conquerors of every pain.

Increasing persecution is the last key item we need to face on this earth before we enter into the Eternal Kingdom. Persecution is an indicator for the "last days" (II Tim. 3:1 – 5, 10 – 14). A sea of people will be found in heaven through our church planting efforts (Rev. 7:9 – 17).

Since persecution is painful, often Christians react in defensive ways. It leads them sometimes even to politicize the issue. A church planter should view persecution through an eschatological lens. Our task is to prepare the Church for persecution; not to prevent it.

Martyrdom and the Mission of God are inseparable, linked together within the Church by unbreakable chains. Jesus forewarns us of this in John 16:1 – 4 so that His people will not stumble when persecution breaks out. The Church must keep witnessing for the Truth even in midst of severe persecution (Rev. 2:8 – 10; 3:8 – 10).

Father, Help me to face persecutions with courage and faith in your Word. Amen.

R. Jayakumar

From the Jungle to Jesus

*And we know that for those who love God
all things work together for good, for those who are called
according to his purpose. ~ Romans 8:28 (ESV)*

READING: Romans 8:18-30

We were planting a new Hispanic church when a man appeared with his live-in girlfriend. In his home country he had fought as a rebel against government forces, suffering many wounds for his cause only to be driven to switch sides because of hunger, and finally fleeing to the U.S.A. Following the Bible Study that night, they both received Christ as their personal Savior. That evening he decided to rent another apartment for his girlfriend and remain separated until they got married. They were later married, baptized, and worked very diligently through a period of discipleship training.

He soon expressed God's calling upon his life to help with the new Hispanic church plant. Together we evangelized, taught, visited and just served our Lord together. Our small group grew steadily and soon we had believers from ten different Spanish-speaking countries! My friend became the leader, pastor and friend to all. It was beautiful to watch him and his wife grow in faith and knowledge as they served together.

My wife and I moved to a different city to begin another Hispanic ministry. We were thankful for the blessing of knowing this fine servant. About a year later I received a call telling me that he had been badly burned in an apartment fire. He died a week later.

Yet he had learned to love and serve. People came to Christ during his funeral and we were reminded of Romans 8:28. He truly loved God and was called to His purpose.

Dear Heavenly Father, Please use our present sufferings for Your glory and help us trust You to accomplish Your purposes. Amen.

Buddy Johnson

Kingdom

*…The people were looking for [Jesus] and when they came
to where he was, they tried to keep him from leaving them. But he
said, "I must preach the good news of the kingdom of God to the other
towns also, because that is why I was sent." ~ Luke 4:42, 43*

READING: Luke 4:31-44

If Jesus had been concerned about just that one group of people, he would
have stayed in that one town. But he kept moving. He had a *Kingdom mindset*.
That is why He felt compelled to preach the good news to other towns, too. That
is why He was sent.

Jesus taught us to be committed to the Kingdom of God. He wants us
to be concerned with more than the one church to which we belong. We must
commit to spread the Kingdom of God throughout our world.

North America seems to have lost much of its *Kingdom mindset*, which
may explain why it is not experiencing rapid growth. However, according
to the Dawn Report, 49% of the people in the world live in nations that are
experiencing the rapid growth of the Kingdom of God. Most of the Christian
leaders in these nations have a pervasive *Kingdom mindset*. They want to see Jesus
come here, there and everywhere.

We saw this at Amsterdam 2000 when many African leaders talked with
us. They urged us to come to Africa to train their leaders, so that more churches
would be planted and the Kingdom of God would be expanded. These leaders
from developing nations had a *Kingdom mindset*.

Let me challenge you to do a personal study of the 'Kingdom of God' in
the Gospels. Your thinking will be transformed. You will see that there is so
much more that Jesus wants for you…The Kingdom of God.

---

*Dear Father, Give me a Kingdom mindset and change my priorities to love what You
love. Amen.*

Paul Becker

Manna Time #1
Recognizing Manna Time

*...thin flakes like frost on the ground appeared on the desert
floor. When the Israelites saw it, they said to each other, "What is it?"
For they did not know what it was. ~ Exodus 16:14b, 15*

READING: Exodus 16:1-15

To date, my husband and I have been in ministry for over thirty years. Church planting frequently takes planters to the razor edge of financial uncertainty. Often we didn't know at the beginning of the month how we'd pay bills due by the end of that month.

At first this used to scare the wits out of me. However, as time passed, I began to realize that we were always held safely within two alternating types of time that I eventually dubbed "Regular Time" and "Manna Time." During *Regular Time* God provides for His own through normal, predictable streams of income like jobs, regular paychecks, financial supporters, investments, inheritance or whatever. During these *Regular Times*, God's provision comes to us <u>indirectly</u>, through the ordinary economic channels that everyone depends on – believers and unbelievers alike.

However, during *Manna Time*, those normal, predictable streams of income dry up, at least temporarily. Supporters don't send what they promised, side jobs end or the bills far exceed our resources to pay them. During *Manna Time* God provides for us <u>directly</u>, using non-traditional methods like serendipities, so-called coincidences, the divinely compelled kindness of others and outright miracles.

Jim and I emphatically testify that God ALWAYS provided what we absolutely needed. It took me a long while to recognize when God had switched us into *Manna Time*, longer still to learn the precious lessons of manna – lessons I look forward to sharing here in the "Manna Time" entries sprinkled throughout the coming months.

Father, Increase my confidence that You will ALWAYS take care of us. Help me to begin to recognize manna when You send it. Amen.

Dionne Carpenter

Manna Time #2
Spotting Manna

When the Israelites saw [manna], they
said to each other, "What is it?" ~ Exodus 16:15

READING: Numbers 11:7-9

Manna usually falls as gently and silently as it did that first morning when it hid beneath the morning dew. It is amazingly easy to miss it.

The first time I knew for sure that we had been in *Manna Time* was during our first church plant. Early in February we found out that we owed an additional $1,000 for federal taxes, due within two short months. For us that seemed an impossible sum to pay. Jim gathered our little family around the kitchen table and explained the situation, affirming that God was going to help us. We prayed in faith for $1,000. Then we collected all our spare cash (about $10) and sent it anonymously to a needy family in our church.

To this day I'm not exactly sure how God provided. We never got an unexpected check in the mail or other obvious help. Mysteriously our bank balance gradually inched higher. Afterwards, bemusedly, we noticed that for those few months our old car didn't need any repairs, neither of our little boys outgrew their shoes or jeans and none of us got sick. Often during those months the grocery store "happened" to drastically discount their prices on the exact items I normally bought.

On April 15, Jim and our two boys and I gathered around the kitchen table once again and cheered loudly as Jim wrote a check for the full payment. We fervently thanked God. It was a pivotal teachable moment for our whole family. As for myself, I resolved to be more alert next time around, to spot more of God's sweet and subtle provisions.

Father, Help me to notice when You send manna, however disguised, and help me to receive it with gladness. Amen.

Dionne Carpenter

Manna Time #3
Complaining About Manna

But now we have lost our appetite; we never
see anything but this manna! ~ Numbers 11:6

READING: Numbers 11:4-6; 18-20

It's tempting for us to feel smug and superior when we read about those grumbling Israelites. *Why I would <u>never</u> have complained if I had been in their sandals!* Yet we church-planters, more than most, find ourselves in remarkably similar circumstances and would do well to learn from their cautionary tale.

Consider this. The Israelites ate manna because they had taken an enormous leap of faith to follow God. It felt noble to leave everything familiar behind. Yet they soon found themselves in unknown territory. Sure, they saw miracles all around, but they couldn't force anything to happen on their timetable. They were reduced to eating the same monotonous food day after day. Sound familiar? On top of that, manna was so humbling, so boring, and so easy to compare against all they had left behind or with all they imagined others enjoying while they suffered on and on.

Financial hardships are a fact of life for most church planters. Like the Israelites we also juggle the grand adventure of faith with the tough times, which, for many of us, include eating mostly humble meals like rice and beans or peanut butter sandwiches.

In the thick of the battle to plant the new church, and far away from home, it's tempting to complain about the small privations, the friends we left behind or the small irritants of pioneer life. It all depends on the way we look at our version of "manna." As it says in Proverbs 15:15, "All the days of the oppressed are wretched, but the cheerful heart has a continual feast."

Dear Father, The next time I eat simple food, help me to savor it as heaven's bread and a gift of grace. Amen.

Dionne Carpenter

God Changes Hearts!

The heart is deceitful above all things and beyond cure. ~ *Jeremiah 17:9*
"I will give you a new heart and put a new spirit in you; I will remove from you
your heart of stone and give you a heart of flesh." ~ Ezekiel 36:26

READING: Ezekiel 36:24-29

My friend Bill (not his real name) was an unlikely candidate for salvation. Tall and handsome, he was both a great athlete and a brilliant student. He married a beautiful wife, and embarked on a career as a test pilot for the U.S. Air Force. From the world's point of view, Bill had everything. I met him knocking on doors, but honestly I didn't expect him to be receptive to the message of our new church.

But both he and his wife were new Christians and became part of the core group of our church plant. I discipled Bill using simple lessons from the Bible with verses to memorize and to obey. Bill and his wife led our children's ministry. It was an amazing thing to see a jet pilot sitting on the floor with little children, teaching them about Jesus.

How could such a change take place, especially since our new church didn't have slick programs, beautiful buildings, or powerful people?

The greatest obstacle to church planting is not our lack of resources or small size. The greatest obstacle to church planting, to the gospel, is the human heart.

But God promises to transform a heart of stone into a heart of flesh! Church planting depends, not on buildings or money or programs, but on the power of God to change people. And He will do this great work!

Lord, Only You can truly save people from their sins. Thank You for saving me. And please change stony hearts into hearts of flesh. Amen.

Jim Carpenter

The Story

I will open my mouth in a parable; I will utter dark
sayings of old, which we have heard and known, and our
fathers have told us. ~ Psalm 78:2, 3 (NASB)

READING: Nehemiah 9

In his prayer, Nehemiah tells the story: "You made a covenant…You did what you promised…You are always true to your word…You displayed miraculous signs…." And so on. Afterwards, the people confess their sins to their Sovereign God. What more could they do after being reminded in their story of the wonderful things he had done and how He had just provided all they needed to rebuild the walls of their city?

Our Epena Pedee friend, Ferne, a missionary to his tribe in the southwest corner of the Colombian jungle, learned the power of telling the story. For seven years he helped translate the New Testament into his native unwritten language. But, not until he attended the dedication service for the new translation at a church in the city, did he understood the impact of God's story. A visiting minister from the United States shared the gospel. Suddenly, everything Ferne had helped produce made sense. This hardened ex-drug cartel and guerilla member repented, along with his family who had come to the city with him. Ferne committed his life to the person and work of Jesus Christ.

We went with Ferne to his jungle home. He shared his story with his yet unreached tribal village. Every one of them repented. Today, Ferne pastors this little church in the middle of the jungle. He shares the gospel story. The lives of the Epena Pedee indigenous people are being impacted.

Our mission is to share the gospel. The story is simple. The story is powerful. The story is God's story.

Father of nations, Burn your story upon the tablets of our hearts and minds so we can share it powerfully unto the salvation of many. Amen.

Christine Cunningham

Believing in Vain?

*Now I make known to you, brethren, the gospel which
I preached to you, which also you received, in which also you stand,
by which also you are saved, if you hold fast the word which I preached
to you, unless you believed in vain. ~ I Corinthians 15:1, 2 (ESV)*

READING: I Corinthians 2:1-5

Recently I attended a funeral where the officiating pastor gave an invitation to salvation. He told us Jesus came to give us abundant life. As we bowed in prayer, he explained that all we had to do to receive this abundant life was to "step over the line" by raising our hands. After the closing prayer, the minister reported that many people had "stepped over the line."

"Whoo-hoo!" he shouted.

We have a great gospel to proclaim. Those who receive it are saved unto eternal life. But Paul adds a disturbing word: "unless you believed in vain" (v. 2). How is it possible to believe "in vain?"

If faith is man-centered belief and not the true gospel, it is in vain. Faith in human response, like a special prayer or raising a hand or walking an aisle, rather than in the saving merit of Jesus' death and resurrection, is in vain.

The minister at the funeral never mentioned who Jesus is, the utter hopelessness of people without Him, the infinite value of His substitutionary death, or the need to repent and believe in Him alone. He only told us to "step over the line."

May God enable us to preach the simple gospel, to proclaim Christ and Him crucified (I Cor. 2:2). And may the faith of those who hear not rest in the wisdom of men but in the power of God (I Cor. 2:5).

Father, Protect me from trying to make the gospel easier. May I preach Christ and Him crucified. I trust You to do the miracle-work of salvation. Amen.

Jim Carpenter

The Two-Pronged Spur to Trust God

I will say of the Lord, "He is my refuge and my
fortress, my God, in whom I trust." ~ Psalm 91:2

READING: Romans 5:1-5

No matter what else God may do in our lives at any given time, once we become Christians God utilizes every circumstance to spur us to a deeper relationship with Him and a fuller dependence upon Him for every aspect of our lives. Sometimes the focus of His maneuvering invites us to trust Him for our public ministry, sometimes for family stresses, sometimes for our personal journey of faith. But secretly or overtly, God continually presses us regarding our trust.

I've identified two main pincers of this relentless focus. God sends us 1) *the lavish evidence of His trustworthiness* from all sides. He uses the evidence found in creation; the evidence of His character as discovered in Scripture; He gives us the evidence of marvelously answered prayer; and He gives us evidence in the satisfaction we find in our growing relationship with the Living Christ.

On the other hand, God regularly sends us 2) *obstacles that threaten our preconceived ideas about God and shake the good or bad things we trust.* When our car breaks down or our daughter gets sick or our denomination cuts the funding for our church plant, it threatens our complacency and tests the depths of our trust in God.

At this juncture, some supposed Christians fall away from faith in Christ (Luke 8:13). Some genuine Christians begin to harbor hidden doubts and reservations about God's character. But true joy is found by those who remember the abundant evidence of God's trustworthiness and rise to the challenge to trust God and find Him present within the struggle of each day.

Father, Help me to cooperate with Your agenda and embrace each obstacle as a new opportunity to deepen my trust in You. Amen.

Dionne Carpenter
Adapted from *Trust Training* © 2008

It's Hard to be a Shepherd

*Be shepherds of God's flock that is under your care, serving
as overseers – not because you must, but because you are willing,
as God wants you to be; not greedy for money, but eager to serve; not
lording it over those entrusted to you, but being examples to the flock.
And when the Chief Shepherd appears, you will receive the crown
of glory that will never fade away. ~ I Peter 5:2-4*

READING: John 21:15-17

Sheep are dumb. They are totally dependent on the shepherd. They don't
have claws, speed, flight or fangs to ward off their predators. The role of the
shepherd is not easy. Sheep are messy and shoveling sheep manure in the sheep
pen is not a fun job. However, those who pastor need to understand they are
"pasturers." They feed the sheep, tend the sheep, shear the sheep (not skin the
sheep) and provide for the sheep.

Those of us who have been bitten by a sheep, butted by a ram, stepped on or
kicked by a mad ewe (female sheep), or pooped on by a lamb, need to meditate
on the words of Peter in I Peter 5. Even with a bold, *Type A* personality, Peter
had a shepherd's heart as the lead pastor on the launch day of the first church on
the Day of Pentecost in Acts 2.

During the hard times when the sheep are hard to manage, persevere.
Hang in there! Remember there is a special crown of glory for the shepherd.

---

*Lord Jesus, I pray that today I will bring honor to you as I tend to the sheep you have
entrusted to my care, in the name of the One who laid down his life for me – a stubborn
sheep. Amen.*

Sam Douglass

Equipping Broken People

I have not come to call the righteous but sinners to repentance. Luke 5:32
And he gave the apostles, the prophets, the evangelists, the pastors and teachers, to
equip the saints for the work of ministry... ~ Ephesians 4:11, 12a (ESV)

READING: Luke 5:27-32

The people our new churches reach are broken people. Jesus said those whom He would call to repentance were the sinners – not those who see themselves as righteous. But saved sinners are still broken people. We are called to "equip" them.

The word "equip" (NIV "prepare," KJV "perfect") is a beautiful word in the Greek language. We get the word "artisan" from its root. An artisan is someone who makes something beautiful and useful. In the first century world, the word "equip" was used of "mending" a broken limb. To reconcile opposing political factions was to "equip" them.

In the Gospels, the verb "equip" was used of mending torn fishing nets (Matt. 4:21). Paul tells those who are spiritual to "restore" a brother who falls into a transgression (Gal. 6:1). *Restore* is the verb "equip." "To equip" means to take that which is broken or torn and so heal and mend and restore it that it becomes beautiful and useful.

Only God's grace can transform broken lives so they become useful and beautiful. And God's word is the only instrument of lasting change. "All Scripture is breathed out by God and profitable for teaching, for reproof, for correction, and for training in righteousness, that the man of God may be competent, *equipped for every good work*" (II Tim. 3:16, 17).

Church planting is not only about finding lost people, but equipping broken ones – through the faithful teaching, reproof, correction and training of God's word.

Father, Grant me Christ's compassion for broken people. Enable me to "equip" them through Your holy word. Amen.

Jim Carpenter

Timing Is Everything

A word aptly spoken is like apples of
gold in settings of silver. ~ Proverbs 25:11

READING: Luke 23:39-43

One of the most practical and helpful bits of advice Jim got in seminary was an off-the-cuff remark by one of his professors who observed that "one hospital visit before surgery is worth ten afterwards." Church planters usually get far more training on the intricacies of how to start a church than how to care for church members in crisis. At first Jim and I followed his advice without really understanding why it was so insightful.

I experienced its wisdom, firsthand, a few years ago. I almost died when a simple out-patient medical procedure went terribly wrong. After a nightmare week of catastrophic pain, doctors rushed me back into surgery, warning my family that I was within about two hours of dying.

In that terrifying moment, lying helplessly on the gurney, life and death hung in the balance. Samuel Johnson is reputed to have said that "nothing more wonderfully concentrates a man's mind than the sure knowledge he is to be hanged in the morning!" I get it now! I desperately needed (and thankfully had) pastoral care to help me face the almost unbearable fear, to say my rushed good-byes and prepare to meet my Maker. Spiritual matters were literally my only concern.

Things changed dramatically after surgery. We knew the outcome – I lived. Praise God! Terror evaporated into the tedium of slow recuperation. I have no recollection of my first few days in post-op recovery and, sure, I appreciated visits after surgery. But I would walk through fire for the wonderful people who prayed with Jim and me on that fateful night.

Want to build loyalty in your people? Sometimes it's a matter of being in the right place at the right time.

Father, By Your grace help me to be there when my people need me the most. Amen.

Dionne Carpenter

Focus on the Fruit

Every time I think of you, I thank my God. And whenever I
mention you in my prayers, it makes me happy. ~ Philippians 1:3, 4 (CEV)

READING: Philippians 1

As a church planter, I often had legitimate reasons for discouragement: difficult people, setbacks, persecutions, fatigue and so on. Staying encouraged has sometimes been a challenge.

The Apostle Paul grappled with the same issue of discouragement. He wrote in II Corinthians 1:8, "We want to remind you, friends, of the trouble we had in the province of Asia. The burdens laid upon us were so great and so heavy that we gave up all hope of staying alive" (GNB). How did he stay encouraged? Our passage tells us that he stayed encouraged by remembering his spiritual children and praying for them.

I have found the same thing keeps me encouraged: when I remember and pray for those who have been saved – those whose eternal destiny was changed from hell to heaven, my joy returns. On the other hand, when I focus on my problems, my spirit languishes and my courage fades.

During the time that he wrote the Philippian letter, Paul was in prison, chained to Roman guards. What a discouraging circumstance! Yet he managed to remain joyful by focusing on the fruit of his ministry.

Recently I again had the privilege of leading someone to Christ. As usual, I left the encounter feeling like I was walking six inches off the ground. Gathering fruit is exhilarating.

What are you focusing on? Focus on the fruit!

But, you may say, how do you stay encouraged when you don't see fruit yet? Stay faithful, keep your eyes on Jesus, and pray *now* for the people who will be the fruit of your labors one day. Focus on the fruit!

Lord, Please help me to focus on what is most important. Help me to focus on the fruit. Amen.

Mark Alan Williams

Witness to the Light

There came a man who was sent from God; his name was John. He came as a witness to testify concerning that light, so that through him all men might believe. He himself was not the light; he came only as a witness to the light. ~ John 1:6-8

READING: John 1:6-9

As his ministry makes clear, John the Baptist was a unique person with a unique ministry. At a crucial time in God's salvation history, John came with the mission of witnessing to the light – Jesus. John was sent by God at a particular moment and in a particular culture with a task only he could accomplish.

Isn't church planting and pastoring like that? Even though none of us can do what only John was called to do, we are also called to witness to the light. In a particular moment and culture, God has called and gifted each of us to witness to the light.

John summarized his ministry this way: "He must increase, but I must decrease" (John 3:30). That's the ministry of church planting, isn't it? Fill in your name: "There came a man who was sent from God; his name was _____!" Read it again. God has called, prepared and empowered you to witness to His Son today!

How might this reality give focus and purpose to your day? Each encounter is an opportunity. Each difficulty becomes an occasion for the light of the world to shine through to a watching world. Time with the family is a chance for Jesus' love to warm and nurture.

Lord, Empower me to witness to the light today. Use me to call attention to Your love and grace to every person and in every circumstance I'm privileged to experience. Amen.

Ross Chenot

The Prayer of Relinquishment

"Abba, Father," He said, "everything is possible
for You. Take this cup from Me. Yet not what
I will, but what You will." ~ Mark 14:36

READING: Genesis 22:1-14

I had the timing all figured out when we transitioned from our second church plant to the third. We prayed like crazy to sell our house by June 30, calculating the sale would be completed in time for us to move by the start of our sons' schools in September.

But no buyer came. I fumed all through July. *God, how could You fail us like this?* By late July, I surrendered the timing of our move to God – dejected but yielded.

We all come to periodic crossroads in our Christian walk. Something suddenly takes center stage: something we dearly love, something we've assumed, or maybe something we've been praying for with all our might. God gives us an unmistakable choice: *Will you lay this down? Will you trust even this to Me, to do with as I will?* This crossroad moment always addresses an issue that, left unchecked, could poison, divert or dilute our single-hearted devotion to Christ. Whatever the details, praying the prayer of relinquishment leaves the taste of death on our tongue because, of course, it always *is* a kind of death.

Sometimes God removes what we surrender, and because He has kindly allowed us the dignity to choose, we find peace. But often He returns to us, in purified form, the thing we gave to Him. Our buyer showed up two weeks after my surrender.

I thought the deadline was June 30. I was wrong. God used that painful delay to teach me to trust His perfect timing, then sent us buyers whose terms gave us plenty of time to move into our new house just in time for the first day of school.

Dear Father, Help me to walk at Your pace. Amen.

Dionne Carpenter

JULY

The Leadership Principle

*Leadership development lies at the
heart of the new church's mission, and
the most important leadership quality
to develop is spiritual maturity.*

Leadership

...if [his spiritual gift] is leadership, let
him govern diligently... ~ Romans 12:8

READING: Romans 12:1-8

What capability does a church planter need more than any other? My answer would be: LEADERSHIP.

A church planter must be a leader of other *people* if he is to establish a single cell church. He must be a person that people are willing to follow. A single cell church is one composed of thirty to eighty people in which everyone knows everyone else. However, if he wants to establish a church that grows beyond a single cell, a church planter must be a leader of other *leaders*.

Leadership is a spiritual gift. Some people are just gifted by God to lead others. Leadership is also a multi-faceted set of skills and attitudes that can be learned. If you are in a position of overseeing others, you need to learn to guide them effectively whether or not you are a talented leader.

The top Christian leadership teacher in the United States is John Maxwell. He offers many resources to empower leaders, including *The Maxwell Leadership Bible*.* This study Bible is filled with hundreds of biblical leadership lessons that flow out of the Word of God. It's a wonderful resource. To become a better leader, I use this Bible in my personal devotions. I am using it to mentor my son, Brandon, in leadership. I use the *Maxwell Leadership Bible* to train my staff in leadership every Monday morning.

Whether you are a gifted or not-so-gifted leader, you can learn to direct your ministry more effectively. This is a lifelong process. Make a resolution: I will learn to become a better leader, starting today. And then, take action!

Lord, Help me to be a good leader to your glory. Amen.

Paul Becker

*You can find *The Maxwell Leadership Bible* on John Maxwell's website at www.injoy.com.

Identifying and Developing Leaders

Paul wanted Timothy to accompany him... ~ Acts 16:3a

READING: II Timothy 1:3-14

Our speaker for the evening service was a new graduate of our EMT course (Equipping for Ministry Training). Eighteen months before, he had been petrified to speak in front of other people. Now he confidently and competently challenged us from God's word. He's a future leader in our church.

How do you equip and deploy the leaders you need in your new church? Very carefully! And there are no shortcuts. You should bring godly, mature leaders with you as part of your church planting team. God may send you ready-made leaders, but growing your own takes time. I know of no "formula," but over the years God has shown me a number of ways that help identify and develop godly leaders.

One-to-one discipleship is essential. I've put together three separate one-to-one training courses: the basics, a focus on our church's values, and a more advanced study of God's character. Working one-on-one with a man helps equip him.

I use *a monthly men's group* as a "fishing pool" for leaders. The stated purpose for the group is to become godly men and to share our lives with one another. We study God's word, read books together and pray. It's very casual. Some of the men show potential for future leadership, others do not, but we all grow spiritually.

We've developed a formal *leadership course* where men commit to 16 months of bi-monthly classes, with practical homework assignments. We try to equip them in one-to-one discipling, small group dynamics, evangelism, and studying and teaching God's word.

And of course there's no substitute for *on-the-job training.* Timothy learned from Paul as he participated in evangelism, teaching, and new church organization. Leadership is both "caught" and "taught."

Lord, Show me your plan to discover, develop and deploy godly leaders. Amen.

Jim Carpenter

Growth Takes Time

*See how the farmer waits for the land
to yield its valuable crop... ~ James 5:7b*

READING: Hebrews 5:12-14

People can only grow so fast. When we are raising up leaders to plant churches in several villages and towns it is easy to get impatient when they don't understand or mature quickly enough for us. We want to see results!

After we eat a meal we need time to digest and allow the nutrition to produce the growth and energy in our bodies. Likewise, we must feed our spiritual sheep on a regular basis, then allow the God-ordained process to take place within them. Giving them too much of the Word or too heavy of concepts too quickly, without providing the processing time, often leads to spiritual indigestion and reduces their desire for the things of God.

Training of leadership for a church plant must take into account the ability of the people to receive the word. During one period of time in our career on the mission field we had young people in intensive training for four months at a time in internship. We found that often the sheer volume of information was not assimilated into their lives and was therefore only head knowledge. Or they would be sent out to assume the leadership of a church in the river villages and fail miserably because they were not of proven character, but just full of head knowledge.

We need to prepare the future church planting leadership for the long term, teaching them the Word of God and church planting principles, and mentoring them in their daily experience to develop and prove their character and test their motivations. They need to put into practice what they have learned and be given opportunity to apply it.

Heavenly Father, Thank you for your patience in our growth in maturity and please help me to have patience with those I am training. Amen.

Ron Thiesen

Things to be Sought First

*But seek first his kingdom and his righteousness, and
all these things will be given to you as well.* ~ *Matthew 6:33*

READING: Matthew 6:19-32

Worldly wealth gives people obvious security and glory. Jesus warned His disciples in Matthew 6:24 that it was impossible to serve both Money and God at the same time. Since monetary blessings are uncertain and often inadequate, as we serve Him, we have a danger of attempting to serve "money" along with Kingdom service.

There is a huge gulf between *given* (v. 33) and *sought* (v. 24). The former is a provision provided by someone, whereas the latter is an intentional hunt by us. Jesus guarantees for a "given" provision. His size and time of supply is based on His sovereign wisdom. When we judge God's provisions insufficient, we choose to hunt for something beyond His provision. This trespass will eventually shift our focus from Kingdom to money.

"First" is not a chronological priority but rather an insistence that disciples set their undivided focus on Kingdom affairs. Consider these two phrases – "money for ministry" or "ministry for money." The first phrase keeps us focused on His Kingdom by the virtue of His given provisions. The second phrase tempts us to gradually exploit our ministry work for personal gain. Exaggerated reports, unrealistic targets, manipulated accounts, betrayal of trusts, and selfish agendas are some of the traits of the seekers of money among the Kingdom workers.

His provision might be insufficient in your scale, but it is His supply. So, my friends, focus exclusively on His Kingdom affairs and "all" these things will be added to you. "Added" means that His supply will increasingly, again and again, unendingly, and adequately be given. Wealth of the world, though glamorous, is not reliable (v. 19).

Lord, Strengthen my firmness to focus only on your Kingdom. Help me to wait upon you for your provision. Amen.

R. Jayakumar

The Nature of a Leader's Presence

He humbled himself, by becoming obedient to the
point of death – even death on a cross! ~ Philippians 2:8

READING: John 13:1-17

Presence is the greatest of all gifts. It is given by parents who are attentive to their children, by waiters who refill empty water cups and by pastors who listen actively to a distraught mother. To be present is to serve; to be present is to die to self. We see presence in its most complete form on the cross. Jesus was so present to us that he literally died.

God calls us to be present in this world, the very presence and reality of Jesus in us. The nature of a leader's presence has a quantity and a quality, that is, a quantity of engagement and attentiveness and a quality of response. How much are you present?

And what is actually present? Our love? Our anxiety? I may think I am present but my presence can be hijacked by my anxieties, and it is no longer I that am attentive and responsive but rather my anxieties. Jesus attends to us without burdening us with an overlay of his own emotions. He does not anxiously react but operates out of a framework of love and true identity.

Your presence is the key to greatness. If you want to be great in God's kingdom, learn to be the servant of all; start by being present. Your presence will allow you to see and respond to opportunities that you previously raced past.

What is the nature of your presence? How much and how are *you* present? Presence is the key to good leadership because to lead is to serve.

Jesus, Even now, I am hardly here. But you are with me and in me, attending to my prayer. In all of my ambitions and desires, help me to consider the nature of your presence. Amen.

Peter Sung

The Goose

…Saul kept a jealous eye on David. ~ I Samuel 18:9

READING: I Samuel 18:5-9

My parents once bought a home in the country that included a little pond just out of sight of the main house. Early the following spring, they bought twenty ducks and one big white goose for their pond. They really enjoyed those ducks! Every morning their goose would herd all twenty ducks up around the bend to my parent's back door. Mom and Dad loved to feed them cracked corn.

But that goose was a cantankerous old bird. He honked and snapped whenever my folks tried to pet the ducks. It was so annoying! That entire summer they tried unsuccessfully to figure out how to get past that goose to pet their ducks. Finally my parents got so irritated that when Thanksgiving Day rolled around, late in the autumn, they butchered the goose and ate it for Thanksgiving dinner.

Within seven short days, all twenty defenseless ducks were killed by predators!

All of which reminds me of church planting. Sometimes an influential lay leader in our church plant can be as irritating and territorial as that goose. However, consider these three questions before deciding to give them "the ax:"

1. Have I missed ways this leader is demonstrating loyalty and courage? (Actually, that goose had served my parents well, valiantly fighting many an unnoticed battle down at the pond. He had faithfully herded the ducks up to the house day after day.)

2. Does my annoyance express godly, shrewd leadership on my part or merely my own pride and carnality?

3. And have I thought through what will happen to the church if I "kill the goose?"

Dear Father, Please deliver me from a jealous spirit and help me to lead all those entrusted to my care with wisdom and maturity, even the "goose" in my flock. Amen.

Dionne Carpenter

By What Authority?

By what authority are you doing these things? ~ Mark 11:28a

READING: Mark 11:1-33

Christ the Lord has all authority to do with us and our church plant according to His good pleasure.

Less than a week before He went to the cross, Jesus demonstrated His authority in three unmistakable ways. To prepare for His entrance into Jerusalem on Palm Sunday, He instructed His disciples to commandeer a donkey (vv. 1-8). *Who does He think He is? – That's private property!* Then He pronounced a withering curse upon an unproductive fig tree (vv. 12-14). *Who does He think He is? – It wasn't even the season for figs!* And before He was through, He cast the moneychangers out of the Temple, calling Herod's magnificent structure, "My house" (vv. 15-19). *Who does He think He is? – He's not even a Pharisee!*

All of this was very offensive to the religious establishment, of course, because it undermined their man-centered equilibrium and forced them to confront the truth of who He is. But when they tried to trap Jesus, He refused to joust with them. Effortlessly He silenced them (and demonstrated His authority!) with His own question.

Jesus' authority *is* offensive – even to us, sometimes. We church planters have a preconceived idea of how our ministries should go, but if the Lord unveils different plans, we might feel betrayed or confused.

But the truth is, Jesus *is* the Lord, and He does have authority in our lives and ministries. Our resources, our private property, our stuff – it all belongs to Him. He has every right to bless (or withhold blessing) on our "fruit bearing." And cleansing our "temples" – our lives, our ministries – is exactly what the Lord will do.

Lord of church planting and Lord of my life, I know Your ways are best. Have your way with me today. You are the King, and I am at Your disposal. Amen.

Jim Carpenter

Life Reverses

About midnight Paul and Silas were praying
and singing hymns to God, and the other prisoners
were listening to them. ~ Acts 16:25

READING: Acts 16:6-24

In Bangalore, India, most of the roads at present are not thoroughfares. Detours are inevitable while numerous flyovers are under construction. Diversions always make journeys longer.

In Acts 16, Paul was precisely led to go to Philippi. The Holy Spirit confirmed this was the target city by leading Lydia's household to Christ. Further, God gave Paul a core team. The team was making good progress until God permitted a regression for a short time, as we read about the cruel imprisonment of Paul and Silas. The description of their agony would tell us that Paul's future seemed to be totally crushed.

We often encounter this experience. William Carey endured difficult hardships in India where he lost his son and his wife became insane. Certainly it would have made him think that his mission in India was doomed.

I do not know what kind of life reversal you were or are right now facing. Remember God is able to make use of your life reversals to move your ministry forward.

How can we change life reversals into our ladder to climb up? Acts 16:25 illustrates three great qualities of Paul, who always moved forward in spite of life reversals. The first one is his *confidence* in the Sovereign work of God in his life. The second is his *courage* to face pains and sufferings for the purpose of His church (9:16). The third is his firm *commitment* to complete the task that God had entrusted to him (26:16 – 18). Remember these three qualities, illustrated so admirably by Paul, as you pass through your own life reverses.

Lord, Strengthen me as I pass through the "Philippi" experience of Paul in my own context. Make me victorious in all my endeavors. Amen.

R. Jayakumar

The Glory of God to Conceal Things

*It is the glory of God to conceal things, but the glory
of kings is to search things out. ~ Proverbs 25:2 (ESV)*

READING: Romans 11:33-36

Church planters want to know things. How can I reach the people in this community most effectively? Who should I invite to join my staff? What facilities can I use for worship services? You'd think it would be easy to find the answers we seek. But "it is the glory of God to conceal things." Sometimes, evidently, the Lord does not answer our questions.

Why does it glorify God to conceal things? Because doing so magnifies His glory as the All-knowing Creator, the Sovereign over all things great and small. Because He conceals some things, it humbles men, forcing them to come to Him for insight, wisdom and clarity. When we bow to His omniscience and beg for His favor to understand something, He is glorified.

The other half of the proverb says the glory of kings – and of church planters – is to search things out. God displays His greatness by concealing, but our "glory" is displayed when we humbly ask God for what only He can give.

Knowing the answers to our questions will never be as important as knowing the God who knows everything. As Paul said, "that I may know him and the power of his resurrection, and may share his sufferings…" (Phil. 3:10).

Church planting is not just a set of skills to learn. It is about relationship with the Head of the church, the Author of salvation, the King of glory. When our questions drive us deeper into seeking the Lord Himself, to know *Him*, then He is glorified, and we are better prepared to lead a church full of people who also need the Lord more than they need answers.

---

*Father, Teach me to seek You above all things, even above answers to my questions.
Amen.*

Jim Carpenter

The Little Engine That Could

Everything is possible for
him who believes. ~ Mark 9:23

READING: Philippians 4:10-20

As a child, when my mother read to me, the book I liked most was *The Little Engine that Could* by Watty Piper. In the story, a long train filled with circus animals, toys and clowns must be pulled over a high and steep mountain. But it can find no engine to pull it.

All the big locomotives refuse, but finally a little engine takes on the challenge. As it pulls with all its might, the engine repeats, "I think I can, I think I can, I think I can." Though it barely makes it, the small-fry succeeds and on the way down the mountain repeats, "I thought I could, I thought I could."

I loved that fairy tale book. But what I love today is the fact that the Lord gives us the same positive perspective related to the major challenges of church planting ministry. This outlook is no children's fairy tale; it is based the rock-solid promises of God.

Though our tasks may seem impossible, we can say with Scripture: "I can do all things, I can do all things, I can do all things." (Phil. 4:13). "All things are possible, all things are possible, all things are possible" (Mark 9:23).

Your church planting trail may be tough, the going may be rough. You may feel like giving up. When you do, remember the Scriptural directive to keep on chugging along with a faith-filled, positive perspective:

"Therefore, my beloved brothers, be steadfast, immovable, always abounding in the work of the Lord, knowing that in the Lord your labor is not in vain" (I Cor. 15:58 ESV).

Lord, Help me to stay strong, even when I am discouraged, remembering that "I can do all things through Christ who strengthens me." Amen.

Mark Alan Williams

Strengthening Ourselves in the Lord #1

*David was greatly distressed because the men were
talking of stoning him; each one was bitter in spirit
because of his sons and daughters. But David found
strength in the LORD his God.* ~ I Samuel 30:6

READING: I Samuel 30

In most church plants, there come crisis moments similar to this episode in David's life when he juggled deep personal distress and the mutinous wrath of followers who wanted to stone him. Setbacks – sometimes staggering setbacks – are a fact of life in church planting. These crisis times test our mettle as leaders.

What saved the day for David and his followers is that David acted like a godly leader instead of getting swept up in the momentary angst. Although David was every bit as distressed as his men, he turned to God and found strength in Him.

What exactly did David do? We can make a pretty accurate guess that he didn't immediately ask God for guidance because it's not until <u>after</u> he found strength (here in verse 6) that he inquired of the Lord (in verse 7). No, if we look for clues in many of David's psalms, it's likely that his was a visceral flight to God as his most trusted comforter and wisest counselor. We know God met David and delivered him from his fears (Ps. 34:4). David remembered God's sufficiency and was able to find his footing again in God's presence. After that deep cleansing breath, David went back to being the clear-headed leader God called him to be.

The next time life punches us in the gut, let's run to the Lord first to find the stabilizing strength that will make us wise, calm leaders during crisis.

Dear Lord, Grant that I may learn to strengthen myself in You, not only for the sake of my people, but also for the enormous blessing it brings to my own soul. Amen.

Dionne Carpenter

Strengthening Ourselves in the Lord #2

The LORD who delivered me from the paw of the lion and the paw of the bear will deliver me from the hand of this Philistine. ~ I Samuel 17:37

READING: I Samuel 17

The story of David's fighting Goliath gives us a clue about how David strengthened himself in the Lord. When Goliath taunted the Israelites day after day, why did Saul and his men cower in fear? And why, by dramatic contrast, did David instantly respond with courageous faith?

Saul probed that very question. David's reply was most illuminating. Many young shepherd boys routinely guarded their flocks against predators, so it was not unheard of that David would have fought bears or lions. However, most boys would have bragged afterwards about their own prowess and cunning.

Not so David. In both fierce struggles, David had come face to face with his own helplessness and then watched God come to his rescue. David gave God full credit, keeping none for himself. Furthermore, during his tenure as a shepherd boy, he had become supremely confident that God would continue to deliver him in every circumstance, no matter how daunting the foe.

Most church planters I've met have great talents and many personal accomplishments. But have those many achievements reinforced our self-confidence and swagger? Or have they revealed to us the surpassing greatness of our God?

Who is the strong one – you or God?

Sooner or later all of us will run into someone or something bigger than we are. Saul and his soldiers certainly did. But if our struggles have taught us something of the length and breadth of God's almighty power, we will never run into anything larger than Him.

No wonder David was unimpressed by a man who was only nine feet tall!

Dear Lord, Give me a humble heart and an unshakable confidence in Your power and Your eagerness to deliver me. Amen.

Dionne Carpenter

Strengthening Ourselves in the Lord #3

*While David was at Horesh in the Desert of Ziph, he learned that
Saul had come out to take his life. And Saul's son Jonathan went to David
at Horesh and helped him find strength in God. "Don't be afraid," he said.
"My father Saul will not lay a hand on you. You will be king over Israel,
and I will be second to you. Even my father Saul knows this." The two of
them made a covenant before the LORD." ~ I Samuel 23:15-17*

READING: I Samuel 23:7-18

Even though David was already mature in the things of God, during
this particular difficulty his friend Jonathan helped him find strength in God.
Jonathan communicated three key things that strengthened David's confidence
in God.

God's perspective: "Don't be afraid." During dark days, even the most spiritual
believer may get bogged down in fears and catastrophic thinking. Jonathan
dispelled David's fear by reminding him of the truth. *David, Saul won't kill you.*

God's promise: "You will be king." Jonathan reminded David of God's
promises. In David's case, God had chosen him to be the next king of Israel. It's
easy to forget what God has promised us; how good to be reminded.

His unwavering friendship: The two of them made a covenant. Lastly, Jonathan
reaffirmed his personal commitment to his downcast friend. Jonathan's loyalty
tangibly reconnected David to God's faithfulness.

Jonathan wasn't always around to encourage David. In I Samuel 30, David
strengthened himself in God unaided by his friend. Sometimes we have to stand
alone. But if we are fortunate enough to have a few trusted friends, it's a blessing
when they encourage us by being Jesus "with skin on." Receive it as a kind gift
from God and from them.

*Dear Lord, How would You like to encourage me right now using these three thoughts?
And show me who needs my encouragement. Amen.*

Dionne Carpenter

Recognizing Repentance

But Barnabas took [Paul] and brought him to the apostles. ~ Acts 9:27a

READING: Philemon I: 8-16

When Barnabas first heard about Paul's conversion, he probably felt some initial scepticism along with other disciples. However, Barnabas stood successful although the Eleven failed.

When Onesimus repented, Paul sent a special letter to Philemon asking him to recognize the repentance of Onesimus. Philemon might have had a strong personality, which made Paul send a note. Paul urged Philemon to accept Onesimus as his colleague in God's mission.

Sometimes we must consider the repentance of someone who has been detrimental for us in the ministry. Paul had the same problem years before when John Mark was proposed by Barnabas to join their second mission trip. (Barnabas had probably heard John's confession, repenting of his earlier misbehavior.) Paul vehemently rejected the proposal, but commended John Mark's reliability some years later.

When David repented, Nathan was willing to recognize it. Jesus recognized Peter's repentance and entrusted the shepherding ministry into his hand. Recognizing others' repentance is essential as we labor in church planting efforts.

Sometimes our judgments might not be correct. Still we need to acknowledge the repentance of others. This is an act of distributing God's mercies. If we lived in a perfect world, no one would injure or abuse or treat unfairly other people. We live in an imperfect world where a perfect Body needs to be built. Ill-doers and immature men and women are sent by God to us so we may demonstrate His mercies and build the Body of Christ.

Recognizing repentance leads to restoration which includes renewal of relationship, comfort and mentoring. This is what Barnabas did for Paul. Legalism, revenge, uncontrollable anger, hurting words and unforgiving spirit are detrimental for a church planter.

Lord, Grant me patience and long suffering. Help me to acknowledge the repentance of others. Make me a distributor of your mercies and grace. Amen.

R. Jayakumar

A Church Planter
Needs to Be His Own Man

"I cannot go in these," he said to Saul,
"because I am not used to them." ~ I Samuel 17:39

READING: I Samuel 17:32-50

I remember several young ministerial students practicing to sound like Billy Graham, the great evangelist. One fellow would stand for hours in front of a mirror with his Bible open, draped over his hand like Billy, and would practice Billy's mannerisms and voice inflection. Quite honestly, he got pretty good and if you closed your eyes and listened to him, you would think he was Billy Graham.

In today's world of resources and gadgets, it is tempting for young church planters to try to emulate the popular preachers of our day. Do not misunderstand, I'm all for borrowing ideas; giving credit where credit is due; and even adapting sermons written by others. However, busy young planters must never slack off in personal preparation or try to be a clone of others. While learning from these great men of God, we shouldn't circumvent the necessity of getting before God and getting our own word from Him.

There is a fine line between desiring the same kind of divine anointing that we see on others, and mimicking them or "lip syncing" their messages – that's IDOLATRY! God has a fresh new work to do in and through you today. Just like David, who refused Saul's armor, so today, go out and face your giants in the power and gifting God has given you.

But you say, "I want to be like…. Their ministry is anointed and mine's not!" Jesus would say, "Take your eyes off of them and onto me. It's none of your business whether I bless them or curse them. BE YOUR OWN MAN!"

Father, I ask for your special anointing on my message and ministry so many will come to know my Lord and Savior. Amen.

Sam Douglass

Equipping

*...to prepare God's people for works of service, so that
the body of Christ may be built up... ~ Ephesians 4:12*

READING: Ephesians 4:1-16

To prepare God's people for works of service: that is the job of the apostle, prophet, evangelist, pastor and teacher. We are to equip Christians to more effectively serve the Lord in their gifts. Usually, people need 'mending' as well as 'training' in order to serve at their best. As a Christian leader, often you will be asked to take a broken person and help him or her become a well-trained worker in God's Kingdom. That kind of preparation builds up the church and helps us all become mature in Christ.

Still, it is easy in the high pressure environment of planting a new church to forget that primary job. There are so many other responsibilities – preaching, problem solving, and pastoring, among many others. Meeting the needs and expectations of people within the church can eat up our time and energy so that we don't have enough left to equip them.

Often, we are so busy DOING the work of the ministry, that we don't have the time and energy to EQUIP others to do the ministry. And, as a result, the Enemy wins. Why? Because, if we did our job of equipping Christians for ministry, our team would accomplish a hundred times more than we could do alone.

Let me urge you to be an EQUIPPER! You can prepare God's people for works of service! Make it a high priority! Stay committed! Do not be distracted! With all the other good things that press for your attention, stay focused on your most strategic priority: Be an Equipper!

You will know God's pleasure as you stay focused on his work. Your people will thank you for it.

---

*Dear Father, Help me to faithfully equip the precious people entrusted to my care.
Amen.*

Paul Becker

Knowing Who I Am #1
Introduction

Wisdom is proved right by all her children. ~ Luke 7:35

READING: Luke 7:18-35

One of the challenges of church planting is that we often bear the full brunt of people's rejection, criticism and cluelessness. Additionally, our church sub-culture may impose its own set of expectations and preconceptions on church planters or pastor's wives. Even godly denominations may subtly favor certain personality types or leaders who most closely emulate the latest Christian fad. It's a given that we should adhere to Biblical standards for godly leadership. But I've sometimes found it difficult to sort out my true identity from all these other competing notions, especially when who I am, as best as I can guess, differs from other people's expectations.

I once worked for a retired Army colonel who turned me down flat when I presented the gospel to him. For some reason his emphatic rejection brought to a head many of my long-standing frustrations and insecurities about how to stay true to the person God had called me to be in the midst of sometimes painful personal rejection.

When I prayed about it, God led me to the amazing story in Luke 7:18 – 35. More than any other passage, this account of Jesus and John the Baptist has given me a framework to process my internal self-doubts against the backdrop of the contradictory or negative feedback given by other people. It has shown me the way of wisdom.

In the coming days we will explore this story and I'm happy to share what I gleaned. But I also encourage you to meditate on this passage, applying its elements to your unique situation.

Dear Lord, Please deliver me from the fear of man and help me to walk in the integrity of my heart. Amen.

Dionne Carpenter

Knowing Who I Am #2
Handling Self-doubts

*Are You the one who is to was to come,
or should we expect someone else? ~ Luke 7:19*

READING: Luke 7: 18-23

If anyone should have known who he was, with absolute confidence, it would have been John the Baptist. How many people do *you* know whose father was visited by the Angel Gabriel? Gabriel pinpointed John's identity as the one great forerunner before the Messiah (Isa. 40:3; Mal. 4:5, 6). John grew up knowing precisely what he had been born to do. When the Pharisees questioned John about his credentials, John responded with confidence. He did his job well. He preached courageously, he baptized the repentant, and, one momentous day, he pointed at Jesus and identified Him as the Lamb of God who takes away the sin of the world.

With that as backdrop, I find it curiously comforting that near the end of his life, John began second-guessing himself. Make no mistake, when he relayed his question to Jesus asking who <u>He</u> was, it was motivated by John's last minute worry that he himself might have accidentally missed the boat.

But John handled his self-doubts in the best way possible: He asked Jesus. Jesus graciously answered him in a way that reassured him and restored his peace of mind. Jesus didn't scold John. Instead He offered John a blessing.

On those days when you question everything you thought you knew about who God has called *you* to be, when the very idea that God called you to plant churches seems most ridiculous, don't be afraid to take your self-doubts to Jesus. He won't berate you. He will understand. And He will comfort and encourage your heart, just like He comforted John.

Dear Lord, You who call every star by name, thank You for welcoming me even on those days I doubt myself. Please give me renewed clarity to serve You with confidence. Amen.

Dionne Carpenter

Knowing Who I Am #3
Handling Other People's Perceptions

What did you go out into the desert to see? ~ Luke 7:24

READING: Luke 7:24-28

After John's disciples left, Jesus turned to the crowd and asked them what they thought of John. Some dismissed John as merely a reed. Others respected him as a prophet. A few clueless folks hoped to be entertained by a man in fine clothes. Jesus identified these widely divergent opinions – the followers, the spectators and the critics.

Like us, John would certainly have run into such wildly divergent perceptions as these about himself. What exactly does a church planter look like, anyway?

But then, remarkably, Jesus gave the crowd the *correct* answer: John is the greatest prophet, and yet, the one who is least in the kingdom of God is greater than he.

More than any other passage in Scripture, this little comment by Jesus has given me peace of mind as I deal with the wildly differing perceptions that people entertain about me. We are all somewhat influenced by how other people perceive us. Some people "get" us although many people completely misunderstand who we are or what motivates us.

Personally, this passage showed me that *nobody* knows exactly who I am except Jesus – not even me. Nobody in that crowd knew the full story. John himself knew only bits and pieces, even though an angel had talked to his dad. The only person who knew the whole story was Jesus.

As I navigate between the often contradictory opinions of others in my quest for godly self-knowledge, this story has taught me to value God's "opinion" above all others, even my own. The more we learn to rest in the confidence of knowing God and being known by God, the less it matters what other people think.

Dear Lord, Help me to find the confidence that comes from seeing myself through Your eyes. Amen.

Dionne Carpenter

Knowing Who I Am #4
Handling Rejection

All the people, even the tax collectors, when they heard Jesus' words,
acknowledged that God's way was right, because they had been baptized
by John. But the Pharisees and experts in the law rejected God's purpose for
themselves, because they had not been baptized by John. ~ Luke 7:29, 30

READING: Luke 7:29, 30

As church planters we frequently run into people who reject us or reject the gospel we present. Rejection can make us feel insecure – how could I have presented it better? What's wrong with me?

After that colonel rejected me, this Scripture comforted me and showed me a way to understand rejection. When people react to us they don't do so as an empty slate; their response reflects the accumulated effects from their many little choices and their many previous experiences.

The folks in John's day who decided to get baptized by John had previously chosen to embrace God's purposes, which, in turn, made them more receptive to follow Jesus later on. Conversely, the Pharisees rejected Jesus partly because they had previously rejected God and previously rejected John's baptism. My boss, the colonel, had closed his heart to God years before we ever met.

It had nothing to do with me.

We should share the gospel and live our lives as winsomely as possible, avoiding any unnecessary offense. But we should also get out of the way. It's really not about us. It is, for each of our hearers, one in a series of solemn choices. It's primarily between them and God.

John did his job well, both for those who rejected him, and for those who accepted his message. For some blessed few, he was a stepping stone in their journey to Christ.

Dear Lord, Help me to rest in the assurance that I am accepted by You and share the good news without fear. Amen.

Dionne Carpenter

Knowing Who I Am #5
Handling Criticism

We played the flute for you and you did not dance;
we sang a dirge and you did not cry. ~ Luke 7:32

READING: Luke 7:31-35

Although both were holy men, John the Baptist and Jesus had entirely different personalities and ministry styles. John was an austere loner who served in the wilderness, preaching a severe repentance. Jesus was the more sociable teacher, interacting with all kinds of people, easily balancing fearless confrontations with tender acts of kindness. Both got criticized – John for having a demon, Jesus for being a glutton and a drunkard.

It's unpleasant to be criticized. It can make us question everything. We want to avoid it whenever possible. But in this passage, Jesus clearly shows us that it's unrealistic to expect we'll always be able to avoid criticism. Blessedly, He does not require from us a criticism-free ministry.

Best of all, in a few transformative words, Jesus takes much of the sting out of getting criticized. After all, think about it – both John the Baptist (the greatest prophet who ever lived) and Jesus (the perfect Son of God) ran into criticism for faithfully doing what they were called to do! And they were the paragons! It's impossible to please everybody all the time.

Of course, you and I are far from perfect and may well deserve some criticism now and then. But criticism, in and of itself, does *not* necessarily mean we're doing the wrong thing or that there is a fundamental flaw within us.

I love that Jesus made this point using two godly men whose ministries and personalities were so strikingly different. God appears to love variety in His choice of servants. Jesus gives us confidence to be ourselves and boldly do what God has called us to do.

Dear Lord, Give me wisdom to discern which criticism to take to heart and which to blissfully ignore. Amen.

Dionne Carpenter

Study to Show Yourself Approved Unto God

Do your best to present yourself to God as one approved,
a workman who does not need to be ashamed and who
correctly handles the word of truth. ~ II Timothy 2:15

READING: II Timothy 3:14-17

Not everyone on a church planting team has been through a systematic Bible training. In fact it has become very clear to me in Peru that there are many who are planting churches who have no formal Bible training but rather have based their ministry on short seminars or conferences which they have attended.

While those seminars are often very informative and anointed, they are no replacement for a systematic biblical training, whether in a traditional Bible school or a systematic video Bible training. Otherwise, although they have knowledge and anointing in leadership principles they lack an overall knowledge of the Scriptures regarding numerous broader topics outside of church planting.

What about you? Have you been trained systematically in the Word of God or are you doing that now? There is no time like the present to begin. Various video courses are available. Does your church have a training plan? Talk with your pastor or mentor for his counsel. Prepare yourself and your teammates to study systematically.

As the Word of God penetrates our lives, we will grow in the Word and in character and be more prepared for EVERY good work. I have talked to many church leaders who feel comfortable in one area of ministry but almost refuse to help out when it's an area that they don't feel particularly "called" to do.

Are you fully prepared for every good work? Do you want to be fully equipped for church planting ministry? Make plans and take the necessary steps to accomplish it.

Dear Father, I admit that I don't feel fully prepared for every good work. Show me what steps I should take to truly be prepared. Amen.

Ron Thiesen

Promises and Pressures

*He lifted me out of the slimy pit, out of
the mud and mire; he set my feet on a rock and gave
me a firm place to stand. ~ Psalm 40:2*

READING: Hebrews 12:1-12

God's promises are not primarily guarantees for success in our church planting journey. Instead they assure us, which helps us complete our journey with optimism. On the journey we face the pressure of sin, fleshly weaknesses, disobedience and trials that would tempt us to withdraw from our commitments. Though Peter was well-known for inconsistency, eventually he became a key shepherding leader. The book of Acts shows how God fulfilled the promise made personally to Peter: "... follow me ... I will make you [a] fisher of men" (Matt. 4:19).

Church planters are not exempted from the same kind of failures that Peter experienced as we strive in God's mission. What can make us optimists? God's Promises, the pledge of God, give us a new zeal and enthusiasm.

Church planters will always have dual encounters: "failures" in life and the "promises" from God. When we fail, we are tempted either to hide or justify our failures. Any unaccounted or unhandled failure will lead us to a spiritual emptiness and an inward defeat.

The list of names in Hebrews 11 encourages us that our God is able to raise anyone from any slimy pit of failures. He is able to set *your* feet on a rock and give a firm place to stand and sing a new song of praise.

Failures of church planters are of various kinds. The promises of God give us a pathway out of every failure that we come across, not by hiding failings but by handling and overcoming them. God's promises are like a book of checks, always available for us to use whenever we become spiritually empty.

Lord, Help us to make use of your promises that give us forgiveness and freshness. Amen.

R. Jayakumar

Fully Prepared for Every Good Work

*Do not be hasty in the laying
on of hands... ~ I Timothy 5:22a*

READING: I Timothy 3:1-7

Churches are raised up by people who have been discipled or mentored ("fully prepared for every good work," II Tim. 3:17). It is too often the case that we are disappointed by someone that has not measured up to our expectations. We place them in a church planting leadership position before they are ready. We get discouraged sometimes when we have to start over. We should be aware that a disciple is someone who has achieved a measurable level of maturity in the standards that the Lord Jesus set forth for his disciples.

What are those standards and what are the characteristics that must be present for a person to be released to head up a church plant? In my experience in the Amazon, three broad qualifications must be present and growing in a church planting pastor in order to expect their church plant to have success.

A disciple must have the proper godly motivation. There are so many different motivations that we see in church leadership, especially in those who have not been tested. Some unworthy motivations, among others, are an opportunity for a salary or a desire for respect and authority instead of the rejection that they grew up with.

They must be of proven character. No church plant will be successful if the testimony of the leadership is lacking. They must have a level of maturity and stability that new believers can count on explicitly.

They must have credibility, which includes knowledge of the Word and an ability to positively influence their congregation of all ages.

Heavenly Father, Help me to be wise in choosing church planting pastors. Forgive me for expecting too much from those who are not yet ready. Teach me how to develop good traits in promising young leaders. Amen.

Ron Thiesen

Seek Them Not

And do you seek great things for yourself?
Seek them not... ~ Jeremiah 45:5a (ESV)

READING: Jeremiah 45:1-5

Who would want to endure a major failure, a terrible national disaster or a "plucking up" of what has been planted (Jer. 45:4)? Such was the situation that kept Baruch, Jeremiah's secretary, awake at night constantly groaning. Yuck! That situation would make me groan, too. I struggle to handle failures, set-backs and disasters. I long for accomplishment, admiration, and success. Don't you?

It is so easy to focus on the wrong thing. But God had an important message for Baruch and for us. God wants us to focus on what is of greatest importance.

What should we seek? We must seek only to know Jesus and to please Him – that alone – whether it brings what people consider success or even failure.

The Apostle Paul briefly recounted his great "successes" in Philippians 3. But his point was not his personal greatness; it was the triviality of all human accomplishments, when compared to knowing Jesus. His conclusion was: "But Christ has shown me that what I once thought was valuable is worthless. Nothing is as wonderful as knowing Christ Jesus my Lord. I have given up everything else and count it all as garbage. All I want is Christ and to know that I belong to him" (Phil. 3:7 – 9a CEV).

Church planting leader, do you seek "great things for yourself?" Seek them not. And don't seek failure and disaster either. Neither of these should be our aim.

If success is our goal, we will end up with "garbage," even if we are "successful." If knowing and pleasing Christ is our goal, we will be filled with His love, peace, assurance, hope, joy, comfort and grace. That is true greatness and success.

Lord, Help me focus on the right goal, which is You. Help me to seek You first and know You intimately. Amen.

Mark Alan Williams

Declaration of War

*And from the days of John the Baptist until
now the kingdom of heaven suffers violence, and the
violent take it by force. ~ Matthew 11:12 (NKJV)*

READING: Matthew 11:1-19

Jesus tells us here that the kingdom of God can only become a reality through violence. Planting a new church takes for God what previously belonged to the Devil; and souls are not won easily. But the soul of the planter is the most critical battleground for the new church.

Paul instructs us in Romans 8:13, "for if you are living according to the flesh, you must die; but if by the Spirit you are putting to death the deeds of the body, you will live." While putting the Devil in his place is important, he is not our greatest threat. Jesus promised the gates of Hades cannot prevail against the church (Matt. 16:18), but many well trained and educated church planters have fallen victim to the weakness of their own flesh.

Peacetime Christian servants will be ill-prepared for their inward battles as they seek to advance the kingdom of God. The deeds of the flesh will wage war to keep the planter from being the leader the task demands. Doubt, unbelief, timidity, pride, vanity, exhaustion, confusion, temptation, lust – all works of the flesh – raise their ugly heads to weaken the planter and kill the church.

Only by the Holy Spirit can we put to death sinful deeds. The church planting pastor must daily fight the pull of the flesh with the weapons of the Spirit: confession, prayer, faith, and the Word of God (Ephesians 6). A cleansed and confident church planter cannot be beaten!

Father in heaven, Give me courage to fight the impulses that surge within me. Cast down any sinful stronghold and deliver me from the chains of sin. Today, I claim victory over my flesh, and declare freedom in the Spirit of Christ. Amen!

Del Loy

It's Time to Plant!

There is a time for everything, and a
season for every activity under heaven: a time to
be born and a time to die, a time to plant and a
time to uproot… ~ Ecclesiastes 3:1, 2

READING: Esther 4

As church planters, now is the *time to plant!* The world cries out for the gospel and we have found that the most effective evangelistic tool for reaching the world is the planting of new churches. Here at DCPI, we know that "today is the day of salvation" and now is the time to plant.

On the local scene it behooves the planter to be sensitive to God's timing. "In the fullness of time" it will come to pass. Just like Queen Esther, you have come to your location for a "time such as this." Pray today for an extra measure of sensitivity to God's Spirit as to the timing and pacing of events in your church plant. There is a sense of God's timing that is ideal for every situation.

Jesus had an uncanny sense of timing in all that he did. He knew when to speak and when to be silent. And when he spoke, He knew what needed to be said, whether words of rebuke, exhortation, hope or comfort. There is a time for everything. Ask God for wisdom to know when to speak, what to speak and His timing for the next step as you lead your church plant.

Father, Today I ask for wisdom and sensitivity to your timing as I lead my flock. Teach me when to speak and when to be silent; when to sit still and when to step up. Please show me the next step in the church planting process. Thank you for hearing my prayers, in the name of the One who had perfect timing and perfect words in every situation. Amen.

Sam Douglass

Distractions

A woman named Martha welcomed him into her house. And she had a sister called Mary, who sat at the Lord's feet and listened to his teaching. But Martha was distracted with much serving. And she went up to Him and said, "Lord, do you not care that my sister has left me to serve alone? Tell her then to help me." But the Lord answered her, "Martha, Martha, you are anxious and troubled about many things, but one thing is necessary. Mary has chosen the good portion, which will not be taken away from her. ~ Luke 10:39b–42 (ESV)

READING: Luke 10:38-42

Jesus came to visit His friends Martha and Mary (sisters of Lazarus). Mary honored Christ by sitting at His feet, while Martha worked hard to prepare an elaborate meal. But Martha became agitated and complained to Jesus, expecting Him to make her sister help her.

Jesus answered Martha lovingly, but firmly. She was upset by many things, He said, but only one thing was truly important – the thing Mary had chosen.

In church planting, it's easy to let our service *for* Christ distract us *from* Christ. The word "distract," used only here in the New Testament, means to "turn aside," to stir up and confuse.

Worry distracts us from worship. Martha's worry kept her from truly honoring Christ. Looking at others distracts us from looking at Christ. Poor Martha's resentment of her sister kept her from enjoying Jesus. Dabbling in many things distracts us from the "one thing." Martha did many things, but she missed Mary's one thing – spending time in the presence of Christ.

Don't let your hard work in serving Jesus distract you from the intimacy of your worship and fellowship with the Lord.

Jesus, Help me always to begin where Mary did – at Your feet – before I rise to serve You. Amen.

Jim Carpenter

The Pain of Losing Key Leaders

...for Demas, because he loved this world,
has deserted me... ~ II Timothy 4:10

READING: I Samuel 20; Colossians 4:14; Philemon 24

The Apostle Paul knew first-hand what it meant to lose partners and key leaders in the ministry. When it comes to parting and severing relationships, it is painful. Whether it be personality conflicts, like Paul experienced between Barnabas and John Mark, or the loss of a fellow partner due to sin and earthly desires, like with Demas, parting ways is difficult.

Some of the most painful memories of my first church plant center around the loss of a praise and worship team leader who "came out of the closet" to pursue an alternate lifestyle. His lack of repentance and defiance of church discipline caused his removal from the body. It was painful for his wife, two teenage sons, and the church when fellowship was withdrawn based on Matthew 18:15 – 17.

Or what about the key leader who left angry because I wouldn't accept the free Country Club membership he offered if I would play golf with him every Thursday afternoon? When confronted by another church member he said, "Our church is getting too big, and my pastor is too busy for me and my family."

Losing key people is always painful and costly. The church planter must determine whether he will be a *man pleaser* or a *God pleaser*. Who is going to set the agenda for the pastor's time and the future of the church? I discovered long ago that people have a "wonderful plan" for your church; Satan has a plan for your church plant; and our Heavenly Father has His plan. Who will set the agenda? Whose plans will be accomplished?

Heavenly Father, Today I choose to be a God pleaser. Please fulfill your plans for this church and comfort my heart as I grieve those I've lost. Amen.

Sam Douglass

Before Accepting That Big Donation

*Then Abimelech brought sheep and cattle and male and
female slaves and gave them to Abraham… ~ Genesis 20:14*

READING: Genesis 20

Have you ever noticed that Abraham accepted many gifts from Abimelech the king of Gerar (a pagan man who acknowledged Yahweh's authority)? Yet, back when the wicked king of Sodom tried to share spoils of war with him, Abram emphatically refused: "I will accept nothing belonging to you, not even a thread or the thong of a sandal, so that you will never be able to say, 'I made Abram rich'" (Gen. 14:23).

We do well to be cautious when people offer us large gifts. Jim and I learned this the hard way when a man in our core group donated some property for our second church plant and then assumed that act of generosity entitled him to run the church as his little fiefdom.

We've also seen amazing Christ-likeness. It was several years before I found out that one of our quiet little widows had donated the property years ago to build the lovely church where we serve now. She never mentioned it.

Godly benevolence blesses us all – giver and receiver alike – causing us to rejoice in God's abundant supply. But it's wise to consider a few questions first before accepting a generous donation: Are there any strings attached? Will this make us indebted to a wicked or carnal person, or imply our approval of their ungodly behavior? Is our potential donor mature enough as a believer to withstand the temptation they'll inevitably encounter afterwards to become prideful or manipulative because they have given such a large donation?

We all need help funding our churches, but let's be cautious to distinguish between God-fearing donors like Abimelech and dangerous ones like the king of Sodom.

Dear Father, Give me great discernment to see the true cost involved when someone makes a generous offer. Amen.

Dionne Carpenter

The Peril of Hasty Hands

*Do not be hasty in the laying on of
hands, nor take part in the sins of others;
keep yourself pure. ~ I Timothy 5:22*

READING: Titus 1:5-9

Our new church was growing, people were being saved, and after about a year I thought we were ready for a church council. Some of the original core members suggested a congregational meeting where men could be nominated for the elder board. Though I felt uneasy about it, I agreed. Five men were elected from the floor. Four were proven leaders who were already serving in various ministries. The fifth, Fred (not his real name), was in his early 20's, was not serving anywhere and seemed to have a critical spirit.

His nomination and election knotted my stomach. I knew in my heart I had just made a terrible mistake. Scripture is clear on the character qualities of an elder, most of which Fred lacked. In fact, the woman who nominated Fred said she did it "to help him get involved."

As a young church planter, I ignored Scripture's warning not to appoint leaders too quickly. I learned the wisdom of that warning the hard way. Fred was a constant problem, and until he resigned, was an ongoing reminder that it's far easier to appoint than to remove an unqualified leader.

By my next church plant I had learned my lesson. Yes, you need leaders. But seek an advisory council of mature leaders from outside the church who believe in you and your church plant – other church planters, elders from the mother church, godly missionaries. Then over the course of several years these "outsiders" can help mentor "insiders" from your church plant. You'll have the benefit of wise, godly counsel without the pressure of appointing too quickly.

Father, Raise up leaders in my new church, and protect me from ever "laying on hands too quickly." Amen.

Jim Carpenter

AUGUST

The Bridge Principle

*Understanding (and communicating
sensitively to) the hearts and minds of people
in the target community is essential to
reaching them with the gospel.*

Bridging the Gap

For through the law I died to the law so
that I might live to God. ~ Galatians 2:19 (NASB)

READING: Galatians 2:11-21

The Apostle Paul was uniquely qualified to bridge the gap between Jewish and Gentile Christianity. He was taught by the famous rabbi, Gamaliel, in Jerusalem. He spoke Greek and was familiar with Greek thought and literature. This meant he could express the doctrines and teachings of Jesus that were based on Old Testament beliefs foreign to the Gentiles in ways the pagan mind could grasp. He preached Jesus as the Christ throughout Asia Minor and Greece and planted churches of Gentile believers.

Paul faced a question that was at the heart of tensions between first century Jewish and Gentiles believers and we face the same question when encountering various cultures of pagan worlds. We continually need to evaluate the question of what is the best way to instill Christian principles of morality in the churches we plant. Paul understood that if merely obeying the law determined righteousness, then he would have been the greatest in the kingdom. Nevertheless, righteousness by personal effort only leads to failure.

We attended a council meeting during our first encounter with new Christians from the Embera Chamí indigenous group. The governor, addressing their newfound faith, expressed deep concern that the identity of their people would vanish if they espoused this new Christianity. We attempted to bridge the gap by gently explaining that God wants to improve what He culturally gave the Chamí, not destroy centuries of culture and identity. God divinely set apart this group of uniquely qualified Chamí to bridge the gap between other Chamí groups and the truth of the love and freedom through Jesus!

Father, Thank you that we are free from the law and that we come to you only by your grace. Let us impart this truth to whatever people group you bring to us. Amen.

Christine Cunningham

God Will Give You a Strategy

I have become all things to all men so that by all
possible means I might save some. ~ I Corinthians 9:22b

READING: I Corinthians 9:19-23

God has established principles in His word for everything we do. Following these principles in our lives will guarantee success in everything that we do (Josh. 1:8). He has also filled our world with many different people groups from many different cultures who need to have the church, the body of Christ, planted among them.

The principles will be the same because they come from God's Word, but what strategy God will give us depends somewhat upon the people group where we are working. It is necessary for us to spend time alone with God praying for the people and to hear from God the next step or divine strategy. The Lord will show us or impress upon us to do a certain thing, then later He will show us more strategy. It is the body of Christ and He, the Head, knows how best to proceed.

In the Amazon, our work ranges from very small villages to towns of three to four thousand. The Lord has given us a strategy to evangelize multiple villages, discover and train potential leadership through Bible training seminars, train key regional leaders and give spiritual support to these key leaders in every way possible. God has blessed His work through these strategies. Praise the Lord!

What are the strategies that God has given to you for your particular community? Are you obedient to the principles in His word and the strategies for your particular area?

Lord, These precious people are your creation. You love them and do not wish that any should perish but that all should come to repentance. Please show me your special strategies for reaching this particular group. Amen.

Ron Thiesen

Christ's Triumph #1

But thanks be to God, who in Christ always leads us
to triumphal procession… ~ II Corinthians 2:14a (ESV)

READING: II Corinthians 2:12-17

When I was still in seminary, God began to call me to church planting. To try to prepare, I did a research project in which I surveyed all the church planters in our denomination. I asked them various questions about the methods they used. The last question was open-ended. What advice would they give me as a future church planter?

One veteran church planter's *only* advice was to claim the promise of II Corinthians 2:14 – 17. I wasn't familiar with the passage, but I began to study it. It has been a major source of encouragement to me for the past thirty years.

Paul, traveling from Ephesus, came to the port city of Troas, a place he sensed was ripe for the gospel. But his plans had included meeting his colleague and protégé, Titus, who was returning from a trip to Corinth. When Titus failed to appear, Paul was filled with concern, both for his young disciple and for the Corinthian church, which had been dealing with many problems.

Church planting is like that. Your best plans may be interrupted. People may disappoint or worry you. And the church(es) you start may struggle. Like any parent, church planters bear the weight of concern for their coworkers and for their congregations.

As heavy as this was upon Paul, it was then that he burst forth in confidence: "But thanks be to God, who in Christ always leads us to triumphal procession!"

He knew, and we must know, that despite sin, setbacks and stalls, Christ, the Lord of Church Planting, still leads us in victory!

Jesus, Teach me to trust that Your guidance is infallible even when my vision is cloudy. Amen.

Jim Carpenter

Christ's Triumph #2

But thanks be to God, who in Christ always leads us to
triumphal procession, and through us spreads the fragrance of the
knowledge of him everywhere. ~ II Corinthians 2:14 (ESV)

READING: II Corinthians 2:12-17

Despite his worry about the whereabouts of Titus and his concern over the new church in Corinth, Paul was confident in Christ "who always leads us in triumphal procession."

When he wrote those words, in the original Greek, he used the image of a "Roman Triumph," the special victory parade for a Roman general. This was a unique honor awarded only to a general who achieved extraordinary acclaim in battle.

This Roman general had to meet three qualifications. First, he must have actually led his troops in combat. Directing safely from the sidelines was not enough. Second, he had to have completely conquered the enemy. And third, he must have advanced the boundaries of the Roman Empire. Simply defending Rome did not qualify.

We are confident in Christ because He far exceeds the exploits of any human conqueror. How we love our Savior, and honor Him, for the greatness of His triumph!

Our Lord Jesus placed Himself in the middle of the battlefield. The eternal Second Person of the Trinity took upon Himself human flesh, entered history, and "has been tempted just as we are, yet without sin" (Heb. 4:15).

Like the Roman general (but so much more!) Christ has conquered all. "For God has put all things in subjection under his feet" (I Cor. 15:27). In His death and resurrection, Christ our King extended the rule of the Kingdom of God to the darkest corners of humanity.

Even when we are discouraged, confused, or weary, our hope and comfort and confidence are in the Triumph of our great God and Savior, the Lord Jesus Christ!

Jesus, Thank You that You are the King and that You are leading me in Your triumph!
Amen.

Jim Carpenter

Christ's Triumph #3

For we are the aroma of Christ to God among those
who are being saved and among those who are perishing, to
one a fragrance from death to death, to the other a fragrance
from life to life. ~ II Corinthians 2:15, 16a (ESV)

READING: II Corinthians 2:12-17

When Paul spoke of Christ leading us in triumphal procession, he used the imagery of the "Roman Triumph," a victory parade honoring a conquering general. The general led his army through the streets of Rome into the arena. For his soldiers, this was a day of highest honor and joyful celebration.

Toward the rear of the parade were the vanquished enemy soldiers. Defeated and downcast, they trudged along in chains, knowing they would be killed when they reached the Coliseum.

Priests of ancient Rome accompanied the processional, twirling censers of burning incense. The sweet smell was a victory fragrance for the general and his army. But for the prisoners, it was the stench of death.

As we follow Christ and proclaim His gospel, there are only two kinds of people we meet: those who are being saved and those who are perishing. For some, the fragrance of Christ is the sweetest aroma they've ever experienced. They believe the gospel and are transformed. Others "smell" Christ and turn away. They are moving inexorably toward eternal death.

Church planting polarizes people. New churches that live for Christ and faithfully teach the Bible begin to "smell" like Jesus. That fragrance wafts through our neighborhoods and into homes, shops, offices and schools. People are either drawn to the Savior or they are repelled.

Lord, Help our new church to be faithful to live for Christ and to share the gospel. And we'll trust You to bring the fragrance of Christ that attracts and transforms. Amen.

Jim Carpenter

Culture Shock!

The true light that gives light to every
man was coming into the world. ~ John 1:9

READING: John 1:1-14

The Son of God was not native to this world. He existed long before He was born in that stable 2,000 years ago. He wasn't from around here! So when Jesus "became flesh and dwelt among us" He was crossing cultural barriers that were greater than what any of us have experienced as missionaries.

After planting churches in two foreign countries, I know what it means to face language studies, strange customs, feeling like an outsider, being misunderstood and trying to act normal in a place that I don't fit. Imagine how strange it must have been for Jesus to leave the culture, relationships and values of heaven to relate with the people He often described as "stiff-necked" and "rebellious." No wonder He took thirty years to acculturate before He began His ministry! Maybe we, too, could be a little more patient with ourselves if we find ourselves called to cross-cultural ministry.

Do you think Jesus experienced culture shock? I believe He did. Hebrews 4:15 says that we have a high priest who can sympathize with all our weaknesses and temptations, "yet without sin." Another strong hint is given in Luke 9:42 where Jesus expresses frustration over human unbelief, "How long shall I stay with you and put up with you?" It sounds to me like Jesus sometimes missed His heavenly home. Even so, Jesus went ahead and healed the boy whose condition prompted His encounter with faithlessness.

The truth is every human culture is counter to God's heavenly culture. Rest assured, the Son of God understands and equips you for this daily challenge wherever you currently reside.

Father, Thanks for sending your Son to experience the pain of culture shock on my behalf. Please empower me to love people and shine as a light in the midst of this culture. Amen.

Scott Last

Power and Truth Encounters

*For indeed Jews ask for signs, and Greeks
search for wisdom… ~ I Corinthians 1:22 (NASB)*

READING: I Kings 18:20-19:13

While in Guapi, a jungle village on the Pacific coast of Colombia, we observed the use of charms and incantations to appease the local gods. The fear that enfolds the jungle culture is fueled by generations of legend and superstition. Conversely, churches in the United States meet for Bible studies and listen to doctors of theology at churches and on local media outlets.

Breaking down people groups into basic cultural concepts is never as simple as the terms we ascribe to them. Cultures fall into two basic categories: power-oriented and truth-oriented. Western culture is predominantly truth-oriented due to the emphasis of the Greek educational systems. Eastern cultures and most third world countries in the western hemisphere are power-oriented largely due to the bold manifestations of demonic power. The evangelist or missionary going to a different culture to share the gospel message should know whether the culture is spiritually power-based or truth-based.

Power cultures say, "If your God is not stronger than the local gods, then I do not want to hear about Him!" Of course the gods they are referring to are none other than principalities of demonic spiritual forces (Eph. 6:12). Truth cultures say, "Give us information based on trustworthy knowledge." These are like the noble-minded Bereans who eagerly receive the word and examine the Scriptures daily (Acts 17:10, 11).

Careful observation before sharing the gospel helps to assess the approach we will take among people groups.

Dear Heavenly Father, As we encounter the bouquet of cultural diversity you take us to, help us to approach people in a way that will assure open hearts and minds to the truth and power of your love and salvation. Amen.

Christine Cunningham

Planting the Church
Where the Church Is Not

It has always been my ambition to preach the gospel where Christ was not known, so that I would not be building on someone else's foundation. ~ Romans 15:20

READING: Matthew 24:9-14

Today I challenge you to 'plant the church where the church is not.' Jesus said, "And this gospel of the kingdom will be preached in the whole world as a testimony to all nations, and then the end will come" (Matt. 24:14). The phrase 'all nations' means all ethnic groups. All ethnic groups must have dynamic, soul-winning, disciple-making churches reproducing within them.

We need to plant churches among unreached and unengaged people groups! As of this writing, 639 unengaged, unreached people groups with populations over 100,000, together numbering over 535,000,000 souls, are still beyond the reach of the Gospel of Jesus Christ. They are spiritually lost and helpless, like sheep having no shepherd.

Will you try to reach one of these groups?

How I thank God for a recent report from one of our Tanzanian DCPI Certified Trainers, Bishop Williams Yindi. "We have just returned from the outreach among those who have never heard about the Saving Grace of our Lord Jesus Christ. It took us about 20 hours on the bus to reach this group near the Mozambique border. We planted a very good church among a previously unreached people group, the Matengo. This brings us to a total of 172 churches planted at this writing." WOW!

Unreached people groups may be closer than you think. European nations are once again unreached, as are large portions of the next generation in the USA. Most cities have pockets of unreached immigrants who have never heard the gospel.

Ask God to open your eyes to see what part he wants you to play to break new ground for the Kingdom.

Dear Lord, Help me to plant a church where the church is not. Amen.

Paul Becker

Are You Loved in Your Community?

*Give everyone what you owe him: If you owe
taxes, pay taxes; if revenue, then revenue; if respect,
then respect; if honor, then honor.* ~ Romans 13:7

READING: Romans 13:1-7

Our purpose for planting a church in a community is to influence the whole community for Christ, to reach all strata of the community. Our ability to influence whole communities or villages for the gospel is greatly enhanced by how we treat the leadership of the community.

In our reality in the villages along the Amazon River and tributaries, it is essential that we "give honor where honor is due" with the village leadership. The very first thing that we do, even before presuming to disembark equipment from the boat, is to converse with the mayor (lieutenant governor), head of the PTA or school principals and get their permission to do our event.

Often they will come to the evangelism event and many times they receive Christ as their personal Savior. When the village leadership receives Christ, or when we simply find favor with them, we have real advantages in planting a church. They are often more prepared to influence their own people and can promote in the process of planting the church. If, on the contrary, we offend them, they are very capable of closing many doors for us and the people of the local community to the gospel.

What about your influence in the target community where you are planting a church? Do you have influence with the *powers that be*? What could you do to befriend them or become an asset to their positive purposes in the community? Get with your team and prayerfully make a plan to obtain the favor of your community leadership.

Our Heavenly Father, We pray for the leadership of the community. Open their hearts to hear your voice. Give us wisdom in reaching their hearts for you. Amen.

Ron Thiesen

Remember the Wind

The wind blows where it wishes and you hear the sound of it, but do not know where it comes from and where it is going; so is everyone who is born of the Spirit. ~ John 3:8

READING: John 3:1-15

As I write I'm sitting in a Starbucks coffee shop. It is very windy outside and the wind messed up my hair as I walked in. I had no control; it blew wherever it wanted. Other customers look windblown and nobody can do anything about it. The wind blows where it wishes. Jesus said that His Holy Spirit is the same: He blows salvation wherever He wishes.

Sometimes I start thinking that ministry success is about me, about my great techniques, strategies, planning, timelines and execution. I may not say it out loud, but I feel it. That attitude is stupid. It is NOT all about me. Salvation is *always* a miracle work of God's Spirit.

I have shared Christ with hundreds of people. Some got saved, others did not. Years ago, when I first started church planting ministry, I remember telling a man I was witnessing to that I believed he was going to be saved. It never happened, at least, not to my knowledge.

But a few years later we started a Bible study group and invited several of our neighbors, including a family that started attending it and our church. The husband seemed a lost cause. He was the "devil's advocate" when we shared Scripture truth. I would have voted him "most likely to never get saved." But today he is pastoring a church he planted. He is leading people to Jesus all the time.

Let's remember the wind today.

> Strive, worry and fret less.
> Pray and trust God more.

Lord, Please move powerfully in "my" ministry through the wind of your Spirit today. Help me trust in myself less and in You more. Amen.

Mark Alan Williams

Donkey Thieves

*Go into the village opposite you, and immediately you
will find a donkey tied there and a colt with her; untie them
and bring them to Me. If anyone says anything to you, you
shall say, "The Lord has need of them," and immediately
he will send them. ~ Matthew 21:2, 3 (NASB)*

READING: Romans 8

Planting churches among the indigenous tribes that have no Christian frame of reference can have unique challenges. Imagine if you will, the mind, not yet indoctrinated to the deity of Christ, tackling this Scripture for the first time.

Jesus instructed his disciples, "untie them and bring them to me. If anyone says anything to you..." Without the presupposing intellectual framework Christians have, it looks very much like Jesus was inciting His disciples to donkey thievery. "If anyone asks you" to our isolated indigenous friends translates to mean: "if you get caught."

We have the context of the whole of Scripture to guide us. Psalm 24:1 says, "The earth is the Lord's, and all it contains, the world, and those who dwell in it." You cannot steal what is already yours.

We work with a local indigenous tribe called the Embera Chamí. The Embera are an ancient warrior people who never surrendered to the Spanish Conquistadors. The nation we call Colombia, they have never officially recognized. Therefore, this land and everything on it belongs to them. Quite often, and understandably, there is opposition when they try to take possession of what they consider to be 'theirs.'

How often as Christians have we faced opposition in taking possession of what is declared to be already ours in Scripture? Donkey thievery to some is obedient faith to others.

Father in Heaven, Help us to take possession of all things you have declared to be already ours. Amen.

Kevin Cunningham

Thirsty for God

Blessed are those whose strength is in You,
who have set their hearts on pilgrimage. ~ Psalm 84:5

READING: Psalm 84:1-5

Recently in one month I was the speaker at a weekend retreat and then took an exhausting trip out of state right before my father died unexpectedly. After the dust settled, emotionally and physically drained, I began aching for a prayer retreat. "My heart and my flesh [were crying] out for the living God."

Some church planters regard prayer retreats mainly as an opportunity to get away to do necessary planning and set the agenda for the next phase of their project. While that's certainly worthwhile; for me, it pales in comparison with my urgent need to connect with the Lord, to bring my inner turmoil, my sorrows, my wounds, my fatigue, my empty hands and my confusion to the only One who can set all to rights. Because it has been true so often in the past, I've become convinced that if only I can steal away to Jesus, He will restore my soul and fill me up again.

The Psalmist might have been in exile, pining away because he wasn't free to take one of the regular pilgrimages scheduled on the Jewish ceremonial calendar. Sometimes we can't stop everything and get away. But the person who *has set his (or her) heart on pilgrimage* looks up, above the bustle of urgent tasks and obligations, to plan and calculate, always searching for creative ways to find that treasured time alone with the Lord.

If that is your heartbeat, then even if you can't go quite yet, you are already blessed, realizing as you do that your strength is in God.

Father, Help me not to give up or shove aside that impulse if I notice that my heart is gasping for a fresh encounter with You. Bless me soon, soon, in Your presence I love so dearly. Amen.

Dionne Carpenter

The Valley of Baca #1

As they pass through the Valley of Baca [weeping],
they make it a place of springs… ~ Psalm 84:6a

READING: Psalm 84:6-9

From time to time, all of us go through seasons that are sad or wrenching. They are impossible to avoid. The Valley of Baca is a place of weeping and grieving. It may be a personal loss such as I experienced recently when my father died. Or it may be a ministry loss such as the church plant that doesn't survive or the person we poured ourselves into discipling who eventually rejects the faith.

But isn't it interesting that the Psalmist notes that true pilgrims "make it" a place of springs?

How do we do that? We do it by reacting and responding well. Each place of grief or humiliation can be transformed into a place of springs if we will humble ourselves before God and receive the pain as from His hand alone. We respond well by acknowledging our pain (if only to ourselves), by refusing to retain any shred of bitterness and by quickly forgiving any who wrong us. We respond well by humbly looking for any life lesson to be gleaned in this valley and taking it to heart as we move forward.

Most of all, we make it a place of springs by steadfastly bringing our grief to God, allowing Him to comfort us when we are most in despair.

Remember, we are pilgrims on a holy journey and don't have to camp indefinitely in our Valley of Baca. Time and distance may soothe the sting of pain we felt while we were there. But what we'll remember most vividly is the precious kindness of God who tenderly and unerringly guided us through sorrow into safety and joy.

Father, Give me the heart of a pilgrim and grace to make my Valley of Baca into a place of springs. Amen.

Dionne Carpenter

The Valley of Baca #2

*As they pass through the Valley of Baca
[weeping], they make it a place of springs; the autumn
rains also cover it with pools. ~ Psalm 84:6*

READING: Psalm 84:10-12

There's an intriguing progression of water in this verse. We start with the *salty tears* of weeping when we encounter unavoidable tragedy or sorrow. The wise pilgrim will make it into a *place of springs* by reacting well and by making the best of a bad situation. And finally, *the autumn rains* also cover it with pools.

What's that about?

Since we don't control the weather this must refer to God's divine blessing and His lavish provision which puts to great use the hard times that we have handled well. Water produces life. The autumn rains nudge our struggling seedlings into a full harvest of spiritual abundance.

Don't you find that to be true for you as well? Admit it, wasn't it in your most difficult circumstances that you grew the most? After your tears subsided, the autumn rains blessed your heart and helped you to grow strong and wise and sorrow-tested.

Although none of us would ever wish for sorrowful times, in retrospect they become the experiences that bless others most reliably. Before going through our Valley of Baca our advice, while sound, may be unwittingly harsh or theoretical. But afterwards, the best advice we give, the most helpful encouragement, the most transformative gifts we share flow directly out of the treasure we discovered at such high cost in our Valley of Baca.

So cheer up, especially if you are stuck in Baca right now. God doesn't waste our pain. The autumn rains will transform even this gloomy place into a healing oasis.

Father, Thank You for Your promise to turn my worst experiences into a place of blessing. Hear my cry, O Lord, and fulfill Your good purpose in my life. Amen.

Dionne Carpenter

Cultural Confusion

*The harvest is plentiful, but the workers are
few. Ask the Lord of the harvest, therefore, to send out
workers into his harvest field. ~ Luke 10:2*

READING: Luke 10:1-12

I was dumbfounded when Pastor Phillip told me I had created a problem, that I was the source of arguments and disputes in his church, and that his congregation was no longer interested in giving their offering because of me. How was that possible?

I had been invited to attend Pastor Phillip's house church in Mysore, India after a productive training in Bangalore. Looking back, I recalled my dilemma when they passed the offering plate. I had no rupees on me at the time so I decided to slip a small US bill among the local currency, a small gesture to help out the fledgling congregation and show my gratitude for their hospitality.

On the train ride back, Phillip explained to me where I had gone wrong. What had seemed to me a modest amount was significantly higher than what that small house church could ever give as offering. This led them to suppose that Pastor Phillip had found a rich patron to support the house church, leaving them little incentive to give out of their own meager means.

My point is not just to be culturally sensitive, but to know that no matter how integrated and aware a foreigner may be, he or she will always be a foreigner. I needed Pastor Phillip's guidance to show me how to channel my good impulse. Long-term, the wisest use of our resources is to look for culturally sensitive and appropriate ways to train and equip local leaders to labor within their own culture. That will produce the most genuine and sustainable results.

Dear Heavenly Father, Teach me to recognize the diversity of the Church and help me to use my own gifts well, while honoring the gifts of others. Amen.

Mark Alan Williams

Despised and Rejected

*He was despised and rejected by men; a man
of sorrows, and acquainted with grief; and as one from
whom men hide their faces he was despised, and we
esteemed him not. ~ Isaiah 53:3 (ESV)*

READING: Mark 14:26-15:47

Rejection hurts, and all church planters know what it feels like. Whether it's a door getting slammed in your face while you're sharing the gospel, a core member bailing out to go to another church or a key leader betraying your trust, church planting brings its fair share of rejection.

Our Savior knows the pain of rejection better than anyone. The story of His arrest, trial, scourging and crucifixion is a terrible reminder of how our Jesus was hated and rejected. One of the Twelve betrayed Him and the rest turned away. The crowd chose Barabbas, a murderer, instead of Christ. Six hundred soldiers (a battalion) treated Him to contempt, humiliation and excruciating torture. He was crucified – a shameful execution reserved only for the lowest of the low. Passers-by reviled Him and the chief priests and scribes mocked Him.

The worst rejection of all, infinitely more painful than all the rest, was when the Father's face turned away. "My God, my God, why have you forsaken me?" (v. 34). No one in all of history has ever faced such hatred and rejection from friends and foes alike.

Church planting is a lonely business sometimes and God calls us to "share Christ's suffering" (Phil. 3:10) through the pain of rejection. But, no matter how bad it gets, we will never experience Christ's deepest pain. Because Jesus died and we belong to Him, we are never totally alone. "I will never leave you or forsake you" (Hebrews 13:5b).

The Father will never turn His face away from us.

Jesus, Thank You for bearing the pain and loneliness, and for being with me in my journey today. I love You most of all! Amen.

Jim Carpenter

Tirelessness

*However, I consider my life worth nothing to
me, if only I may finish the race and complete the task
the Lord Jesus has given to me… ~ Acts 20:24a*

READING: II Timothy 4:1-8

Betrayals, repeated failures in our strategies, unproductive core team, toxic colleagues, an uncooperative spouse, political opposition and financial deficiency are among the common challenges that can drain the determination of the church planter.

The rebelliousness of the people of Israel made Moses tired. The wickedness of Jezebel triggered Elijah to think about retirement. When God directed Jonah to a place contrary to his choice, it disturbed his vigor to serve. King Saul's wickedness could not affect David's determination for God's program. Jesus was impeccably obedient to the Father in fulfilling His will in spite of various disappointments. The trials of Paul made him work tirelessly for God.

Are you fatigued and stranded somewhere in your church planting journey? If so I would remind you of Paul, a man who fought his good fight with an unceasing determination. What made him to be an untiring man of God's Mission? Passion for people and energy from prayer are the two great power sources that continually recharged his energy. If you have real passion for your target community you won't easily lose your grip. Passion for perishing people will make you a loyal, patriotic soldier in His Kingdom mission.

Sometimes, though we have a genuine passion, the density of trials may wear us down. I urge you to run to the power room as quickly as possible and stay there as long as possible. You are an ambassador for Christ, a good soldier under the Captain, a flawless athlete, a hard working farmer, a royal priest, a good shepherd and a co-worker of the Lord. Serve Him tirelessly – it is worth it.

Lord, Give me your energy so I may do your will at all times. Amen.

R. Jayakumar

All Means All

*All authority has been given to Me in
heaven and on earth. Go therefore and make disciples of
all the nations, baptizing them in the name of the Father and the
Son and the Holy Spirit, teaching them to observe all that I
commanded you; and lo, I am with you always, even to
the end of the age. ~ Matthew 28:18-20 (NASB)*

READING: Matthew 9:1-13

In Colombia, doctors make house calls. Jesus made house calls. He went to the sick where they were. Although he also spent time ministering in the religious 'clinics' of His time – the Temple and the local synagogues – the majority of His ministry was in the marketplace.

His unconventional ministry practices and personal associations with the spiritually afflicted put Jesus at odds with other contemporary professionals. He dared to eat and drink with sinners. He went into places where prostitutes and tax collectors gathered. Jesus made house calls.

In today's religious society we encounter the same shortsighted mindset. We build bigger and better 'clinics' and wait for sick sinners to stagger in off the street. Our emergency rooms are state of the art, our people well-trained to handle all kinds of incoming cases. Yet, it appears that the sick are not coming. They are dying in their homes, in the bars and gambling casinos while our staff waits in antiseptic halls. Some do venture out, offering on-site evangelistic events at local stadiums or gathering places. There we employ the same 'come to us' strategies, presenting a mobile version of our fine facilities.

It is not working. Jesus demonstrated the need to attack spiritual death and decay. He was not worried about possible contamination or damaged reputation. When he said 'all,' he meant all; all authority, all nations, all that I commanded, always. He knew that to stop the disease you must go to the source.

Father in heaven, Help us with all of this. Amen.

Kevin Cunningham

Manna Time #4
Elasticity

Here is a boy with five small barley
loaves and two small fish, but how far will
they go among so many? ~ John 6:10

READING: I Kings 17:7-16

We don't discover one of the most amazing characteristics of manna until we are down to the last scrap of food in our cupboard. Manna showcases God's delight to supernaturally stretch tiny resources to meet gigantic need. Manna is incredibly elastic.

We see it over and over again in Scripture – the manna that supplied millions of meals for forty years, the widow with her ever-refilling jar and jug (I Kings 17), another widow who repaid her enormous debt from one little cruet of oil (II Kings 4), and the stories of Jesus feeding more than five thousand and more than four thousand with heaping baskets left over. We see it as well in modern times in the holy experiments of saints like George Mueller.

(On a sobering note, on occasion God may do the opposite, and dry up the wealth people trust in, transforming their bulging wallet into a purse that has holes in it. See what I mean by checking out Haggai 1:1 – 11.)

If we are willing to learn, manna can teach us powerful lessons of faith. It can teach us to look beyond the limits of our checking account balance or how few coins we have in our wallet and see our wonderful God who lavishly supplies our every need out of the treasury of "His glorious riches in Christ Jesus."

All these stories have one other thing in common. In each case, the manna arrived when people yielded the little they had to God, or to His servant, and asked for help.

Dear Father, I give You what I have and ask You to give me this day my daily bread.
Amen.

Dionne Carpenter

Manna Time #5
Peaceable Manna Gathering

Each morning everyone gathered as much as he needed,
and when the sun grew hot, it melted away. ~ Exodus 16:21

READING: Exodus16:19-30

There is no such thing as leftover manna. It's really disconcerting! Manna is the simplest, most literal answer to prayer when we ask God to "give us this day our *daily* bread."

It's enough to make you chuckle to watch the Israelites in their bumpy adjustment to manna. Many of them gathered too much on weekdays only to find their hoard riddled with maggots the following morning. Then they felt skeptical when Moses instructed them to gather double on Sabbath Eve. But even Sabbath manna lasted only two days.

None of us gathers manna peaceably from the start. We all struggle to synchronize with God. Manna-gathering is a holy exercise that teaches us visceral, moment by moment dependence upon Him. We may assume we will grow in our knowledge of God mainly through the grand, public adventure of planting our new church. But, looking back, I see now that some of the deepest and most foundational lessons of faith are taught through the mysterious way God supplies in those hidden, tiny increments that give us bread and water and shelter, the humble necessities.

Peaceable manna-gathering exudes confidence that God will provide for today's every need. Ask for *today's* expense without borrowing worry for all the times in the future we'll need the same thing or other things. Wait expectantly. Be wise in the meantime. Receive and be generous to share all your manna without fear.

And take courage. Don't be afraid when you see that ungathered manna melt away in the noonday sun. Tomorrow morning He will once again send you all the manna you need.

Dear Father, Help me to synchronize my steps to Yours and to rest in the assurance of every day's supply. Amen.

Dionne Carpenter

Manna Time #6
Manna for His Disciples

*At that time Jesus went through the grain fields on
the Sabbath. His disciples were hungry and began to pick
some heads of grain and eat them. ~ Matthew 12:1*

READING: Matthew 12:1-8

Why did Jesus pick that particular route to travel on that particular Sabbath? Well, He noticed that His disciples were hungry and they needed to eat. It couldn't have been far from where they had slept the night before because the ever-critical Pharisees did not accuse Him of disobeying their picayune Sabbath travel regulations, just their Sabbath labor laws.

The entire public ministry of Jesus fell under the umbrella of what we have dubbed *Manna Time*, inaugurated by His forty-day fast which symbolically mirrored and redeemed the forty years the Israelites wandered in the Wilderness. He answered one of Satan's temptations using a manna quote. "Man does not live on bread alone but on every word that comes from the mouth of God" (Mt. 4:4). Then He provided "manna" for His disciples for three solid years under various guises: free lunches at the homes of new believers and community leaders; the patronage of wealthy friends; wedding banquets; memorable hillside meals of bread and fish; and these occasional morning strolls through ripened fields of grain.

Those of us who forsake all to follow Christ into ministry can take great comfort from His spirited defense to the Pharisees here in Matthew 12. The logic of His argument reveals a practical grasp of what people need – the human body needs food and regular Sabbath rest.

Had you noticed this before about Christ's ministry? Look back over your own story and notice the many times that God has steered your path so that you, too, found yourself walking waist-high through "coincidental" daily provision and timely supply.

Dear Father, Thank You for knowing exactly what I need and for taking such good care of me. Amen.

Dionne Carpenter

Treasures of Heritage

To the weak I became weak, that I might win the weak;
I have become all things to all men, so that I may by
all means save some. ~ I Corinthians 9:22 (NASB)

READING: Acts 15:11-19

During stateside visits, we stay with my mother-in-law, Wanda, a gentle influence of blessing. At seventy-nine, she manages a small antiques business that keeps her busy getting out to thrift stores and garage sales. She sells her antiques and collectible findings at a local antique mall. She likes making a little money, but her real joy is finding the timeless pieces and then researching their history and value.

Wanda's tidy, unpretentious home is filled with fascinating antique pieces. When relaxing in the peaceful ambience her world offers, it is intriguing to tour these corridors of history. What are most precious about these treasures of the past are the historical truths of life we can glean from them.

When engaging unexposed people groups with the gospel message, we do well to express the same curiosity and intrigue toward their unique cultural perspectives. A key concern of native people groups is the danger of losing their cultural identity and tribal significance. It is vitally important that they sense our genuine and informed respect for their worldview, for who they are and where they've been. We all embrace our cultural heritages. It is our inner fiber. God told the Israelites to tell their story to their children and their children's children to instill a deep understanding of who they were and where they came from.

The primary message of Jesus is love and transformed hearts, not lost heritages. Our challenge is to honor God within diverse cultures as we communicate truths that empower the gospel message to grow.

Father, Fill us with perfect love and an understanding of diversity that breathes transforming life into each new community you give us. Amen.

Christine Cunningham

God's Redemptive Purpose

*And we know that in all things God works for the
good of those who love him, who have been called according to
his purpose. For those God foreknew he also predestined to be
conformed to the likeness of his Son, that he might be the
firstborn among many brothers. ~ Romans 8:28, 29*

READING: Romans 8:18-39

In the economy of God, God makes all things work together for the good. Not all things are good. In fact, our world is filled with restless evil and heartbreaking circumstances. But God promises to make all things work together for the good. Our God is a redeeming God.

When good things happen, this does not prove that we did the right thing. It reveals that God is a powerful, redeeming God who works good things out of anything, good and bad. Of course the premier example of this is the cross. If God can transform an instrument of death and curse into a symbol of life and salvation, surely he can redeem us now.

The same Spirit that raised Jesus from the grave now works within us. But God's redemption is not purposeless. The end picture of our redemption is to transform us into the image of his son, Jesus.

God's good and perfect will is not primarily for your church to grow or for you to enjoy personal success as a pastor. God's redemptive purpose is to transform you and your church into the image of his son, Jesus. Jesus is the firstborn among many siblings, and he wants you and yours to join the family. To that end, in the seasons to come, there is a place for suffering and confusing times and conflicts and disappointments. But God's economy is perfect, and you will not shed any tears in vain.

Father, I lay down my agendas and plans. In every circumstance make me more like you. Amen.

Peter Sung

The Promise for Loneliness

*"I tell you the truth," Jesus replied, "no one who has
left home or brothers or sisters or mother or father or children
or fields for Me and the gospel will fail to receive a hundred times
as much in this present age (homes, brothers, sisters, mothers,
children and fields – and with them, persecutions) and
in the age to come, eternal life." ~ Mark 10:29, 30*

READING: Psalm 68

Without a doubt, the biggest challenge I faced as wife of a catalytic church planter was an ever-present, sometimes bone-crushing loneliness. We were always the new folks in town, the strangers in a strange land. This can hit us wives especially hard. Making new friends takes time and effort, not to mention bravery to open our hearts again and again to unknown and untested people. I had to be cautious not to rely too heavily on church folk or to expect them to meet my emotional needs.

Also, church planting is plain hard work and there usually wasn't much time left over after church or family demands were met to cultivate my own friendships and a support system outside the church. Incidentally, wives often face loneliness even in the preferred team model.

By our second church, I sort of made my peace with the fact that I would probably always be lonely, that loneliness was part of the cost I paid so my husband could fulfill his high calling and so that precious souls would find Christ.

That's when I found this promise in Mark 10. It comforts me that Jesus sees the friends I left behind, and my long stretches of loneliness, and that He will compensate when the time is right.

Dear Lord, Help me to keep a sweet spirit if I am lonely today, to be willing to endure hardship for Your sake, and to let it be enough that You see my pain. Amen.

Dionne Carpenter

How Our Loneliness Can Help

For I was hungry and you gave me something to eat,
I was thirsty and you gave me something to drink, I was
a stranger and you invited me in... ~ Matthew 25:35

READING: Matthew 25: 31-46

Loneliness can be a crushing burden to bear. But, in a curious way, our painful loneliness can uniquely prepare us to become effective church planters. It gives us deep empathy for the strangers who tentatively attend our church services for the first time or for folks in our community who are going through transitions of their own and, thus, are more open to the gospel message.

Isn't God good? He doesn't waste our pain, especially not this pain. God graciously allows us to go through the experience of moving to a new community, of getting lost on our first field trip to the new market, of feeling nervous or shy the first time we attend a new church, of sitting at a social event while people ignore us and talk only with their friends, and of desperately missing the loved ones we left behind.

Then, lo and behold, we start a church and run into many lonely people just like us. Those displaced people are usually the ones most receptive to our new project, precisely because they haven't already locked in with their own group of friends or their own full social calendar.

It's astonishing how quickly a growing church can become ingrown and inwardly focused. Even brand new church plants aren't immune from this temptation to exclude or ignore the strangers in our midst. Thank God for allowing us to know firsthand the excruciating pain of loneliness so we can set a good example by our warm welcome of visitors.

Dear Lord, Thank You for redeeming my loneliness. Help me to recognize Your sacred presence hidden within the face of every stranger I welcome. Amen.

Dionne Carpenter

Mission Field

During the night Paul had a vision of a man of Macedonia standing and begging him, "Come over to Macedonia and help us." ~ Acts 16:9

READING: Acts 16:6-10

Pastor Ken Eze (pronounced 'easy') is the Nigerian leader of a team of eight church planters who work among Muslims in northern Nigeria. I asked him, "Would you call church planting among Muslims a very difficult ministry?"

He replied, "It is difficult, but not very difficult. Our church planters show Muslim people the love of Jesus. The people come to Christ and a church is born."

I asked him, "Have you ever been in danger because of your faith?"

He said, "On September 10th, the day before 9-11, our city was attacked by Al-Qaeda. My leaders and I had to literally run for our lives. We have since returned to our homes."

Later, a gathering of international church planting leaders shared their hearts and their needs. Finally, with passion, Ken Eze looked at me and other leaders from the States and simply said, "HELP US! We need your help."

His words "HELP US!" burned into my soul, reminding me of Paul's Macedonian vision. I asked Ken, "What kind of help is needed?"

He said, "In Africa, we have a lot of zeal, but we have very little information and training."

Where is your mission field? For many older churches the mission field is 'there'...across the oceans in places like Africa. For many new churches, the mission field is 'here'... as we plant a church in our city or region.

In Acts 1:8, Jesus defines the mission field as here, there AND everywhere. That should be our definition of the mission field, too! As a church planting leader, you have something to offer other church planters around the world. How is God leading you to impact your mission field? Regionally? Nationally? Internationally?

Father, Make me faithful to respond to the cry, "Help me!" Amen.

Paul Becker

Safe and Holy

*For the law was given through Moses; grace
and truth came through Jesus Christ. ~ John 1:17*

READING: Luke 7:36-50

One of the most amazing facts about Jesus' ministry is that he commanded and ministered to a broad spectrum of people: Jews and Gentiles, men and women, young and old, sick and healthy, strong and weary, poor and rich, sinner and saint, clean and unclean. How did he accomplish this great feat?

Jesus was a safe and holy person. Jesus was full of grace and truth. Safety and holiness do not tend to mix very well in the real world. Non-Christians usually do not feel very safe with religious people. They fear judgment, condescension, or just plain irrelevance. It is also easy for Christians to not feel very safe with non-Christians. Christians feel easily threatened by the people of this world.

Jesus was a safe person precisely because he was such a holy person. His holiness was never threatened by those who were less holy. Pharisees had proximity rules about lepers for fear of becoming unclean. When Jesus touched a leper, instead of Jesus becoming unclean, the leper was made clean. Jesus' holiness was strong and infectious, and therefore he was also a safe person.

A church plant has a unique opportunity to start fresh in culture as a safe and holy place – safe, not because the holiness is diluted, or holy at the expense of people feeling safe. A church can and should be a safe place because it is a holy place. A truly holy place is a safe place.

Are you a safe and holy person?

Heavenly Father, Help me to boldly approach the throne, just as I am, so that I might find grace and mercy to help me in time of trouble. Amen.

Peter Sung

Dealing Gently

Brothers, if someone is caught in a sin, you who are
spiritual should restore him gently... ~ Galatians 6:1

READING: I Thessalonians 2:1-16

God deals with His weak children as "a father disciplines" (Heb. 12:7 – 9). So Paul dealt with his people in Thessalonica (I Thes. 2:11). Church planting is a team effort. In every team men like inconsistent Peter, short-tempered John, doubting Thomas, timid John Mark, undependable Onesimus, betrayer Judas Iscariot, coverts Ananias and Sapphira, wealth-lusting Demas and prominence-lusting Diotrephes are common. Church planting is not merely making people come together. Leading clueless individuals to a Christ-like population is the crux of planting.

Paul's strategy in Thessalonica was "encouraging, comforting, and urging to live lives worthy of God." He used a different method as he faced disappointments with John Mark (Acts 15:38). John needed more seasoning and was not ready to join the team for Paul's intended second journey. I believe Paul deliberately put John under the mentoring leadership of Barnabas whose journey was not as dangerous as Paul's.

Disciplining weak brethren in a church planting team demands a commitment to mentoring, encouraging, comforting and urging. Church planting does not merely demand a "team" but a "team of people who live lives worthy of God."

Being gentle does not mean compromising, though. In 48 AD, Paul rejected Barnabas' suggestion to add John Mark to the team. But after twelve plus years, John Mark was again close to Paul as a trusted colleague, "helpful to me in my ministry" (II Tim. 4:11; cf. Philemon 24; Col. 4:10). Barnabas, a gentle and comforting mentor, encouraged, comforted, and urged John Mark to live a life worthy of his calling. John Mark who was unfit to be a partner in a risk-taking team was made a fitting candidate by the gentle dealing of Barnabas.

Lord, Give me patience to accept problematic weak men and women, and the wisdom to season them for my team. Amen.

R. Jayakumar

The Sabbath Rest

*Six days you shall labor and do all your work, but the seventh
day is a Sabbath to the LORD your God... For in six days the LORD
made the heavens and the earth, the sea, and all that is in them,
but he rested on the seventh day. ~ Exodus 20:9-11*

READING: Hebrews 4

Church planting leader, are you taking a Sabbath Rest?

When God created the universe, He rested on the seventh day. Do you think that He *needed* to rest? No. God was not worn out from speaking the universe into existence! Rather, He set a divine example that once a week we are to rest our bodies, refresh our minds and renew our spirits in worship.

While we shouldn't be legalistic in keeping the Sabbath, let's remember it was so important to God that under the Old Covenant, the penalty for breaking the Sabbath was death! (See Ex. 31:14, 15.) Let's not brazenly ignore what God has so clearly shown us is so important.

Under the New Covenant, it is left up to our discretion to choose which day to set apart for rest and worship. "Therefore let no one pass judgment on you in questions of food and drink, or with regard to a festival or a new moon or a Sabbath" (Col. 2:16 ESV). Make your Sabbath whichever day works best for you and your family.

And don't try to pretend that Sunday is a "day off." It is probably your most exhausting day. Choose another rest day and guard it religiously. Your ministry will be more fruitful, your body more healthy and your family happier as you follow this Sabbath rest principle.

Lord, Help me to honor the Sabbath principle of Scripture. Help me to rest in You, trusting that You can do more through me in six days than by myself I can do in seven. Amen.

Mark Alan Williams

Freedom

*The Spirit of the Lord is on me, because he has
anointed me to preach good news to the poor. He has sent me
to proclaim freedom for the prisoners... ~ Luke 4:18*

READING: Isaiah 61

I'll never forget the day Eric Helmbold, Jeffrey Jackson and I were given a tour of Elmina Castle, the infamous Slave Castle on the Atlantic Coast of Ghana. We walked through the cramped rooms that held hundreds of male and female slaves. The facilities for food and sleep were awful. In this castle, the slaves experienced disease, beatings, rape and death. We saw the iron shackles that bound the slaves, and *The Door of No Return* through which slaves passed to board the ships that took them from their homes forever and made them slaves in the Americas.

The slave trade is a prime example of man's inhumanity to man. This was truly a tragedy caused by greed. For centuries, white people enslaved black people. Jeffrey thought about his own African ancestors who passed through a place very much like this one on their way to slavery in North America. Eric and I grieved with Jeffrey for the sins against these precious people whom God had created.

Why were our DCPI trainers in Ghana? We were not there to enslave people. Exactly the opposite! We were there to bring true freedom...freedom in Christ. We were in Ghana to equip leaders to plant dynamic churches to bring freedom in Christ to people.

Are you in a season of perseverance or discouragement or crisis in church planting? Remember that you are called to a noble purpose. YOU ARE THERE TO BRING FREEDOM IN CHRIST to the precious people in your church, in your community and in your world. It is worth the fight. It is worth the sacrifice.

Dear Father, Help me to remember that to bring freedom in Christ is worth the investment of my life. Amen.

Paul Becker

Sharing the Vision

*I will give you every place where you set
your foot, as I promised Moses. ~ Joshua 1:3*

READING: Joshua 1:1-11

Are you in confusion about your own vision? We always have multiple questions in our heads about our own vision, our calling and even the plan of God. Well, here is my advice: Start connecting with people and share your vision with them. God will start imparting your vision into the people you meet.

I will never forget one particular Saturday night when Pastor Sohail and I were at Pastor Mansha's house. I shared with him my calling and vision and for almost six hours we all talked about fulfilling the Great Commission. The anointing of the Holy Spirit was growing stronger as the night went along.

The next morning, I asked Pastor Sohail for permission to preach in the Sunday service. We were still in the anointing from last night's discussion when this fresh wave blessed us more. Pastor Masha was excited about what God had started in his life and ministry overnight. Twelve members of his church said YES to the altar call to fulfill the Great Commission by immediately starting an outreach to the nearest villages.

I suggested that Pastor Mansha make a list of ten villages around Hyderabad which they had never reached before. Immediately after the service, five of us (Sohail, myself, Masha and his one Elder and Deacon) rode on two motorbikes and visited four villages that day. Without drawing attention to ourselves, we did a prayer walk at one village (Kali Mori). This is where Pastor Mansha planted a church, which is growing strong.

Heavenly Father, Thank you for connecting me with my co-workers. I surrender and depend on your ability. Please use me as you want. Amen.

Amir John Williams

SEPTEMBER

The Magnet Principle

*When God plants a church there should be
widespread community awareness and interest.*

Ice Cream Church

*Jesus said, "Let the little children come to me,
and do not hinder them, for the kingdom of heaven
belongs to such as these." ~ Matthew 19:14*

READING: Matthew 18:10-14

My heart was pulling me to plant a church in a particular village and so my team and I began to pray every day that God would provide a way. After many days of no answer I saw a vision of ice cream in front of me.

"Weeks of no answer and now you show me ice cream! I want a church, not ice cream!" I cried. Yet my team and I continued to pray, not understanding what that vision might have meant or if perhaps we were being divinely mocked.

Several days later, while praying with the team, we were distracted by the ringing of a bell. We looked up to see a young man pushing an ice cream cart and ringing his bell to attract customers. My mind flashed back to my vision of ice cream a few days earlier. Aha!

After asking the salesman how much for the entire cart, we bought the remaining ice cream and took it to the village, passing it out to the children. On the third consecutive day of handing out free ice cream, we brought along an elder and a Sunday school teacher.

Together we asked the kids: "Who is giving you free ice cream?" After hearing a variety of responses, our team explained that it was Jesus who will give them free ice cream.

This first introduction to Jesus was given to eighty children and now more than sixty families attend what has become known in the community as the *Ice Cream Church.*

Dear Lord, Thank you for answering the prayers of our ministry team and for giving us creative ideas to stir widespread community awareness and interest in our new church. Amen.

Saleem Sadiq

Blinded by the Blessings

Beloved, think it not strange concerning the
fiery trial which is to try you, as though some strange
thing happened unto you. ~ *I Peter 4:12 (KJV)*

READING: I Peter 4:12-19

Maybe we don't actually say it, but we may think this: "God and I are really close and I am doing His special work in church planting. Therefore, things are bound to go wonderfully and I expect no difficulties in life."

So, this warning by the Apostle Peter is for beloved church planting leaders. The fact is that bad things happen to good church planters. It isn't strange; it is supposed to happen.

Some time ago I was emotionally overwhelmed by several major trials – a family member's suicide, a problem child, a parent's Alzheimer's disease and financial disappointments. This "bad news" verse encouraged me. It helped me break through the "betrayal barrier" which is the feeling that God promised me a rose garden, but gave me only thorns.

Before then, my life had been virtually "problem free" and I assumed life would continue that way. Then the "fiery trials" came and began to burn. The pain was intense, made worse by my mistaken notion that God had somehow reneged on His promises.

Eventually I realized that Jesus never promised a problem-free life, that all the twelve original church planters, except John, died horrific martyr's deaths and that our Savior Himself suffered incomprehensibly. Oops, I had been blinded by all the blessings.

Am I hopeful, encouraged, trusting, joyful? Yes, but not because I expect to have no suffering. Now I am rejoicing, despite trials, as instructed in verse 13, "But rejoice, inasmuch as ye are partakers of Christ's sufferings; that, when his glory shall be revealed, ye may be glad also with exceeding joy" (KJV).

Lord, Thank you for how you teach and grow me through trials. Help me to rejoice in them. Amen.

Mark Alan Williams

Playing Favorites

My brothers, as believers in our glorious Lord
Jesus Christ, don't show favoritism. ~ James 2:1

READING: James 2:1-11

In context, James addresses the dangers of favoring rich believers over poor ones. But church planters do well to apply this conscientiously toward everyone who comes to their baby church. Especially in the early days, when core group members and new converts are getting to know one another, the pastor and his wife hold enormous power to elevate one and "demote" another in the newly forming group. Any hint of personal favoritism has a destructive effect on this fragile new church.

It didn't take me long to discover that the women were always watching me, the pastor's wife, if only subconsciously, and many were keeping strict tally of what I did for whom. More than one woman has left in a huff because of some perceived inequity. This social dynamic is true of women the world over.

Consequently, I've hammered out several personal ground rules, offered only to spur your thinking and adaptation within your context. Around here, in-home parties to sell products proliferate. I don't attend any because I can't attend all. Also, although I'm a weaver, I stopped making *hand-woven* gifts for church-sponsored baby and wedding showers because I can't realistically weave a gift for every baby and bride.

At congregational gatherings, I take care to greet <u>every</u> woman warmly and attentively, and avoid chatting longer with ladies I privately like better. I don't habitually sit with any regularly-attending woman. If a solitary woman visits, I may sit with her once or twice, but quickly introduce her around helping to jump-start her friendships with other church women.

It's wiser and more Christ-like to deliberately wield our God-given influence to welcome newcomers into the group and to help social misfits feel included.

Father, Alert me to any hint of partiality. May I use my unique position to bless others.
Amen.

Dionne Carpenter

Shine

Let your light so shine before men, that they
may see your good works, and glorify your Father
which is in heaven. ~ Matthew 5:16 (KJV)

READING: Matthew 5:14-16

Over several long years, my first church plant, Emmanuel Baptist Church, slowly grew from a small home fellowship to a body of believers large enough to require its own building. Growth was slow and went all but unnoticed by our community. In fact, about that time my long-time mentor came to town and eagerly tried to look me up. Unfortunately, he had lost my phone number and only came with the name of our church to go by.

He asked around. To his surprise, it seemed that no one knew who we were! We were not listed in the phone book or newspaper and our existence was unknown by most of the people in town. Needless to say, when he finally found me I was in for a bit of a scolding. I had forgotten the 'Magnet Principle,' and it was evident by our lack of presence in the very community we wanted to impact.

Seven years later when we began our second church plant, I had learned from my mistake. We called thousands of people, put ads in the newspaper, went door to door, and did everything we could to let people know what was happening. As a result, the launching of our first service was attended by over 200 people and was able to touch many more lives!

By spreading the word of our work in humble and culturally appropriate ways we will see God reach the greatest number possible.

Dear Heavenly Father, Thank you for your blessings that you have given us and remind us of the many ways you have shown us favor. Please give us wisdom to know how to properly share these blessings with others and boldness to make the most of every opportunity. Amen.

Mark Alan Williams

Thy Kingdom Come

And he said unto them, "When ye pray, say:
'Our Father which art in heaven, hallowed be thy name.
Thy kingdom come…'" ~ Luke 11:2 (KJV)

READING: Luke 11:1-5

The church is *the* chosen presence and authority of God here on earth. The church is the kingdom-come of God. This fundamental truth is easy to forget when we are working hard to plant a new church. Jesus taught his disciples to pray for the lifting up of God's name, the propagation of God's will, the increase of God's kingdom, the fame of God's name.

God uses our particular gifts, our specific vision, and our gathered resources but the church and her ministries belong to God and God alone. At best, we are called as God's servants to do his work, in his time, in his way. My way is not Yahweh.

Jesus taught his disciples that we can do nothing apart from him. Sometimes it does not feel this way. We have power and gifts to do many things well. But activity, productivity, and even results are not the same thing as fruit, fruit that remains. Do we want to be fruitful planters or just busy, hardworking and "successful" planters?

The truth is that God truly is the source of all good things. He is the miracle worker behind it all. We are mere conduits. And in the end, when we are standing before our Father, we will give him all of the honor and the glory and the praise, not because he's a glory-hog but because he truly deserves it.

God's kingdom shall reign forever and ever! And he alone is worthy!

Heavenly Father, May your kingdom come! May your will be done! May your name be lifted up that all may draw near to you! Amen.

Peter Sung

A Taste of Heaven

Give us this day our daily bread. ~ Luke 11:3

READING: Luke 11:1-13

After an intense and intentional focus on God's name and God's kingdom, is Jesus merely teaching his disciples to pray for food? A more literal translation would read: *Give us today our coming day's bread.* The word that is translated *coming day* or *daily* is a word that is rich in connection to the end times or last days. The word is eschatological. What Jesus is teaching are the particulars of how God's kingdom is built on earth. It is an imperative for churches and Christians. Pray, Jesus is saying, to taste today of God's coming kingdom.

The whole mission of a church plant is to give to people today a taste of the heaven that is to come. In heaven, God's name is praised; in heaven, people listen and love; in heaven, justice reigns; in heaven, racism and classism is extinct; in heaven, children are safe; in heaven, sermons are really good; in heaven, music melts your heart again and again.

Church planters need personal reminders that God cares for them as people and not just as planters. Church planters need to taste of God's coming kingdom on a regular basis or discouragement and fatigue can set in. Flesh acts and human ambition can sneak up on us.

And church plants need to taste of God's coming kingdom on a regular basis. It reminds us that the things we are doing and standing for are eternal and true.

Father, Give us today a taste of our coming day's bread. We are hungry and thirsty and weary. You who are meek and humble in heart, give rest to our souls. Amen.

Peter Sung

A Church's Reputation

*And day by day, attending the temple together and
breaking bread in their homes, they received their food with
glad and generous hearts, praising God and having favor with
all the people. And the Lord added to their number day by day
those who were being saved. ~ Acts 2:46, 47 (ESV)*

READING: Acts 4:13-36

"I'll never go back to church. They're all a bunch of hypocrites!"

The man who told me this was very bitter about Christianity in general
and the church in particular. Years before, his car had broken down while he
was traveling far from home. He found a church where revival services were
being held, and sat through a sermon encouraging Christians to love everyone.
Afterward he approached church leaders for help, and was turned away. For him
that was proof that all Christians are frauds and all preachers are charlatans.

A church's reputation in the community is a delicate matter. It can be ruined
by pride, gossip, immorality and other kinds of sin within the congregation. It
can also be tarnished by unfortunate mistakes.

Recently a single mom began attending our church. A new Christian, she
chose us because, when she was a child, our congregation had brought Christmas
gifts to her family when her father was in prison.

We have a young man attending for a similar reason. He had been in a
juvenile correction facility, and his mother was looking for a church that would
love and disciple him when he got out. She knew of ours because of the same
gifts-for-children-of-prisoners program.

We will always offend some people, but let it be the "offense of the cross."
May it never be because we're trying so hard to avoid being ripped off that we
turn away people with genuine needs.

*Lord, Grant that our new church will have a reputation of Calvary love in the
community. Protect us from pride and from fear. Amen.*

Jim Carpenter

Seeking the Lost

*For the Son of Man came to seek
and to save what was lost. ~ Luke 19:10*

READING: Luke 19:1-10

One way I've created widespread community awareness and interest in planting churches has been through community saturation – knocking on literally every single door in a community, regardless of whether the building is residential or commercial or industrial, regardless of whether the occupant is rich or poor, regardless of the perceived receptivity of the people behind that door.

As a result, I've experienced a lot of rejection, contact with unexpected people, and some "interesting" situations. At times I've found myself speaking God's truth and grace to people typically shunned not only by Christians but also by unbelieving pillars of the community. In one city, we found ourselves actually leading Bible studies inside brothels.

Zacchaeus is an example of a fellow known by the community to be corrupt and avoided as a tax collector. Though it raised eyebrows, Jesus invited himself into Zacchaeus' home and spent some real time sharing with him. Zacchaeus' repentance led him to more than repay what he had plundered over the years.

My experience has shown me something of the heart of God who sees and loves the ones who have been rejected by society and the people who have failed most spectacularly. It is a privilege to be used of God to extend the love of Christ in a personal way by seeking those who are lost.

Father, I hate to admit it but I need to be reminded that Jesus came to save the lost. He came to heal the sick. Help me to love the people I want to draw back from, and to value the people I want to write off. Amen.

Chris McKinney

Friends Let Friends Come Drunk

*Jesus said to him, "Today salvation
has come to this house, because this man,
too, is a son of Abraham." ~ Luke 19:9*

READING: Luke 19:1-10

In one small town, our church planting team was showing the *Jesus* film at night, with evangelistic preaching in between reels. The movie got everybody's attention, and gathered a crowd for our preaching. Afterwards, one man staggered over to me. "I want to join your religion," he confided, his words slurring together. Not wanting to engage in a serious conversation with someone obviously drunk, I promised to visit him in the morning.

I doubted the man would follow through sober what he had started while drunk. He would likely be embarrassed after having made a spectacle of himself. My companions shared my evaluation but came along anyway.

The man was not expecting us, but he invited us to come in and share with him. Very matter-of-factly he claimed to have accepted the gospel and said he intended to join the church. His wife and mother-in-law gave us "Don't look at us!" looks. Having extended the invitation to all to come to Christ, we had no good reason to refuse this one who came, so we walked down to the river and baptized him. Leaving him with instructions on joining with the other Christians for training and fellowship, our team crossed the river and we were on our way to another province, expectations low.

When I revisited that town several months later, I learned that the "town drunk" hadn't been seen drunk since the night of the *Jesus* film. So changed was his life that several people had given their allegiance to Christ since then, starting with his wife and mother-in-law. I was ashamed that I had such little faith in the power of God for salvation of *all*.

Father, Thank You for saving sinners of whom I am chief. Amen.

Chris McKinney

The God of All Grace #1

*And now the God of all grace who called you to His eternal
glory in Christ after you have suffered a little while will Himself
restore you and make you strong, firm and steadfast. To Him
be dominion forever and ever. ~ I Peter 5:10, 11 (ESV)*

READING: I Peter 5

Peter wrote at a time of great suffering for Christians. The Roman Emperor, Nero, had begun a terrible persecution to stamp out faith in Jesus. Christians were dipped in tar and burned as torches to light Nero's garden parties. They were torn apart by wild beasts in the arena.

So Peter wrote a letter of encouragement for the suffering saints. And as he concluded, he penned the words we read above. There are at least five encouragements in those two verses. We'll cover two today and three tomorrow.

First, *God's character:* He is "the God of all grace." Not some grace, partial grace or occasional grace. *All* grace. In tough times, we can always count on God's grace. Someone has said "grace is *everything* for *nothing* to those who don't deserve *anything*."

Second, *God's plan:* He has definitely "called you to His eternal glory in Christ." When you're in the middle of a storm, all you can think about is the present moment. Suffering does that to us. But God has made us for eternity. He has *foreknown, predestined, called, justified and glorified* His children (see Rom. 8:28 – 30).

Church planting will periodically bring us into seasons of suffering. But whatever we face, we can depend upon God's character and trust in His plan.

Lord, Thank You for Your grace. In whatever trials You call me to face, grant me an eternal perspective that trusts Your wisdom and relies on Your power. Amen.

Jim Carpenter

The God of All Grace #2

*And now the God of all grace who called you to His
eternal glory in Christ after you have suffered a little while will
Himself restore you and make you strong, firm and steadfast. To Him
be dominion forever and ever. ~ I Peter 5:10, 11 (ESV)*

READING: Psalm 90

The Apostle Peter gives us five great encouragements for troubling times. His first two (from yesterday) are about God's character: "the God of all grace," and His plan "who called you to His eternal glory in Christ."

Third, he speaks of *God's mystery:* "after you have suffered a little while." God reveals many things to us, but there is still much that is "mystery." Peter writes as if suffering is to be expected, but the timing is mysterious. What is "a little while?" Obviously God doesn't measure time the way we do. "A thousand years in Your sight are like a day that has just gone by..." (Ps. 90:4).

Fourth, *God's promise:* "will Himself perfect, confirm, strengthen and establish you." How we rejoice when we read these words! The God of all grace, who takes note of our troubles, who measures time in a way mysterious to us, still gives us this blessed guarantee: He Himself will use the hard times to work for eternal benefit in our lives.

Finally, Peter speaks of *God's glory:* "To Him be dominion forever and ever. Amen." Christianity is not a man-centered religion. "Dominion" means God's "manifested strength." In the end, whatever sufferings we endure will work for our eternal blessing. But even more important, they will display the greatness and power and glory of our King.

God of all grace, Strengthen me to endure and to bring You glory in all the seasons of my life. Amen.

Jim Carpenter

Possessiveness in Ministry

*The man runs away because he is a hired
hand and cares nothing for the sheep. ~ John 10:13*

READING: John 10:1-13

There are times during the process of planting churches in a city or, as in our case, along the rivers, that we have to back up and remember whose kingdom we are building. Oftentimes other ministries come along that want to build a church building, sometimes with open hands to bless the body of Christ there.

At other times it would appear that their intention is to build their own kingdom. They make promises to believers you have been working with for years. We may get the idea that these are "our" people and all other outside influences are bad for them. Many times these other offers and influences will divide the church body. But we also have to be careful not to get too possessive of God's people. After all, it is the Kingdom of God that we are building.

Not allowing "our people" to go to another church event for fear that they might like it better there, or not encouraging fellowship with others, can come from fear. There was a time that I wanted to hold onto "my leaders" with a closed fist. But the Lord spoke to me that not everyone that comes through your front doors is going to stay and be God's choice for your church leadership. This Scripture talks of *hirelings,* people who are with you for some benefit, pay, etc., but might not stay if things get tough financially or otherwise.

Those who have been tested and proven to be with you in tough times are priceless in a church plant.

Dear Heavenly Father, Help me to remember that this is your kingdom that we are building and serving, and that you have a plan for us. Help me to trust you for the right leaders and give me wisdom to train them. Amen.

Ron Thiesen

When Your World Shakes

God is our refuge and strength, an ever-present help in trouble. Therefore we will not fear, though the earth give way and the mountains fall into the heart of the sea, though its waters roar and foam and the mountains quake with their surging. There is a river whose streams make glad the city of God... ~ Psalm 46:1-4a

READING: Psalm 46

There are days in church planting that rival any Hollywood special effects depicting the earth giving way and the mountains collapsing into the sea. A key family decides to leave. The money isn't enough for the bills. You have to move your worship location. Someone in your family struggles with a serious illness.

Pick your catastrophic spiritual warfare.

In the midst of it all, the psalmist sees a river, a river in the middle of a dry city. The river brings healing, refreshment, life and vitality right into the center of the devastation. The river is God and His blessings of grace and sustenance. It is no wonder the writer can say "God is my refuge and strength."

What has you anxious and worried today? Are you dealing with one of the things mentioned above? Are you concerned that you say something significant on Sunday? Has one of your significant supportive relationships hit a rough patch?

There is a river. There is a river of God's empowering presence to drive out the fear and bring visions of refreshment and life. As we take refuge in Him, there is a river of blessing.

Lord, Even though the earth shakes around me, my trust is in You! Though the waters roar, I will not fear. Please be my strength. Let me splash in Your river of blessing. Amen.

Ross Chenot

Rejecting the Pastor's Wife Stereotype

Each one should use whatever gift he has
received to serve others, faithfully administering
God's grace in its various forms. ~ I Peter 4:10

READING: I Peter 4:7-11

One of the biggest blessings of church planting ministry didn't dawn on me until about five years into our first church. In a church plant, more so than in the vast majority of established churches, the church planter's wife has freedom to be herself and serve the Lord the way God has wired her.

For the longest time I didn't realize that. I brought a head full of baggage and stereotypical expectation into our first church. I felt inadequate to measure up to that ideal of a regal, extroverted lady who teaches Sunday school, runs the Women's committee and plays the piano. Yikes!

Periodically, awkwardly shy and up to my elbows in tasks that didn't fit that stereotype, I'd express my chagrin to this woman or that in the church, apologizing for not measuring up as a pastor's wife. It took me a long time to notice that they always responded with a blank stare. *"What on earth do you mean? What are you supposed to be doing? We love you just the way you are."*

For most of the women in our church plant, I was the *only* pastor's wife they had ever known; many were brand new Christians. (Don't you just LOVE that about new churches?) They had no expectation of me other than what they saw me do. Additionally, church plants tend to give everyone grace to start small and "grow into" their spiritual gifts.

One happy day, I gratefully threw off that pastor's wife stereotype once and for all. I can't be that mythical lady. But, with God's help, I can be myself.

Jesus, Help us to give our brand new Christians a great first impression of what pastors and pastor's wives are like. Amen.

Dionne Carpenter

Renew Your Mind

…casting down imaginations, and every high thing
that exalteth itself against the knowledge of God, and
bringing into captivity every thought to the obedience
of Christ… ~ II Corinthians 10:5 (KJV)

READING: II Corinthians 10:1-5

There are places we might not be comfortable or safe: a mosque, a bar, a dark alley, a séance. There are also places in our thoughts we shouldn't go. Thoughts of discontentment, faithlessness, focusing on failures, resentment, lust, worry and others are dangerous to our mental and spiritual health and must be avoided. Church planting leaders must guard against visiting these dangerous thought locations.

How can we avoid them? One key is to remember that our minds cannot run in a vacuum. We must *replace* our negative thoughts with positive faith thoughts. Philippians 4:8 tells us what to think; "Finally, my friends, keep your minds on whatever is true, pure, right, holy, friendly and proper. Don't ever stop thinking about what is truly worthwhile and worthy of praise" (CEV).

We live in a negative, fearful, faithless, sinful world. God's instruction is to be different; "And be not conformed to this world: but be ye transformed by the renewing of your mind, that ye may prove what *is* that good, and acceptable, and perfect, will of God" (Rom. 12:2 KJV).

So resist the temptation to think like the world. Renew your mind in the power of the Holy Spirit. Take your thoughts captive. Meditate on the Word of God. Focus on God's blessings. Contemplate Christ. Ask the Holy Spirit to help you "bring into captivity every thought to the obedience of Christ." Doing so will protect you from dangerous mental and emotional captivity.

Lord, Help me not to allow my mind to wander into negative territory. Instead, help me think on what pleases You. Amen.

Mark Alan Williams

The Ram in the Thicket

And Abraham lifted up his eyes and looked, and
behold, behind him was a ram, caught in a thicket by his horns.
And Abraham went and took the ram and offered it up as a
burnt offering instead of his son. ~ Genesis 22:13 (ESV)

READING: Genesis 22:1-19

The story of Abraham and Isaac in Genesis 22 is a beautiful image of sacrifice and substitution. All church planters ought to rejoice in the truths of this great chapter. It would bless and encourage our people if we preached them every year.

Here is Abraham, a father whose son means everything to him. But in the excruciating drama of Mt. Moriah, he puts his all on the altar – literally. As Abraham's knife rises above the beating heart of his son, we cannot fail to see the shadow of Calvary's cross.

And here is the innocent son, willingly carrying the wood for his own altar. "Father," he says, "I see the fire and the wood, but where is the lamb for the burnt offering?" Yes, we see there the ram caught in the thicket. Isaac was spared because a substitute took his place.

But within this eternal drama is another twist. The One who stayed Abraham's hand, who spared Isaac and revealed the ram – He was the Angel of the Lord (vv. 11, 15). And He was not just an angel. We know Him as the pre-incarnate Christ, who, 2,000 years after Abraham, staggered up a lonely hill carrying the wood of His own cross.

For Him there would be no substitute. He came as the Lamb slain before the foundation of the world.

What must our Lord have thought on that day when Abraham named Him *Jehovah Jireh* – the Lord will provide – knowing one day *He* would be the sacrifice God provided?

Lord Jesus, May I never forget how You took my punishment. Keep me near the cross today. Amen.

Jim Carpenter

Organic Growth

...praising God, and having favor with all the people. And the Lord was adding to their number day by day those who were being saved. ~ Acts 2:47 (NASB)

READING: Isaiah 49

One drop of blood under a microscope reveals details of hundreds of blood cells. Our body is composed of trillions of microscopic cells, living organisms with complex components. Each cell does its part to keep our body functioning properly as a whole. Our body is organic. So is the body of Christ.

There is a divine side to the expansion of the church that keeps it functioning properly as a whole. God works through human hearts and hands. We must ask what human factors contribute to the spread of the gospel and the growth of the church.

Spiritual life is possible because God invaded time and space to redeem humanity. The good news of salvation is too wonderful to keep private. It compels us to share the gospel.

Second, the gospel satisfies a universal need in the hearts of people. The Christian movement proves that the active love of God makes the Christian life possible and gives Christians newfound consideration for the needs of others.

Third, the practical expression of Christian love is among the most powerful causes of Christian success. Tertullian reports pagans saying, "See how these Christians love one another!" They witnessed Christian love finding expression in the care of the poor, of widows, orphans, those in prison and those who need compassion.

Finally, persecution helps to publicize the Christian faith. The body of Christ grows exponentially when Christians display courage in the face of torment, courtesy toward enemies and a joyful acceptance of suffering.

God, the giver of life, is active in the deeds of his children and in those to whom his children witness. Organic growth is divine!

Father, Make me mindful of the intricate involvement you have in the expansion of your church. Amen.

Christine Cunningham

Momentum

*In this way Hiram kept Solomon supplied with
all the cedars and pine logs he wanted.... ~ I Kings 5:10*

READING: I Kings 5:1-12

My desire for you is to have momentum in your ministry. According to the definition in the *World Book Dictionary*: "Momentum is the force with which a body moves. For example, a falling object gains momentum as it moves. Momentum is impetus resulting from movement. For instance, the runner stumbled just before the end of the race but his momentum carried him over the finish line."

Momentum is a Latin word literally meaning "moving power."

Recently, one of our new Vice Presidents said, "Joining DCPI has been like getting on a moving train." That is what I want for you – a ministry that is like a moving train.

Consider King Solomon and how he accelerated the momentum of his reign. Solomon made this written request of King Hiram, "And behold, I propose to build a house for the name of the Lord my God, as the Lord spoke to my father David, saying, 'Your son, whom I will set on your throne in your place, he shall build the house for my name.' Now, therefore, command that they cut down cedars for me from Lebanon" (I Kings 5:5, 6a).

Here are three steps for you to take in order to capture or accelerate momentum in your church plant:

1. PRAY. Ask God to move in power in your ministry and show you what He wants you to do.
2. LOOK. Where is God moving in power? Join Him.
3. DO SOMETHING. Take top priority actions in line with your vision, values and plan.

John Maxwell says that momentum is the leader's best friend. Once you succeed, it is easier to continue to succeed. May you and your team be swept forward in God's moving power!

Father, Give me godly forward momentum in my ministry today. Amen.

Paul Becker

Manna Time #7
Training for Leadership

Jesus replied, "They do not need to go away.
You give them something to eat." ~ Matthew 14:16

READING: Matthew 14:13-21

Matthew, Mark and Luke's Gospels all record the story of Jesus leading His disciples through the grain fields *before* they tell the story of Jesus feeding the five thousand. From a training standpoint, this is significant. The disciples had been enjoying *Manna Time* for awhile before they looked with dismay over those hillsides thick with people urgently in need of food.

It must have been quite a shock when Jesus told them, "You give them something to eat."

Yet that was a crucial milestone in the training of the twelve: *Now that you have seen Me provide for your needs, go out and become channels of provision to those under your care.* Our *Manna Time* lessons of confident faith and reliance must not remain merely a personal comfort but rather the springboard for our confident trust in God to provide for the needs of the many.

The truth of the matter is that none of us is adequate to meet even the simplest needs of our people. No matter how many seminars or seminaries we have attended, or how many resources we can gather, when weighed against the crush of humanity's spiritual and emotional brokenness and physical need, we are – all of us – just bumbling novices clutching a little borrowed lunch bag.

Our sufficiency comes, always and only, from our nearness to Christ.

And that's an enormous comfort!

So, pay close attention to your precious private occasions of *Manna Time* provision and learn from them the larger vocational lessons of confident dependence on God. It's the only way any of us can ever hope to obey Jesus' command to feed His sheep.

Dear Father, Make me a channel of Your provision to those You have placed in my care. Amen.

Dionne Carpenter

Manna Time #8
Provision During Judgment

*...if this is so, then the Lord knows how to rescue godly men
from trials and to hold the unrighteous for the day of judgment,
while continuing their punishment.* ~ II Peter 2:9

READING: II Peter 2:4-10

Although I had noticed the periodic appearances of *Manna Time* quite early in our church planting career, I recently began to study manna in earnest because the economy of my country and my state is stuck in a particularly severe recession. What defense do Christians in general, and church planters in particular, have in the midst of such widespread misery? Can we expect God to provide our minimum daily needs in times like these?

It astounded me to notice in the Bible how often seasons of *Manna Time* overlap with seasons of widespread (often national) punishment or judgment. All the Israelites received manna for forty long years (instead of a few weeks or months) precisely because the adults grievously sinned at Kadesh (see Numbers 13 and 14). God's daily provision came, even for those under judgment, for the sake of God's glory and because their innocent children needed it. Isn't that incredible? Elijah experienced *Manna Time* provision the entire 3 ½ years while his countrymen in Israel suffered through God's judgment by drought. And Peter gives us several examples of God's pinpoint protection of His people while a wider judgment swirled around them.

The study of Scripture has increased my confidence. God will surely provide what we need even in the middle of widespread unemployment and foreclosures and despair. With Paul, we can rest content, "whether living in plenty or in want" (Phil. 4:12), knowing that God will use the lean times to purify our hearts and teach us deeper lessons of daily trust.

Dear Father, I trust You to see my situation now and provide whatever I need, no matter what is happening around me. Amen.

Dionne Carpenter

Manna Time #9
Instructive Helplessness

*You shall drink from the brook, and I have
commanded the ravens to feed you there.* ~ I Kings 17:4

READING: I Kings 17

We may feel terribly helpless in times of financial hardship. It's tempting, during that uncomfortable uncertainty, to fixate on someone we assume should help us. Thoughts like this might trouble our mind, "Why, Mrs. Jones just spent thousands of dollars to build a pool. She owes me a favor. Surely, she should help me out!" Such bitterness can befoul our soul.

The Lord wisely guides our path through periodic *Manna Times* precisely to wean us off of such ugly carnal attitudes. With laser-like precision, *Manna Times* can target our ungodly insistence to stay in control at all costs, our latent covetousness or an impulse to manipulate people who are well-to-do.

Jesus says, "Blessed are the poor in spirit [the ones who humbly acknowledge their utter helplessness, their lack of resources], for theirs is the kingdom of God" (Mt. 5:3). Fix your eyes upon Jesus. Look to Him to provide for you, in whatever manner He deems best, and resolutely refuse to entertain resentment toward any other would-be benefactor.

Therein lies the path of joy, because when we submit to God, He commands provision to come our way. The ravens had no choice but to obey Him. Neither did the unwitting but fortunate widow later on in I Kings 17. God delights to display His irresistible power when we have no control at all.

If God commands Mrs. Jones to help you, then she will certainly obey. But, meanwhile, surrender to God and forget about Mrs. Jones and her potential largesse. Don't let your fixation on the solution you've imagined spoil the pleasure of watching God's chosen solution unfold.

Dear Father, Thank You for taking care of me in Your own infallible way. Give me humbleness of heart to enjoy watching You take charge. Amen.

Dionne Carpenter

God Gives the Growth

I planted, Apollos watered, but God
gave the growth. ~ I Corinthians 3:6 (ESV)

READING: I Corinthians 3:1-9

Truly Jesus Christ is Lord of church planting.

One of the ways God taught me this truth was through my efforts at reaching new people with the gospel. In several of my church plants I spent many hours knocking on doors. I concentrated on homes where people had recently moved to the area, and I used a simple survey (that I created) to gain information and to find anyone who had an interest in our new church.

Using this survey, I compiled a list of people who had expressed openness to our new church plant. Then in the months that followed I would regularly visit these people who initially had seemed most interested. My aim was always to build a relationship with these people, to share Christ with them, and to involve them in a Bible study.

Sometimes God blessed these efforts. But sometimes He didn't.

But here's what I almost always noticed: if I was faithful to reach out to new people, to spend significant time praying for the lost and trying to build friendships, God would inevitably bring new people to our church and to Himself. *But sometimes it seemed to have nothing to do with the efforts I was making!* Sometimes people would just show up out of the blue.

God gets the glory! We *are* responsible to "plant and water," but the gospel seed that grows does so because of God's grace and power, not our efforts.

How grateful we are to Christ for leading, supplying and being our Lord in the church planting adventure!

Thank You, Lord, that "You give the growth." Help me to faithfully plant and water, and then to trust You for the results. Amen.

Jim Carpenter

Collateral Damage

If your brother sins, rebuke him, and
if he repents, forgive him. ~ Luke 17:3b

READING: Luke 17:1-5

For months, Jim dealt with a particularly disagreeable man (I'll call him Bob) in the core group of our church plant. Night after night I witnessed firsthand the terrible toll it took on my dear husband to wrestle through their difficulties and hammer out a workable relationship. I worried and prayed, my stomach in knots, helpless to intervene and distracted from my own responsibilities.

And then, praise the Lord, Bob had a change of heart. He and Jim had a wonderfully cathartic meeting in which Jim was able to articulate, at least a bit, how Bob had hurt him. Bob apologized for sinning against Jim. Jim freely forgave him and was able to move on.

I, however, was left with that knot in my stomach and my raw unfinished business.

Without knowing it, Bob had turned my world upside down, too. His behavior disrupted the peace of our whole family. Try as I might, I could think of no way to broach the subject with Bob. He would have just stared at me blankly – oblivious that I'd been devastated, too, in agonies while he attacked the one I love.

Where do I go to find closure when Luke 17:3 doesn't seem to apply?

Pastor's wives often find themselves in this kind of conundrum. As I've matured, I've accepted the fact that I must take responsibility to resolve this privately. It helps enormously that I can talk with Jim, and that he has become sensitized to my need for "second-hand" closure. Often he's the only one who knows. I've also learned to take my private pain to the cross, allowing Jesus to set my heart free before bitterness sets in (Heb. 12:15).

Father, Help me to find closure and healing, and to forgive freely those who know not what they do. Amen.

Dionne Carpenter

Church Planting Idols

Then Jesus said to his disciples, "Those who want to
come with me must say no to the things they want, pick up
their crosses, and follow me." ~ Matthew 16:24 (GW)

READING: Matthew 16:21-28

Do church planting leaders worship idols? It sounds preposterous, yet they surely do. Jesus set the bar for discipleship quite high: a cross, the ultimate symbol of suffering and loss.

John Calvin called the human heart an "idol factory." The truth is that we manufacture idols all the time when we elevate anything above God in our lives. An idol is anything we elevate above God. Our hearts fashion idols out of all sorts of things. Do you relate to any of these idols?

- *persons:* my children, my heroes, some "winner," anyone I will not confront or witness to because of fear, myself
- *places:* home, work, church, the gym, a vacation spot
- *attitudes:* selfishness, pride, discontent, anger, success
- *things:* status, my goals, bank account, investments, recreation, food, productivity, progress

Ask yourself, "What has first importance in my life right now?" If it is the Lord, He is your God. If it is anything else, that is your idol. Many of the items on the list above are good things, in and of themselves. But they become idols when we put them above God in our affection, goals and desires. Fill in this blank—My biggest temptation to idolatry is: _____.

Here is the bottom line: Living to please others is "people worship;" living to please myself is "self worship;" but true worship means living to please Jehovah God.

Lord, Help me to put You above all in my life. Amen.

Mark Alan Williams

Suffering Is Necessary

Was it not necessary for the Christ to suffer these
things and to enter into His glory? ~ Luke 24:26

READING: Luke 24:13-35

Sometimes I wish that I was demonized! I daydream that it'd be easier to just cast out a demon than to work through a deeply personal and painful issue over the course of months, years or even a lifetime. Why go *through* the valley of the shadow of death when I can just fly above it or sidestep around it or, better yet, be teleported instantly to the other side?

This kind of short-term, arrival-survival, escapist thinking is immature, counter-productive, and at best, naive. And, unfortunately, all too common.

Why was it necessary for Jesus to suffer? Why does suffering come before glory? There are many responses to these questions. I submit one here: When humanity shook her fists at God the Father and demanded an answer to the question of suffering, God gave us his Son and his Son gave us himself as an atoning sacrifice for our suffering.

Suffering is inevitable. Suffering is necessary. Suffering leads to glory. Jesus suffers with us and in our stead. Suffering has helped me to believe that this is enough, that God's grace is enough.

Church planting is a glorious task because it is accomplished in the crucible of suffering with Jesus, so that we might know him in life and in death. Suffer well, dear church planters. Do not be surprised at the painful trial you are suffering, as though something strange were happening to you. But rejoice that you participate in the sufferings of Christ, so that you may be overjoyed when his glory is revealed.

Dear Father, I confess that I have been using my faith as an escape from reality and that I have avoided and over-simplified. You laid down your life of your own accord. Help me to do the same. Amen.

Peter Sung

Lighting a Candle

*I turned around to see the voice that was speaking to
me. And when I turned I saw seven golden lampstands,
and among the lampstands was someone "like a son of man,"
dressed in a robe reaching down to his feet and with a
golden sash around his chest. ~ Revelation 1:12, 13*

READING: Revelation 1:12-20

On the day after our church went public, my daily Bible reading landed me in Revelation 1. I had anticipated the launch for months. There is always a letdown after a major event, so I asked God to encourage me.

Revelation opens with an encounter with the Risen Christ. In heaven today, Jesus is so awesome and powerful that John actually fell at his feet as though dead. "Here is a God worth serving!" I decided. I had my encouragement for the day! I worshiped Jesus as he is pictured here in this passage.

As I closed my Bible, the Lord whispered to me, "Hal, notice where I am in this picture."

"You're walking among the lampstands in heaven, Lord."

"Yes, and how did those lampstands get there?"

Instantly it struck me – one of the most encouraging revelations of my life. The lampstands of Revelation 1 are lights in heaven that shine to God's glory. They are real objects. Jesus walks among them, receiving honor from their flicker and glow. According to Revelation 1:20, these lampstands represent churches on earth – churches planted by people like me and my team.

Only church planters get the privilege of lighting a candle in heaven. From my brief conversation with the Lord that day, I concluded that there is no greater privilege than being called by God to plant a church for his glory.

Lord, Thank you for using someone like me to plant a church to reach the lost on earth and light a candle in heaven to give you glory. Amen.

Hal Seed

Not Just a Crowd but a Community

*We continually remember before our God and Father your work
produced by faith, your labor prompted by love, and your endurance
inspired by hope in our Lord Jesus Christ. ~ I Thessalonians 1:3*

READING: I Thessalonians 1:1-10

The congregation of Thessalonica was a community of people who remained partners in the gospel and in suffering; they were imitators of Christ, and a model to all believers.

Church planting is not merely producing a crowd. Rather it is a challenge to raise men and women of faith, love and hope. Faith is pictured by Paul as an internal property; love is pictured as a manifested virtue; and hope, a driving force for saints in Thessalonica. Church must consist of men and women like this.

The Encyclopedia Britannica and Oxford Universal English Dictionary defines *ecclesia* as originally a selected civil body, summoned or convoked for a particular purpose. *Purpose* distinguishes a constructive "community" from a "crowd."

A crowd can come from "man-made" growth dynamics. This growth is static and technically built. A constructive community grows by itself and its growth is organic and dynamic. Applying man-made techniques impairs the organic nature of community. Fruit that is ripened artificially loses its flavor. Although "static-build" is sometimes necessary, church planters must plant constructive communities rather than being ambitious merely for a crowd.

One of the defining features of the "missional church" is that of being salt and light. The Lord's message rang out from the church at Thessalonica, and their faith in God became known everywhere (I Thes. 1:8). Their faith produced work, love prompted labor, and hope inspired endurance of the church at Thessalonica, which is a great model for a constructive community committed for God's purpose.

God, Help me to raise a constructive community that may remain the salt of the earth and the light of the world. Help me to plant churches like the Church in Thessalonica. Amen.

R. Jayakumar

The Child Inside Everyone

A father of the fatherless and a judge for the widows
is God in His holy habitation. ~ Psalms 68:5 (NASB)

READING: Galatians 4:1-7

One day, while walking, I saw a small child run up squealing and giggling. His little hands were raised and his baby fat fingers motioned as if he was trying to catch something out of the air. Instantly I knew that there must be a daddy nearby. Looking ahead of the little boy, a man with a big daddy smile was kneeling down ready to snatch up his baby as soon as he reached him.

As a parent, I remember the pleasure of seeing elation in my little ones when I would return home. It was poignant. Their bright innocent eyes wide and twinkling, their hair bouncing behind them, all are sweet recollections.

However, I have no memory of running to an earthly father joyfully waiting for me with arms wide open. So many children experience the absence or indifference of their fathers. Life's dysfunction brings disappointment and disillusionment to the fatherless in the world.

For me, sometime along life's way, a restoration of my broken heart began when someone told me about the love of our heavenly Father. God, from His holy habitation, came into my bitter hurting heart and began a process of healing and liberation.

The child inside everyone is fatherless and waiting for someone to tell them. Their Father is waiting to rescue them from the dagger of hurt that plunges ever deeper into their heart and soul. The body of Christ offers a sanctuary where tears are wiped away. Our heavenly Father is ready to lovingly envelop the hurting child within all of us. Let us invite someone to our Father's house of rest, acceptance and love.

Father, Awaken my heart to empathize with the pain of the fatherless in the world. Help me to lead them to you. Amen.

Christine Cunningham

Saul's Armor

*Then Saul clothed David with his armor… And he
tried in vain to go, for he had not tested them. Then David
said to Saul, "I cannot go with these, for I have not tested them."
So David put them off. ~ I Samuel 17:38, 39 (ESV)*

READING: I Samuel 17:32-40

Recently I was faced with a tough decision. It was time for a member of my staff to find another position, but he was reluctant to leave. I thought about how other leaders would make this change. I've read books, gone to seminars, and listened to tapes of top leaders, and I had a pretty good notion that they would force the staff person to leave, and quickly.

But I decided to do it "my" way. I prayed about it, and encouraged the staff person to put out his resume, but didn't make any plans to shove him out the door. I admit it took longer, but when the timing was right he found another position and left the church on good terms with me and with the congregation.

When I was a young church planter, I tried hard to be like the "great leaders" I read about. Like David, I was trying to wear Saul's armor. It just didn't fit. You and I need to learn from gifted leaders. But God created each of us to be unique. We must fight the battle with the weapons He has given us.

Facing a giant with only a sling shot and no armor might have looked silly. But David knew God had equipped him to fight in a different way than Saul fought. And in the end David's sling shot and his five smooth stones worked just fine.

Father, Thank You for making me the person I am. Help me be the best I can be, according to Your specific design for me. Amen.

Jim Carpenter

Rejecting the Pedestal

Therefore rid yourselves of all malice and all deceit,
hypocrisy, envy, and slander of every kind. ~ I Peter 2:1

READING: Luke 12:1-3

I grew up in an extended family of "professional Christians" including missionaries, pastors and church planters. From an early age it was drilled into me that congregants would put their leaders on a pedestal, expecting them to model every spiritual virtue to perfection. I was told more than once to foster this impression, and, if I fell, to hide that weakness or sinfulness from the folks "out there." To make matters worse, my one and only seminary class on "how to be a good pastor's wife" used a book by a well-regarded pastor's wife who echoed the same advice!

Although some of my family members were truly godly and well-intended, my closest role models were deeply dysfunctional and used that flawed rationale to cover up gross iniquity.

Needless to say, I went into my first church anxious and stressed, with my defenses high, all primed to be just as big a hypocrite as my worst role models. It was pretty miserable and enforced an artificial barrier between me and the women in our early church plants.

Over time, God helped me tackle the dysfunction of my childhood, and as I found true healing and mind renewal I resolved that I would deliberately climb down off that pedestal and live to the best of my ability without guile or hypocrisy. It was a wobbly transition figuring out what portion of my journey of faith is rightly private.

But my conscious decision to reject hypocrisy has paid wonderful dividends. It has encouraged our church women to lower their own masks. Nowadays, if I notice someone putting me on a pedestal, I chuckle, promptly confess to her my latest spiritual pratfall, and welcome her as a fellow-traveler.

Only Jesus deserves the pedestal.

Jesus, Help me serve You with unfeigned simplicity. Amen.

Dionne Carpenter

OCTOBER

The Balance Principle

*The church planter's walk
with God, family life, and ministry
must be in biblical balance.*

As Christ Loved the Church

*Husbands, love your wives, just as Christ loved
the church and gave himself up for her...* ~ *Ephesians 5:19*

READING: Ephesians 5:21-33

Years ago I heard a young church planter admit that he had planted his first church "on the back of his wife." He meant that he had neglected her and allowed her to take second place to the congregation he was starting.

Most church planters are highly motivated. We are often unusually dedicated, determined and devoted. But sometimes our spouses and children pay an unfair price for our calling.

Of course any family in ministry makes sacrifices. But when God calls us to church planting, we must not impose ungodly sacrifices on top of the costs that are already part of our ministry.

When a wife is expected to work as hard as another pastor, as well as taking care of the home and the children, it can be too much. The husband is a husband first, before he is a church planting pastor.

The Bible says that husbands are to love their wives with the tender, sacrificial love Christ displayed for His church. How tragic it is that the church itself can become the cause for husbands to neglect or mistreat their wives!

Take a day off. Spend time with your family. Treat your wife with respect, love, and kindness. Show her the affection and attention she deserves. The Lord will bless your marriage and your church.

In the end, you'll have both a happy wife and a healthy church. And your marriage will become an example for others in the churches you plant.

Lord Jesus, Help me love my wife as You love Your church. And help me to demonstrate Your loving sacrifice in caring for my family. Amen.

Jim Carpenter

Arrows in the Quiver

Sons are a heritage from the Lord, children a reward from
Him. Like arrows in the hands of a warrior... ~ Psalm 127:3, 4a

READING: Psalm 127

How does a church planter nurture his children effectively as Solomon exhorts? The warrior needs to season, prepare, and process his arrow for its purpose. He sets precise targets in order that the arrow may shoot accurately.

Undivided commitment is an important requirement for every church planter, as planting is a 24/7 affair in reality. But undivided commitment leads some church planting parents to be uninvolved in the affairs of their children. Several years ago, while I was visiting with a church planting family, I observed that the father did not know what grade his children were in at school. Undivided ministry commitment should not lead us to neglect our God-given parental responsibilities.

God expects us to be faithful both to our ministry and to our nurturing responsibilities. Our intimacy with God and ministry cannot be justifiable if, in the process, we fail to build closer intimacy with our children. Eli was close to the altar but far away from his children. Isaac, on the contrary, was able to distinguish between Esau and Jacob by smelling them. He knew each son's distinct smell!

A quality, impacting, and loving intimacy with children should be the highest priority for every church planting parent. Sons and daughters of the kind Solomon describes will be an incentive for our church planting efforts by being a model to all the families connected to our church plants. By making their children a top priority, many planters have won their children as close vision partners.

Lord, Give me wisdom to remain a good friend, counselor and guide to my children. Help me, Lord, to please you by fulfilling my parental responsibilities in the midst of my hectic church planting commitments. Amen.

R. Jayakumar

Finishing Well

They chose Stephen, a man full of
faith and of the Holy Spirit… ~ Acts 6:5b

READING: Acts 6:8-15

Many people, church planters included, start well but finish poorly. You and I want to finish this earthly race with no regrets and great glory to God. Stephen finished well. Though not a church planter, he was definitely part of the "launch team" for the new church in Antioch. His death propelled the Jerusalem Christians to evangelize new territory and ultimately to plant the Antioch church. How did Stephen, Christianity's first martyr, finish well?

He was faithful in small things. At first Stephen wasn't a great evangelist or preacher. He took care of the widows in his church. Your ministry may be small, but it is divinely appointed. Be faithful.

He was known for his character. Stephen was first chosen, not because of his gifts and abilities, but because he was "full of faith and of the Holy Spirit." He could be trusted; he was a godly man.

He had courage to speak the truth. When Stephen was arrested for preaching, he was falsely accused (vv. 11 – 13). The high priest who presided at his trial demanded "Are these things true?" (7:1). Stephen could have denied the charges and possibly avoided execution. But he saw his trial as an opportunity to tell the truth of the gospel.

He forgave the people who hurt him. His last act on this earth was to forgive his persecutors (7:60). He followed Christ to the end.

He gave other people courage. Stephen's life, and death, empowered others and led to a church planting movement that continues to this day (8:1, 4). One of his fellow deacons from Jerusalem, Philip, went to Samaria to preach the gospel (8:6f).

May we finish well and hear our Father say, "Well done, good and faithful servant."

Father, Thanks for the race I've run so far. Help me to finish well. Amen.

Jim Carpenter

Take Temple Time

Or do you not know that your body is a temple of the Holy Spirit within you, whom you have from God? You are not your own, for you were bought with a price. So glorify God in your body. ~ *I Corinthians 6:19, 20 (ESV)*

READING: 1 Corinthians 6:12-20

Pastor and author, John Maxwell, admits that he lied to himself for many years before having a heart attack. His lie was that *others* needed to eat right, exercise and take care of their "temples" but he was an exception. Because he had not missed a preaching or teaching commitment due to illness for many years, he thought he was the exception to the rules of health maintenance. Then one day, as he lay in a hospital wondering if this was the end, he admitted the truth. His "clay pot" (II Cor. 4:7) was as fragile as anyone else's.

Many church planting leaders make the same mistake and take their health for granted – until they lose it. We lie to ourselves thinking that since we are in God's Work, He will negate our physical health sins of commission and omission. Here are some of those "sins":

- Health sins of *commission*: overworking, overeating, eating unhealthy food, worry, overstress, alcohol abuse, drug abuse, sexual sin

- Health sins of *omission*: neglecting exercise, neglecting sleep and Sabbath rest, not taking advantage of available checkups and healthcare, ignoring medical advice

Sure, you may have an amazing ministry, a fantastic family and a wonderful devotional life, but if you neglect "temple time" you may pay a heavy price. John Maxwell survived his heart attack but many don't.

Take the temple time you need to care for your one and only body.

Lord, I confess that I have abused Your temple, my body. Please help me to invest the time and effort to maintain my health. Amen.

Mark Alan Williams

Teach Them Diligently to Your Children

Hear, O Israel: The LORD our God, the LORD is one. You shall love the LORD your God with all your heart and with all your soul and with all your might. And these words that I command you today shall be on your heart. You shall teach them diligently to your children, and shall talk of them when you sit in your house, and when you walk by the way, and when you lie down, and when you rise. ~ Deuteronomy 6:4-7 (ESV)

READING: Deuteronomy 6:1-9

Your family is your first congregation. If you don't win them for Christ, who will? If you don't shepherd them, who will? Church planting is so demanding that some church planters neglect spouse and children. But God's plan is for our family to be our first ministry.

The famous *shema* passage of Deuteronomy 6 establishes the pattern: First, know the Lord *personally* (vv. 4, 5). You shall love the Lord with all *your* heart, *your* soul, *your* might (v. 5). If you don't love the Lord personally, you'll never share His love with anyone else.

Then make sure you share that love with your family: teach the word of God "diligently to your children" (v. 7a). Don't leave it to your spouse, Sunday school teachers or youth leaders.

And share your faith with your children during the course of your daily life: "when you sit in your house and when you walk by the way, and when you lie down, and when you rise" (v. 7b).

We can't change our children's hearts. But we can make sure that they have our affection, our attention and our prayers.

Father, Help me draw close to You each day, so I can shepherd my family and teach my children. May each one of them find and follow Christ. Amen.

Jim Carpenter

The Church Planter's Children #1
Founding vs. Catalytic?

Fathers, do not exasperate your children; instead, bring them
up in the training and instruction of the Lord. ~ Ephesians 6:4

READING: Ephesians 6:1-4

Jim planted our first church assuming he'd be the founding pastor and we'd stay in Chino forever. The project consumed Jim's complete attention and it seemed self-evident that many truly worthy things could – temporarily – dip to lower priority because that task was so demanding and time-sensitive. We were just learning how to balance the competing demands of ministry and family.

Within three years that church plant was up and running. Jim had discovered he enjoyed being an attentive father. He was more unapologetic about making fatherhood a high priority even in the massive push to plant church #2.

By our third church, Jim realized he was a catalytic church planter, not a founding pastor. We noticed it affected the way we raised our sons and how we viewed them within a church planting context.

Children in our catalytic pastor's family became significant members of the travelling troupe of church planters, not just stragglers. It was far more important for them to be on board with the vision for church planting in each new location. And though it's always vital to disciple church folk, we regarded our two boys as the *most* strategic people to disciple and mentor within each catalytic project.

Think about it this way. We had only a brief season within each church planting project to evangelize and disciple the people in that community. Even valued team associates co-labored with us for only a few years. We gladly poured our lives into those people.

But we began to realize that our boys were the only precious souls we might have the luxury to disciple for eighteen years or longer.

Dear Father, Please help me to disciple my own precious children and make them a high priority. Amen.

Dionne Carpenter

A Neglected Orchard

*And let us not be weary in well doing for in due
season we shall reap if we faint not. ~ Galatians 6:9*

READING: Habakkuk 3:17-19

I'm watching my forty year old son water citrus trees on the moshav where he lives in the Galilee. He's caring for an orchard of oranges, olives, grapes, pomegranates, tangerines and grapefruit, planted about forty years ago. Late last year, my son began restoring the neglected property. By extensive clearing, pruning, cultivating and watering, David has given the place new life and created an inspiring haven.

There are two obvious factors at work here. Factor #1 is that these are old trees and vines with deep roots and thick trunks, mature enough to bear substantial fruit. It takes time to see a lot of fruit. When we expect "over night" success, large numbers of people responding, numerous new works being planted quickly, we set ourselves up for frustration. A productive orchard doesn't happen in a year or two or even five.

Factor #2 is the thoughtful attention and patient labor this young man has invested in the property. Our role in nurturing the spiritual communities we plant strongly resembles David's work in the orchard. Not in a flash, but as days become months become years, by patiently tending the vineyard of the Lord, we are creating a robust, fruit-bearing environment.

Are you looking at the years you've poured into the Lord's vineyard, perhaps in an inhospitable location, wondering "What do I have to show for it? Where's the fruit?" I confess to needling myself with this type of question.

Be at peace, in God's vineyard, we will reap if we faint not.

Father, I confess my discouragement and self-condemnation and draw near to you whether I see fruit or not. I now shift the focus from my efforts and evaluation to your greatness and your grace. I choose to rejoice, knowing that the fruit will come. Amen.

Eitan Shishkoff

Under Divine Protection

*...he who was born of God protects him, and
the evil one does not touch him. ~ I John 5:18b*

READING: Psalm 27

Church planting puts us in direct conflict with the kingdom of darkness, so it's wonderful to know that God is our strength and protection. Recently I had to confront a church member named Rob (not his real name) on a pattern of ungodly behavior. When I asked him to step down from his public ministry, he became furious and stormed out of my office.

For weeks he remained angry, unrepentant and prideful. Following Matthew 18:15ff, I brought in two other elders. We were moving toward church discipline but all the while we were praying.

One Saturday night I had a dream. The phone rang and the angry voice I heard was Rob's. He was just outside my window, talking on his cell phone, and he was intending to enter my house by force. I looked out the window and saw him getting out of his car, beginning to walk toward my front door.

But as he moved toward the house, five burly men appeared and took his arms. Though they were not aggressive, they were firm. They stopped him and moved him back to his car. One of them looked at me, smiled, and said, "Rob is having a bad day. We need to help him calm down."

That's when I woke up.

When I told the dream to my wife, she was convinced the Lord was showing me how He had posted angels to protect me and our church. The next morning at church Rob humbled himself and apologized. Breakthrough!

When dealing with people problems, be prayerful, humble and loving. Follow God's word, and don't be afraid! He will strengthen and protect!

Lord, Grant me a loving and humble heart when confronting sin. And thank You that You are my strong tower of protection! Amen.

Jim Carpenter

Your Children Are Your Co-Laborers

Blessed is the man whose quiver is full of
[children]. They will not be put to shame when they
contend with their enemies in the gate. ~ Psalm 127:5

READING: Psalms 127

Church planter's children must be a positive part of the church plant or they may become a casualty of it. Many times our hard work for God in church planting can be perceived as abandonment or rejection of our children when we don't have their needs in mind. They feel like we don't give them quality time so they feel rejection. They will try to cope by spending more time with friends. They may begin to hate the church or anything to do with it for taking away their parents.

In our church planting, we travel away from the central church to plant churches along the rivers. One time our teenage daughters told us they didn't want to go with us this time because they missed all their youth activities at church. It was a crucial moment in our family life but God gave us wisdom. Instead of not taking only our family members on the trips, we let them invite some friends, too. They became involved in the outreaches. What a blessing that decision has been!

Our children and their friends do most of the evangelism with dramas, children's ministry, music and one-on-one evangelism. They are rewarded with the joy of leading people to Christ on trips as well as at home. They caught God's heart for the lost. We saved our family unity and gained powerful co-laborers in the harvest.

How do your children view your ministry? How can you help them catch your vision and passion for souls and church planting?

Thank you for my children, Heavenly Father. They are a blessing that you have given to us. Give us wisdom as to how we can help them catch your vision for the lost. Amen.

Ron Thiesen

A Little Leaven
Leavens the Whole Lump

*...you are to deliver this man to Satan for the destruction
of the flesh, so that his spirit may be saved in the day of the Lord.
Your boasting is not good. Do you not know that a little leaven leavens
the whole lump? Cleanse out the old leaven that you may be a new
lump, as you really are unleavened. For Christ, our Passover
lamb, has been sacrificed. ~ I Corinthians. 15:5, 6 (ESV)*

READING: I Corinthians 5

When I was a boy, I fell down at school and scraped my arm. I knew if I told the teacher she would apply disinfectant, and that would hurt. So I just ignored the scrape. I didn't tell my mother. After several days my arm was swollen and hot, and I developed a fever. My body had a serious infection, and I was very sick for several weeks.

Sin, left untreated, can affect the whole church. And a sick church cannot produce a healthy witness for Christ. Gossip, a bitter spirit, immorality – these infections will hurt the church. The cure, discipline, is painful, but nowhere near as traumatic as letting an infection grow.

The church at Corinth had an infection. A man in the congregation was involved in immorality with his own stepmother. He was unrepentant, and though the sin was well-known in the church, the congregation was taking no disciplinary action.

Paul exhorted the church to practice church discipline – expel the man (vv. 3-5).

Like yeast in a lump of dough, sin will spread if we let it. Christ, our Passover Lamb, died to take away sins. We honor Him by leading a pure life.

A church that truly loves Jesus will practice church discipline.

Lord Jesus, Protect Your church from sin, and grant me the courage to confront it when it appears. Amen.

Jim Carpenter

The Church Planter's Children #2
Vision Casting

Fathers, do not exasperate your children;
instead, bring them up in the training and
instruction of the Lord. ~ Ephesians 6:4

READING: I Corinthians 12:21-26

Since catalytic church planting usually requires a nomadic lifestyle, it became very important that our sons feel good about each move. Being a pastor's kid is hard enough on any child, and the upheavals of moving can often create additional stress.

When Jim and I felt called to uproot our family to plant our third church, we prayed fervently that our sons (age 10 and 13) would also get excited about the move. We let them in on the decision-making process quite early on. We told them we were praying for God to guide us and asked them to join us in prayer so we would all hear from God. We made multiple family trips up to the Antelope Valley and debriefed together on each drive home. They did not feel pressured either to stay or to move. They noticed that Jim did not commit our family to a move until after they felt enthusiastic.

By the time God led us to Iowa, our oldest son was off to college so Zachary (age 15) came alone. At that pivotal time in his life a huge move could have given him animus for much teen angst. Right before we moved, Jim and I needed to make a quick trip to Iowa to find housing for our family, select a school for Zach, and begin preliminary church plant site selection. God mercifully gave us the brilliant idea to send Zach along instead of me. That "man's man" trip with Jim gave Zach a sense of project ownership, and our demonstrated respect for his input helped our California son in his bumpy adjustment to the Midwest.

Dear Father, Please give me patience to allow my children time to also catch our vision. Amen.

Dionne Carpenter

The Church Planter's Children #3
Sharing the Joys

Fathers, do not exasperate your children;
instead, bring them up in the training and
instruction of the Lord. ~ Ephesians 6:4

READING: Philippians 4:8, 9

Because the church planting lifestyle creates such an overlapping experience of home and church and work, it's almost impossible to completely shield our children from observing our frustrations and sorrows in ministry. Relational shakeups can affect even young children: *"Daddy, why doesn't my friend Billy come to our church anymore?"*

Therefore, it's doubly important to make the effort to educate our children on the joys and blessings as well so that they can see why we love doing what we do.

Jim did this in a number of ways with our two boys. One enjoyable strategy involved letting one or the other son tag along, every once in a while, on Jim's regular outing to go door-to-door calling in the community. This was a win-win situation. It gave him a companion between houses – people were usually less resistant when they saw Jim with a youngster in tow – and it made good, lasting memories of father/son bonding.

Another memorable time, our son Andy was serving as a greeter in our third church. A gentleman asked Andy to find his dad, which he did. The man told Jim that he was ready to pray to receive Christ. Andy stood right beside his daddy as Jim led this precious man to Christ. Andy and Jim were so excited!

As a regular habit, we found it important to verbalize often and in specifics the reasons why we were so happy to be doing what we did. Children take their cues from us because we set the emotional tone for the household.

Dear Father, Please help me to model a positive attitude before my children. Amen.

Dionne Carpenter

A New Commandment

Love never gives up. Love cares more for others
than for self. Love doesn't want what it doesn't have. Love
doesn't strut, doesn't have a swelled head, doesn't force itself on
others, isn't always "me first," doesn't fly off the handle, doesn't keep score
of the sins of others, doesn't revel when others grovel, takes pleasure
in the flowering of truth, puts up with anything, trusts God
always, always looks for the best, never looks back, but keeps
going to the end. ~ I Corinthians 13:4-7 (The Message)

READING: I Corinthians 13

In Jerusalem, the Church of the Holy Sepulcher sits on a location believed to be the hill of Calvary. An altar marks the spot thought to be where the cross of Christ was placed. It is perhaps the most sacred location in Christianity. Yet seven branches of the Christian church bicker over ownership of the site and church building. At times the controversy among clerics has erupted into physical altercations resulting in injuries requiring hospitalizations. The keys to the only entrance have to be kept by a neutral party, a Muslim family!

Before we shake our heads let's ask ourselves if we too are not sometimes quite loveless. I Corinthians 13 shines a spotlight into our hearts revealing our love level. The verses above are from *The Message* paraphrase. As you read each description about love, give yourself a letter grade for each one – A (for most Christ-like) to F (least like Christ).

Love is much more than an emotion, it is ACTIONS! Right now:

1. Thank God for the areas you scored high.
2. Determine what you will do today to begin to correct low scoring items.

Lord, Help me to love, not just in word or theory, but in deeds. May people recognize that I belong to You by my love for others. Amen.

Mark Alan Williams

Iron Sharpening Iron

As iron sharpens iron, so one
man sharpens another. ~ *Proverbs 27:17*

READING: Exodus 18:5-27

The second year of the church plant was grueling. We were in front of the timeline with exponential numerical growth. As lead pastor, the demands were great, with nightly visitations into homes of prospective core group members to hear their story. It was time consuming to shepherd this congregation. Many had religious backgrounds and baggage, but as yet no life transformation. Averaging about 90-100 hours per week on the job was taking its toll physically and impacting my marriage and family in a negative way.

His name was Kyle. Even though we didn't have official Elders, he was on my Pastoral Assist Team. After one of our multiple services, he said, "We need to talk... NOW!"

I said, "Sure, what's on your mind?"

He said, "Not here...out back, behind the building." The look on his face told me he was serious. Once out back, he took his finger and poked it in my chest raising his voice with a stern look, and said, "It's gotta stop. You can't keep burning the candle at both ends. Your health is suffering, your marriage is suffering and your children don't even know their Dad. You can't sacrifice your children on the altar of your church plant."

I tried to push back, but to no avail.

Kyle finally said, "If you drop dead tomorrow, we'll have a new lead pastor within six months, but your wife won't have a husband and your children won't have a father. You must get your priorities right because the message you are preaching with your life actions is not good."

Thank you, Father, for putting godly men in my life to hold me accountable. Even though confrontation is painful at times, please use them and their loving exhortation to shape me into the man of God you desire me to be. Amen.

Sam Douglass

Suitable Helper

Your wife will be like a fruitful
vine within your house… ~ Psalm 128:3a

READING: Genesis 2:15-25

God so thoughtfully created everything in advance for man. He never said "it was very good," until woman – the suitable helper – was made. Man was made complete by having a woman that God made. Since the omniscient God made Eve, apparently she must have been perfectly suitable for Adam.

"A wife of noble character who can find?" (Prov. 31:10). Although God created women with the potential for perfect suitability, not necessarily every woman exhibits the fruits of their God-given virtue.

The woman you have is God-given and the perfectly suitable one for you. She has a God-given "perfect-suitable" ability to stand with you in every way possible, if not now, at least in the future. If your wife is like Manoah's wife, praise God. Make full use of her counsels and contributions. If she is like Sarah, keep working with her – do not say she is useless. She is a little weak but faithful. If she is like Sapphira, pray for her but do not dishonor her and don't yield to her as Ananias did. Instead, lead her into maturity through your godly example and your tender love and care. If she is like Job's wife, take time to tutor her to understand your calling, commission and purpose.

The psalmist says that blessed is the man who fears the Lord (Ps. 128:1). This reverential fear is the fertilizer, which will cause her inbuilt "suitability" to bear fruit. Let your call and vision be made hers. Communicate with her convincingly. Bind her with your love. Be her hero. You will see how blessed you are because of her. She is just made for you and for your calling.

Lord, Help me to see the potential of my wife. Make us mutually complementary as we serve You. Fulfill Psalm 128 in our lives. Amen.

R. Jayakumar

The Art of Giving

For by the grace given me I say to every one of you:
Do not think of yourself more highly than you ought, but
rather think of yourself with sober judgment, in accordance with
the measure of faith God has given you. ~ Romans 12:3

READING: John 5:1-20

How weak is my human nature! Paul warns us that even in our doing of good, sin is present and able to infect. For instance, when I give I can be tempted not just to under-give but to over-give. God gives each of us a measure of faith and if we give beyond that measure, we become more susceptible to stumble.

I once heard a pastor share about his financial struggles and felt convicted to give more to the church. I tore up my prepared check and wrote a new one for a larger amount. Later I found myself being unduly attentive to things I had not noticed before: the pastor's shoes, the number of coffee brewers, lights being left on in vacant rooms. I had given above and beyond my faith and now a critical and judgmental spirit ruled my heart.

Arrogance can always be found within self-deprecation as well as self-exultation. In both cases, Jesus' view and value of me is not enough. I am disappointed in myself because I *should* do better, or, on the other hand, I credit myself rather than Jesus. Pride is a tricky thing.

There is great temptation to over-serve, over-give, and over-work when planting a church. In us resides a reservoir of complex and mixed motives and rationale. Rather than simply trusting God, we may look for spiritual and generous ways that attempt to control God and put others in our debt.

Jesus, Save me from both my goodness and my badness. Make me like Jesus who only did what he saw his Father doing. Give me wisdom and faith to give well. Amen.

Peter Sung

Lest I Myself Be Disqualified

But I discipline my body and keep it under control, lest after preaching to others I myself should be disqualified. ~ I Corinthians 9:27 (ESV)

READING: I Corinthians 9:24-27

I've met many church planters in my life but one of the best I ever knew was Justin (not his real name). A gifted evangelist, he easily made friends with unchurched people, and often led them to the Lord within a short time. Justin was also a very effective preacher. His sermons were interesting, thoughtful and personal, all the while remaining true to the meaning of the text.

The church Justin was planting was doing well. Many lost people had come to Christ and many others had begun a renewed walk with the Lord. He had assembled a committed team of leaders who were eager to reach the community for Christ.

But then Justin faced some personal challenges. A death in the family hurt him deeply. He was criticized unfairly by some people in the church. He began taking time off and would be gone for hours without explanation. I could tell he was depressed and I wondered if he was hiding something. Finally his secret was revealed – he had become involved in an inappropriate relationship with another woman. His wife and children were deeply hurt and the church was devastated. Within a few weeks Justin resigned as pastor. Eventually, the church itself was forced to close.

Although the Apostle Paul was a godly and effective church planter, he knew that he was capable of falling into sin. He disciplined himself to stay focused. My friend, Justin, fell and was "disqualified." Though he is still saved, he is no longer in ministry.

May God help us to stay close to Christ, obedient to His word and faithful to our families!

Protect me, Lord, from sin. Show me how to run the race – and finish – in holiness. Amen.

Jim Carpenter

The Church Planter's Children #4
The Family Farm

Train a child in the way he should go, and
when he is old he will not turn from it. ~ *Proverbs 22:6*

READING: I Corinthians 12:4-11

I found the model of the family farm to be a helpful analogy as we pondered how much to involve our children in the ministry. On a family farm, everybody pitches in and helps with chores; even the youngest can gather the eggs.

Church planting is a lot like a family farm because the church planter's wife and children become an integral part of the functioning new church enterprise. In the long run, we found that our sons benefited from our reasonable expectation that they pitch in and help. This began with a light hand when they were about school age of us encouraging them to befriend newcomers who were their own age.

As they grew older, we gave them plenty of leeway to pick ministry "chores" around the church that they felt interested in exploring, and gave them freedom to fail within a safe environment. In Rosamond, our gregarious Andy (age 14) picked greeting as his niche. It cultivated his social skills and gave him confidence in group settings. Zach (11) thought he'd enjoy learning how to run the sound system. He became a dependable technician and had literally years of first-rate experience by the time he enlisted in the Army Signal Corps.

We found that our children rose to the challenge when our expectations took into account such factors as their maturity level, personality, giftedness and changing school obligations.

Come to think of it, what I've just described sounds pretty much the way I'd mentor any new believer or core group member!

Dear Father, Please help me to spot the unique personality and giftedness within each of my children and tailor my expectations to meet their individual needs. Amen.

Dionne Carpenter

The Church Planter's Children #5
The Family Farm

Train a child in the way he should go, and
when he is old he will not turn from it. ~ Proverbs 22:6

READING: Proverbs 22

There's at least one other way that church planting resembles the family farm. All the children can be well-respected co-laborers on the family farm, helping the family to earn its collective living. But, as with farming, there comes a day when each child should be given the opportunity to make an adult decision about whether to make farming – or church planting – his or her own calling.

So it's good to discuss the appropriate boundaries of our expectations for our church planter children. Let me begin with an observation about this verse in Proverbs. Some overbearing parents down through the years have misinterpreted this verse to imply that by our zealous training we can force our children to adopt our beliefs or our career. I was a preacher's kid myself, raised in this type of manipulative environment. It repelled me, making it more difficult for me to wholeheartedly embrace an adult commitment to Christ, let alone full-time ministry (even though I had, in point of fact, been called to ministry).

Rather, this verse wisely observes that as parents we should train our children in "the way <u>he</u> should go" – a uniquely tailored way – and thus prepare each of our children to fulfill their God-given potential in a healthy way.

Although we made no apology for expecting our two sons to chip in and help out at church while they lived under our roof, we never pressured them to become church planters. We prayed for them to discover God's call for their lives and to follow Him wholeheartedly into whatever career He directed.

Dear Father, Please bless my children and give me wisdom to train them in such a way that they will gladly follow You wherever You lead them. Amen.

Dionne Carpenter

Set Yourself up for Hope

Who hopes for what he already has? ~ Romans 8:24b

READING: Romans 8:24, 25

In our business of raising up disciples and working with all the diversity of peoples' problems, we have many opportunities to be discouraged or disheartened with seemingly hopeless situations. We put so much time and effort into the growth and progress of potential leaders that oftentimes we will feel let down. We are aware that this could happen, but still it takes something special, some meaningful moments that give us the will and desire to go on and fulfill our calling.

Thank God for those moments, where we are so filled with joy and satisfaction that it gives us a new infusion of resolve to continue confronting difficult attitudes or issues that arise.

I have found that if we give ourselves something to look forward to, that pleasant anticipation gives us the grace to go through our other difficult times. We work better when we have a hope set before us.

My parents were very wise that way. We always had to work hard as a family in the field or around the house, sometimes to make ends meet, but mostly to teach us to work. But we always had a hope set before us, perhaps a special family trip to the beach or mountains, or a picnic down by the creek where mom and dad spent special time with us. That gave us the will power to continue working hard with joy.

It is the same with the ministry. We need to set ourselves up with regular seasons of hope to look forward to with joy and be encouraged to go on to the next season. Do you have a day off to look forward to each week or other special events to count the days?

Heavenly Father, Help me to celebrate the good moments so that the hard moments will be bearable. Amen.

Ron Thiesen

Contentment

*I rejoiced in the Lord greatly that now
at length you have revived your concern for me.
You were indeed concerned for me, but you had
no opportunity.* ~ *Philippians 4:10 (ESV)*

READING: Philippians 4:10-13

Are you content as a church planter? Suppose those who pledged to support and encourage you did not follow through with their help. How content would you be? Paul says, "I have learned" to be content. He wrote as a prisoner in Rome, chained to a soldier. He expected to be executed. Still he was content.

Philippians is a letter to a church he had started. Finally, after a lengthy delay, they expressed their concern by sending Paul financial support. But how long had it been since they had last helped him? Ten years! He had not received any help from them in a decade – ten years of labor, heartache, exhaustion, loneliness, and, ultimately, imprisonment.

Some church planters might have become bitter. But Paul says, "You were indeed concerned for me, but you had no opportunity." One key to his contentment lies in the Greek word translated "no opportunity." Literally it means "no time." In New Testament Greek there are two words for time. One (*chronos*) is simply time as a measurement. The other term, the word Paul uses here, *kairos*, refers to *a strategic time, the opportune moment.*

"I know you were concerned, but the strategic moment to help me had not yet arrived." And who controls the strategic moment? Almighty God!

Paul saw the delay and apparent neglect of a supporting church as under the good, wise, and all-powerful hand of God. He came to believe that though God is sometimes mysterious, He always acts with compassion, faithfulness, and kindness, for His own glory and our good.

Lord, Teach me to be content, no matter what the circumstances, to Christ's glory. Amen.

Jim Carpenter

Loving Your Spouse

*Husbands, love your wives, just as Christ
loved the church and gave himself up for her to
make her holy, cleansing her by the washing with
water through the word... ~ Ephesians 5:25, 26*

READING: Ephesians 5:22-33

Church planters must have strong marriages. You must love your spouse. This is foundational to your life and church planting mission. It is the number one predictor of ministry success.

When God prepared the way for the birth of his precious son, Jesus, God gave Jesus a loving mother and foster-father. God is deeply committed to the institution of marriage.

I have been appreciating my wife more and more. We are very different. We give each other depth and balance. It hasn't been easy, but we are life partners and ministry partners.

How can we plant a healthy church if we don't have a healthy marriage? Our life, marriage and family are to be an example to those who find Christ in our new churches.

God isn't asking you to give up a happy marriage for the sake of your mission. He wants you to have both a happy marriage and a productive mission.

I am not currently pastoring a church, but attend a fine local church. When I think about my own pastor and his wife, I think of a couple who are very different in their gifting, but who have been committed to one another and have been faithful in their commitment to the ministry of our church through the years.

As a church member, knowing that my pastor has a strong and devoted relationship with his wife brings a security to me in my church relationship that I could not have if they weren't happy together.

Father, Help me to love my wife well. Amen.

Paul Becker

The God Who Sees

*And he saw that they were making headway painfully, for
the wind was against them. And about the fourth watch of the
night he came to them, walking on the sea. ~ Mark 6:48*

READING: Mark 6:30-52

It had been an exhausting but fulfilling day of ministry. Jesus multiplied
loaves and fishes, fed five thousand, and stretched the faith of the Twelve. But
then He dismissed the crowd, sent His disciples off across the sea and went up
on the mountain to be with His Father.

Did His disciples wonder why He left them? Were they experiencing
confusion? Disappointment? Whatever they felt, their voyage certainly didn't
feel like a victory cruise. The wind was against them and it was tough going.

But even while He was praying, even in the darkness before dawn, and
even at a distance to make human sight impossible, Jesus was watching and saw
their trouble. "He saw that they were making headway painfully." And He came
to them, walking on the sea.

Church planters often experience a let-down after the exhilaration of
ministry. Multiplied miracles on Sundays often lead to storm-tossed Mondays.
After victory and blessing, things get harder. Sometimes it feels as if the Lord
has left us. But He hasn't.

He is praying, but He is also watching. He sees all our difficulties when the
wind buffets and the waves roil. He sees all these things because He is *El Roi*,
the God who sees (cf. Genesis 16:13).

And He will come to us, Master of it all, walking on the sea. Nothing can
stand in His way.

---

*Lord Jesus, There are days when I feel like I'm all alone, in the middle of a storm. Thank
You that You see where I am and what I'm going through. I trust You as I wait for
You. Amen.*

Jim Carpenter

The Church Planter's Children #6
The PK as Qualifier

An elder must be blameless, the husband of but one
wife, a man whose children believe and are not open
to the charge of being wild and disobedient. ~ *Titus 1:6*

READING: Titus 1:5-9

I grew up in a dysfunctional pastor's home. It's tough to be a pastor's kid (PK). But my parents made it harder by constantly telling my brothers and me that our behavior (as a six-year old or whatever) directly affected our father's qualification for his livelihood. *Your daddy could lose his job if you don't obey us!* It was a staggering burden for little ones to carry. They exploited our fear of financial disaster to coerce us into rigid submission – or at least enough outward compliance to hoodwink the church folk. That dysfunctional message caused a great deal of damage.

Meanwhile, I married Jim, an exceptional father and elder. He handled this issue in an entirely different way. He gave our sons unconditional love and consistently disciplined them with a firm and patient hand. At first, it astounded me that he remained calm when our little boys messed up occasionally, as little boys do, even publicly, and didn't harangue them. He never mentioned how their misbehavior might impact his career.

Jim gave our sons room and grace to struggle through the challenges of each stage of childhood, allowing them space to articulate their occasional questions about Christianity without reproach. And, almost every night, he stole into their bedrooms after they fell asleep and prayed over each precious boy.

By God's abundant grace, our grown sons both love the Lord.

Jim had greater success fulfilling those elder qualifications because he understood that the lion's share of responsibility rested on *his* shoulders to be a wise and godly parent, not on our sons to be perfect children.

Dear Father, Have mercy on my children and help me parent them well. Amen.

Dionne Carpenter

The Church Planter's Children #7
When To Protect

Look! Your disciples are doing what is unlawful on the Sabbath. ~ Matthew 12:2

READING: Matthew 12:1-8

One day in our first church, we gathered at a home to baptize several new converts in a backyard pool. Fifty or sixty people informally surrounded the pool to watch, singing an enthusiastic spontaneous rendition of "I have decided" before we meandered indoors for a potluck luncheon. Afterwards, one irritated couple button-holed Jim and criticized our son, maybe five years old at the time, for playing quietly with his playmate in the nearby wading pool during the solemn occasion.

One of the hazards of being a pastor's kid is that, more so than regular children at church, many adults take liberties to criticize or opine on their behavior – notice, they didn't confront Aaron's folks. Jim calmly but firmly defended our son. Surely when John the Baptist baptized people little boys played in the shallows. Zach was being a normal child and Jim defended him from attack.

Of course Zach didn't always get a pass. Sometimes we thanked our "reporters" for spotting something we missed. We insisted that our boys apologize and make amends when they did wrong. Children need appropriate discipline and we were grateful for well-intentioned help.

It's a double-edged sword, this notion among the adults that pastor's kids are somehow communal property. Done well, our children benefit from kindly communal wisdom and attention. Done poorly, that ever-present threat of criticism and disapproval may discourage a child, sometimes irrevocably.

As parents we must discern when to defend our vulnerable pastor's kids from unreasonable attack, and when to agree with their critics, endorsing due discipline. We must make it clear to the church that we will protect our children appropriately; that they are not fair game for mean-spirited cranks.

Dear Father, When they need us most, may our children know they can count on us. Amen.

Dionne Carpenter

The Anger of Jesus

Be angry and do not sin… ~ Ephesians 4:26 (ESV)

READING: Mark 11:15-17

What makes you angry? Church planters often have short fuses. When our plans are thwarted or people stand in our way, disappoint us or betray us, we may get angry. We may justify our anger because we're doing God's work. We may even use anger to "motivate" people to do what must be done. Anger is not automatically a sin. After all: "Be angry, and do not sin." But is our anger *righteous* anger?

Jesus did get angry. But why? He got angry when His disciples kept little children from His blessing. His disciples thought they were guarding Him from time-wasting interruptions. But Jesus was "indignant" – much displeased (v. 14).

He was angry at the tomb of Lazarus – "deeply moved in His spirit and greatly troubled" (Jn. 11:33). The Greek words mean He was agitated and upset. When our Lord overturned the tables of the money-changers and drove out the vendors, He was angry (See Mark 11).

So Jesus got angry when people were hindered from coming to Him. Trying to stop the parents from bringing their children to Him was wrong. The money-changers and other vendors set up their booths in the only part of the Temple to which Gentiles had access. That was wrong.

And the terrible toll that sin takes, including the inevitability of death, is what angered Jesus at the tomb of His friend Lazarus – even knowing that He would soon raise him from the dead.

But Jesus did *not* get angry when His plans were opposed, when His disciples failed, or even when He was betrayed, falsely accused and sentenced to death. Often our anger is selfish, because of something done to us. Jesus' anger was on behalf of people who were shut out and broken by sin.

Lord, Forgive me when my anger is all about me and not about others. Amen.

Jim Carpenter

The Courage of Jesus

*Jesus answered them, "Did I not choose you,
the Twelve? And yet one of you is a devil." He spoke of
Judas the son of Simon Iscariot, for he, one of the Twelve,
was going to betray him. ~ John 6:70, 71 (ESV)*

READING: Luke 22:47-53

We must admire our Savior's courage. And because He was so strong in facing His trials, He can give us courage to overcome the challenges of church planting. He knows what it feels like to enter foreign territory, to trust untested co-workers, to work hard, to be disappointed and betrayed, to suffer, and to triumph in the end.

He placed the future of His church in the hands of twelve ordinary men, and one of them was a traitor. Jesus' courage in choosing these men is wrapped up in the mystery of His sovereign will. It's beyond us to fully understand. Judas' duplicity came from his own stony heart, but it also fulfilled the divine plan (cf. John 13:18).

Jesus knew about it from the beginning – as God had always known it – but as a Man, the drama of His betrayal was as real, as terrifyingly sequential, as an avalanche. The very events He planned and set in motion, eons before, broke His heart when they unfolded in time. His close "friend's" treachery played out face to face, the kiss felt sharp as a spear, as cold as a tomb.

And again, Jesus knew it all going in – the purse pilfered, the secret conspiracy and Garden arrest, and on to the cross.

Church planting can be daunting. It takes brave disciples to start a church. But our Savior has walked this road, His victory gives us hope and His Spirit fills us with courage beyond ourselves.

Lord Jesus, Thank You for Your courage! Strengthen me to follow You today, and to rely upon Your Spirit. Amen.

Jim Carpenter

Be Anxious for Nothing

Be anxious for nothing; but in everything by prayer and
supplication with thanksgiving let your requests be made known
unto God. And the peace of God... ~ Philippians 4:6, 7a (KJV)

READING: I Corinthians 3:5-9

We forget sometimes that this kingdom we are building is the Kingdom of God and not our own. We get so caught up in how things are going and so worried about the results that we get carried away with cares. We sometimes let the apparent lack of results or problems get us discouraged and we take that discouragement into our relationship with our spouse and children.

Yes, it is good that our spouse understand our concerns and the work that we do even to the point of being intimately concerned together; however it is NOT right to let our concerns upset our family and marriage to the point that we live in turmoil. We need to learn how to separate our ministerial lives from our private lives.

We are encouraged by Peter's wise counsel to "cast all [our] anxiety on Him because He cares for [us]" (I Pet. 5:7). As the Scripture says in today's reading in I Corinthians, we are laborers together with God but He is responsible to give the increase.

We are responsible to be obedient and to whole-heartedly do whatever God asks of us. When we have done our best in the power of the Holy Spirit and ministered His word to the people, we can rest in faith that God's word will not return void but will have the effect for which God sent it.

Dear Lord Jesus, Help me learn to separate my pastoral cares and problems from my personal life with my spouse and children. Help me find the right balance of letting them participate in the work you have called me to do without upsetting my family's peace of mind. Amen.

Ron Thiesen

Be Sure Your Sin(s) Will Find You Out

But if you fail to do this, you will be sinning
against the Lord; and you may be sure that
your sin will find you out. ~ Numbers 32:23

READING: Joshua 7:1-10; Acts 5:1-11; I Timothy 3:2

If the first New Testament church had sin in the camp, with a married couple like Ananias and Sapphira, surely the 21st century church plant is not exempt. The church planter must be ready for the unexpected and at the same time be "above reproach" personally. Statistics prove that if a lead pastor has a supportive spouse, is assessed properly and has a coach, 90% of the time they will have a successful church plant.

But you say, "What about the other 10% that don't make it?" All too many of the other 10% have sin somewhere in the camp like Achan in the days of Joshua. Let's focus here on the seriousness of sin in the lives of the leadership team. As a coach of church planters, I tell them "keep your hand out of the money pot and your britches on" and you will have a healthy church plant if you have a spouse on board and a good coach.

Many are the horror stories of church leaders who have secret sins that are exposed to the ruination of the church plant. Whether it is a staff member coming out of the closet as a practicing homosexual or a lead pastor addicted to internet pornography, in either case, sooner or later the secret sin will surface. A church planter must live a life above reproach and he must strive hard to put in place accountability measures and accountability partners to protect against the lust of the flesh.

Lord Jesus, Please help me live a life above reproach, in the name of One who gives victory over the flesh, Amen.

Sam Douglass

Lean into the Wind

...they shall mount up with wings like eagles. ~ Isaiah 40:31 (ESV)

READING: Isaiah 40:9-31

For my 50th birthday, my wife gave me an unusual present – a paragliding lesson. A paraglider is a fabric wing attached by suspension lines to a harness. You strap on the harness, run forward, the sail fills with air – and you're flying!

For four hours my instructor taught me how to fit into the harness, climb up the hill to varying elevations, and then run downhill as the sail behind me popped open to catch the wind. I was tethered to my instructor like a human kite.

Finally, exhausted from hours of climbing up the hill, he told me I was ready to solo. Actually he was far more confident than I that I was ready. But we climbed the 750 feet to the top of the hill, and I ran for the edge. I could feel the wing fill and suddenly I was airborne!

I had a walkie-talkie strapped to my chest, and my instructor gave me instructions as I sailed high above the ground. For ten minutes I glided through the air like a giant bird. It was exhilarating! My instructor's voice guided me to start my descent for an easy landing at the bottom of the hill.

My paragliding adventure reminded me of church planting.

Church planting is exciting, dangerous, and a little bit crazy. You won't succeed without the support and encouragement of others. (Without Dionne's enthusiasm, I would never have tried this!) When the time comes, you have to "launch." Lean into the wind and trust the Holy Spirit to "lift" you. And remember – obeying your "Instructor's" voice (through His word) during your "flight" is essential.

Lord, Fill me with Your Holy Spirit today. I depend upon His lift and power to make this church planting all You want it to be. Amen.

Jim Carpenter

A Natural High

*Or do you not know that your body is a temple of
the Holy Spirit within you, whom you have from God?
You are not your own, for you were bought with a price. So
glorify God in your body. ~ I Corinthians 6:19, 20 (ESV)*

READING: I Corinthians 6:9-20

Church planting is intense. The strain is multi-faceted: spiritual, emotional, mental and physical. It is not unusual for planters to suffer breakdowns in any of these areas. Sometimes moral breakdowns occur as well.

One fundamental antidote is the God-mandated Sabbath.

Another important stress release is the joy of physical exercise. Recent studies in physiology have revealed that moderate exercise releases endorphin chemicals (internally-produced pain killers) into the brain. These endorphins produce a natural high of positive emotion that assist in stress release. Most researchers agree that the greatest increase of blood endorphins come from moderate-intensity exercise lasting at least twenty to thirty minutes.

Modern inventions have contributed to a more sedentary lifestyle. Instead of walking we often ride in easy chairs on wheels (cars, taxis, busses, trains and planes). In Biblical times people usually walked. Machines have replaced most of the manual labor that was commonplace. Coupled with an abundance of food, we can become walking time bombs with every tick of our heart bringing us closer to the heart failure that could end our lives prematurely.

Paul's admonition, here in I Corinthians 6, is often ignored by church leaders: This passage is a call to healthy living in all its aspects.

God created a natural high. Go and get high on some exercise today.

Lord, Help me to be a steward of my body, for the sake of the Gospel. Help me to be like the Apostle Paul who wrote, "But I discipline my body and keep it under control, lest after preaching to others I myself should be disqualified" (1 Corinthians 9:27 ESV). Amen.

Mark Alan Williams

NOVEMBER

The Multiplication Principle

Healthy churches will reproduce, and daughter church planting should be envisioned and planned from the new church's beginning.

Banyan Trees

*News of this reached the ears of the church at
Jerusalem, and they sent Barnabas to Antioch. ~ Acts 11:22*

READING: Acts 11:19-25

The banyan, the national tree of India, is a huge structure with long, deep roots. The enormous tree acts as a shield, which is why these trees are planted near homes, temples, villages and roadsides. With its many large aerial roots, a mature banyan looks more like a forest than an individual tree.

Located in the Indian Botanical Gardens, spreading by the River Hooghly from Kolkata, *Howrah* the Great Banyan was the widest tree in the world in terms of its collective canopy. The area occupied by the tree is about 14,500 square meters. The present crown of the tree has a circumference of about one kilometer and the highest branch rises to about 25 meters. At present it has 2,880 aerial roots reaching down to the ground. This tree now lives without its main trunk, which decayed and was removed in 1925.

The church in Jerusalem had "aerial roots" and thus became a great blessing to the Jews and Gentiles in the first century – extending its reach first to Samaria (Acts 8:5), then to Phoenicia and Cyprus; some from Cyprus to Antioch (Acts 11:19), and from Antioch to worldwide.

The first and primary trunk of the Great Banyan tree is not huge but its spread is remarkable. Church planters should have similar visions for aerial roots from their simple and small church plants. Sometimes the first church plant, like the first trunk of the Great Banyan tree, might disappear for one reason or other. Still, as the dead trunk enjoys pride of its canopy, church planters can be proud of their first fruit bearing but ceased church plants.

Father, Help me plant a Great Banyan Tree Church Plant; a plant that spreads every day; a single church plant that becomes a forest of mature churches! Amen.

R. Jayakumar

It's Always Right to Multiply

And the things you have heard me say in the
presence of many witnesses entrust to reliable men who will
also be qualified to teach others. ~ *II Timothy 2:2*

READING: II Timothy 2:1-4

As church planters we naturally wonder when it is the right time to birth new churches and even if it is worth it. For me, the sacrifices of church multiplication seemed huge when our church sent some of our biggest donors and best leaders to help start new churches.

Therefore, it is inspiring to hear about the church planting movements catalyzed around the world. For example, between 2004 and 2008, DCPI church planting trainers first launched and then expanded their work in Kenya. During the summer of 2008, a research team was sent to Kenya to evaluate the results. In less than five years, more than 100 Master Trainers and Certified Trainers had been equipped in Kenya. They trained more than 1,800 Kenyan leaders who planted more than 3,700 churches for Kenya!

According to three separate research projects in Kenya, Ghana and India, the average number of new believers who come to Christ per church plant is 46.7. This means that over 150,000 precious people have become followers of Jesus in the churches these Kenyan leaders started! The Kenyan Master Trainers also became a missionary force by opening more than ten other countries for DCPI, including England, Egypt and Pakistan.

My conclusion is this: it is ALWAYS the right time to multiply. Churches that multiply churches reach more people in more places and more quickly than ministries that stay self-focused. Often the multiplying church grows more rapidly as well.

Dear Lord, Help me to envision and practice the multiplication of churches and church planting movements for your sake. Amen.

Mark Alan Williams

No Clone Churches

*I know your deeds, your hard work
and your perseverance… ~ Revelation 2:2a*

READING: Revelation 2

Several families in the core group of our second church plant had moved out en masse from a city about a hundred miles away to retire in Temecula. They really wanted us to recreate for them a clone of their beloved home church down to the tiniest detail like the format of our Sunday bulletin. We couldn't. Temecula was a different place. It wasn't possible to transplant that exact church. As our church grew, new people came and totally changed the group dynamic.

I confess Jim and I have hoped a time or two to clone successful projects, or wished, by religiously following the advice of some expert or other, to clone their model. It didn't happen. In fact, although Jim and I were the common denominator in all four of our church plants, each congregation developed an entirely different personality. Strategies that worked great in one church fell flat in the next and vice versa.

That's the nature of groups. Every class at school develops its own identity; ask any teacher. Even two fifth-grade classes at the same school will differ from each other.

It's always struck me, when reading Revelation 2 and 3, how different those seven churches were, even though they'd been planted around the same time, all within 150 miles of each other. Jesus knew each one, uniquely and specifically.

We do well, as under-shepherds, to leave our pre-conceived ideas about people at the door and discover the unique personality, struggles and giftedness of each new group. May we value the distinctive redemptive gifting of each congregation and strive to help each church bring glory to God.

Dear Lord, I love that my church family, with all our quirky personalities and challenges, is known to You. Have mercy on us all and help us serve You well. Amen.

Dionne Carpenter

Never Give Up

Therefore, my dear brothers, stand firm. Let nothing move you.
Always give yourselves fully to the work of the Lord, because you know
that your labor in the Lord is not in vain. ~ I Corinthians 15:58

READING: II Corinthians 4

Can you name this person?

- He was dismissed from a school in Munich because he lacked interest in his studies. But he did not give up.
- He failed to pass an examination for entrance to a polytechnic school in Zurich. But he did not give up.
- He later applied for an assistantship in teaching but was rejected. But he did not give up.
- He did become a tutor for boys in a Zurich boardinghouse, but was soon fired. But he did not give up.

These facts are from the life of Albert Einstein. He refused to give up and today his name is a household word and a synonym for genius.

Carole Hyatt, co-author of *When Smart People Fail,* says that the way to distinguish between smart people and stupid people is that smart people move on after a failure, job loss, rejection or embarrassment. But stupid people get stuck and say, "Failure is the only option for me." Smart people look at what went wrong and correct it.

Have you wanted to give up? I sure have – many Mondays in my earliest years of church planting. But the church we started will soon celebrate its 30th anniversary. Good thing I didn't listen to discouragement and give up.

God's repeated instruction is clear: "Therefore we do not lose heart" (II Cor. 4:16); "Therefore, my dear brothers, stand firm. Let nothing move you" (I Cor. 15:58a); and "We must run the race that lies ahead of us and never give up" (Heb. 12:1b GW).

Lord, Help me to persevere when the days are hard and success seems minimal. Please help me to never give up. Amen.

Mark Alan Williams

Keeping Our Channels Clean

*...and teaching them to observe everything I have
commanded you. And surely I am with you always,
to the very end of the age. ~ Matthew 28:20*

READING: II Timothy 2:2

When you fly over the Amazon River in a small plane or navigate the rivers, you can see clearly the natural phenomenon of the river channels and lakes constantly birthing and dying. When the water changes course and a channel loses its connection with the flow of the current, it begins to close up at what was once the entrance and exit of the lake. We have gotten stuck on just such sandbars many times when traveling the rivers in the river launch.

Churches, and even our personal lives, are the same. If we get out of the flow of the Holy Spirit in our church services or personal relationships, the "dirt" starts to accumulate at the intake and output of our lives. We become stagnant and accumulate other unwanted things in our lives. If this continues too long, like the river channel, we will become closed off and dry up, ceasing to produce good fruit in our lives.

One of the devil's strategies to sabotage the fruitfulness of a church is to cause strife within, which causes the vision to stagnate. Then the outreach dies. When this happens the church will likely eventually die. Matthew 28:20 tells us that we should teach people to obey *immediately* what they are being taught and promptly share it with someone else, thus keeping the blessing flowing like the river.

What about your church? Do you have a church outreach project? Is there a church plant nearby where your people can experience the joy of serving and winning others to Christ?

Dear Heavenly Father, Please help me to instill in my church the vision for reaching others so that we can keep our channels open to your Holy Spirit. Amen.

Ron Thiesen

You Don't Have to Be
Big to Make a Big Impact

*And after this there arose war with the Philistines at Gezer. Then
Sibbecai the Hushathite struck down Sippai, who was one of the descendants of
the giants, and the Philistines were subdued.* ~ *I Chronicles 20:4 (ESV)*

READING: I Chronicles 20:4-8

Today's passage shows us that you don't have to be a David or even a
Goliath to make a big impact. Like David, the giant killers listed in I Chronicles
20 were normal sized men. But they took on giants and won! Sibbecai, Elhanan,
and Jonathan the son of Shimea don't get as much press as King David, but they,
too, were giant killers.

The wonderful truth is that all of us can be giant killers for the Kingdom if
we step out in faith to multiply churches. You don't have to have a megachurch
to make a mega-impact through church multiplication.

When my church of 200 daughtered a church of 200, we doubled overnight.
As that daughter church has grown, it has multiplied the size of the mother
church many times over.

When my church of 200 birthed a different church of 15, the impact seemed
minimal. But that church, in a remote community with a small population, has
grown to equal the size of the mother church.

Too many church planters want to be the Goliath and not the David,
Sibbecai, Elhanan or Jonathan. But let's remember who won those skirmishes.
And let's remember that megachurches are called that because they are genetic
mutations of normal-sized churches. I am not against megachurches, just against
thinking you have to be a megachurch to make a mega-impact.

Be glad for whatever size church you have, multiply it and watch God
bring a mega-harvest!

*Dear Lord, Help me to remember, even when I feel small, that I can make a huge
impact for You as I multiply churches. Amen.*

Mark Alan Williams

Mother Church Gives
Birth on Her Death Bed

...I saw a great many bones on the floor of the
valley, bones that were very dry. He asked me, "Son
of man, can these bones live?" ~ Ezekiel 37:2b, 3

READING: Ezekiel 37:1-14

The old Bethel Church was over 100 years old with only 26 remaining members. The youngest member was 76 years old and the offerings could barely pay the utilities. The old church was in crisis mode. With seven acres of land, buildings and a prime location (the state had just mandated that the little county road be widened into a four-lane feeder artery to the largest corporation headquarters in the county), what were they to do? The church leaders explored several options, such as whether to sell the property or put it on the auction block.

Finally, after much discussion, they decided to turn over the property and all their assets to a new church IF someone would help them make the transition. While serving as pastor of a local traditional church, it became my privilege to organize a small launch team of five families to work with this dying church to give birth to a daughter church. Yep, an old Mamma church gave birth to a young thriving baby while on her death bed. It was a difficult delivery and the baby looked much different than the Mamma. Some might even say that the baby was born by caesarean birth, to save the life of the baby before the Mamma gave up the ghost.

Whatever the case, by God's grace, a beautiful daughter church was birthed, and now, several years later, the daughter church has now birthed a granddaughter church.

Heavenly Father, Even as I grow older and get more set in my ways, please keep me pliable and teachable so your Kingdom's work can be accomplished. Grant that I may be fruitful even in old age. Amen.

Sam Douglass

The Happy Church Planter #1
Poor in Spirit

*Blessed are the poor in spirit, for theirs
is the kingdom of heaven. ~ Matthew 5:3*

READING: Matthew 5:1-12

The most famous sermon ever preached was Jesus' Sermon on the Mount. And the opening to His messages was the best introduction ever given – the eight beatitudes. The beatitudes are our Lord's instructions on how to be truly happy. "Blessed" means happy.

Church planting is a high calling, but our happiness as church planters does not depend upon how quickly our congregations develop or how abundant is the harvest of souls.

The world cannot produce real happiness. No one can buy it, earn it or discover it. Happiness comes from God alone. If we learn the lessons of happiness, our congregations will be filled with happy people, too.

First, Jesus said, "Blessed, truly happy, are the poor in spirit, for theirs is the kingdom of heaven." "Poor" means destitute – like a beggar crouching down with his empty hand extended. Christians are blessed because they start by knowing they are poor in spirit. They are happy because theirs is the kingdom of heaven. They live under the rule of God and depend totally upon His grace.

Coming to God every day, mindful of our spiritual poverty, leads to submission to His agenda, rather than demanding our own. It brings contentment with the life He gives. It leads to adoration of the great God who has loved us and saved us, apart from any works of our own. And it teaches us to be grateful for what we have, rather than resentful of what we don't.

The Lord told Isaiah, "...This is the one to whom I will look: he who is humble and contrite in spirit and trembles at my word" (Isaiah 66:2).

May you be a happy church planter!

Father, Thank You that in my poverty of spirit You have made me rich in Christ! Amen.

Jim Carpenter

The Happy Church Planter #2
Mourning for Sin

*Blessed are those who mourn, for
they will be comforted. ~ Matthew 5:4*

READING: Psalm 6

What kind of happiness shall we teach in our new churches? Jesus' words run counter to what the world teaches. The world regards mourning as the opposite of happiness, preferably a short season of life and quickly forgotten.

But Jesus is talking about more than grief over the death of a loved one. After all, God doesn't comfort all mourning. Amnon mourned because he had lustful designs on his own sister (II Sam. 13:2), and Pharaoh was grieved after he let the children of Israel go (Ex. 14:5). People who end up in hell mourn for all eternity.

Our Lord spoke of mourning for the sin in our lives, not because of sin's consequences, but because sin grieves our Savior and offends the holiness of Almighty God. It's the kind of mourning Paul expected of the church at Corinth: "Ought you not rather to mourn?" (I Cor. 5:2).

Although we're forgiven, we Christians still struggle with sin. Happy is the Christian who hates his sin because he loves his Savior. That Christian is blessed because he continues to receive the comfort of God while he continues to fight for holiness.

We are happy as we continue to bring our sin to Him and experience His grace. After we have confessed God comforts us. "Comfort, comfort my people, says your God. Speak tenderly to Jerusalem, and cry to her that her warfare is ended, that her iniquity is pardoned, that she has received from the LORD's hand double for all her sins (Isa. 40:1, 2).

The book of Ecclesiastes says there is a time to mourn and a time to dance (Ecc. 3:4). Real mourning for our sin leads to the dance of grace and forgiveness.

Holy Father, Teach me to hate my sin because I love my Savior. Amen.

Jim Carpenter

The Happy Church Planter #3
Meekness

Blessed are the meek, for they
will inherit the earth. ~ Matthew 5:5

READING: 1 Peter 3:1-17

The world equates meekness with weakness. But that's not true. Only two people in the entire Bible are described as meek. One is Moses (Num. 12:3). But Moses was certainly not weak. He was a strong and passionate leader who brought an entire nation out of Egyptian captivity.

The other is the Lord Jesus. "I am meek and humble in heart" (Mt. 11:29). But though *meek*, Jesus was never *weak*. He threw money-changers out of the Temple, faced angry crowds, stood up to demons and storms and enemies and death and sin and hell and defeated them all!

Jesus said happiness is for meek Christians – whose strength is under control. Meekness toward God means accepting His ways without complaining or murmuring. Meekness toward others means being loving and patient and kind, free from malice or bitterness or the desire for revenge.

Church planters are usually assertive personalities whom God has gifted to lead. But meekness is not a personality issue, it is a character issue. Strong leaders can and should be gentle and humble like Jesus. Meekness is not absence of assertiveness; it is the absence of self-promotion. Meekness is not about being subservient. But it is about being submissive toward God.

Jesus said happiness starts with poverty of spirit, which leads to heartfelt mourning for sin, and then produces meekness – strength under the control of God's Spirit.

The meek Christian will inherit the earth in two ways: first, here and now, he is content. He looks to God and has enough. But second, there is a new day coming, a new heavens and a new earth, which Jesus has prepared just for us.

Lord, As I lead my church plant, teach me meekness. May the strength You have given me be always under the Spirit's control. Amen.

Jim Carpenter

The Happy Church Planter #4
Hungry and Thirsty for Righteousness

Blessed are those who hunger and thirst for
righteousness, for they shall be satisfied. ~ Matthew 5:6 (ESV)

READING: Psalm 63

Have you ever been desperately hungry? Or thirsty? Many people around the world struggle just to find food and clean water every day. Jesus said that the happy Christian is actually a hungry and thirsty person. And He meant a deep, painful, and ongoing hunger and thirst.

But Jesus was not talking about physical food or water. He said the blessed person has a spiritual hunger and thirst *for righteousness*. To be hungry and thirsty for righteousness is to desire God above all things. That's the kind of hunger we church planters want to impart to our congregations. *Righteousness* in Scripture means *justification* (being declared righteous because of Christ's sacrifice) and also *sanctification (*growing in personal holiness).

True happiness, Jesus says, means you desire God above all people and all things. You want to be right with Him, and you want to grow more like Him. The world's hunger and thirst only produces more hunger and thirst. But Jesus promised that this hunger and thirst would be satisfied.

So why are some Christians not hungry and thirsty for righteousness?

A person may lose his appetite because of sickness. Spiritually, if you're sick with sin, you won't have a desire for righteousness. Or maybe you're full of "junk food" which bloats but does not nourish.

Another reason: perhaps you're not getting enough spiritual "exercise." Obedience stimulates your appetite for God. One last suggestion: Maybe someone isn't hungry and thirsty for righteousness because he has never truly "tasted" the sweetness of God. King David said in Psalm 34:8, "Taste and see that the Lord is good."

Father, Please give me a deep, abiding, and ongoing hunger and thirst for You alone. Amen.

Jim Carpenter

The Happy Church Planter #5
Merciful

Blessed are the merciful, for they shall receive mercy. ~ *Matthew 5:7 (ESV)*

READING: Luke 10:25-37

Desperate, broken people cried out to Jesus for mercy, such as two blind men: "Have mercy on us, Son of David" (Mt. 9:27); a Canaanite woman with a demon-possessed daughter: "Have mercy on me, O Lord, Son of David…" (Mt. 15:22); and blind Bartimaeus: "Jesus, Son of David, have mercy on me" (Mk. 10:47). People tried to quiet him down, but he just kept screaming for mercy. Christ called for him and gave him back his sight.

Jesus is the most merciful person who has ever lived. He healed sick people, gathered little children in His arms and forgave a woman who was going to be stoned because of her adultery. And our Lord said mercy is one of the keys to being a happy Christian.

Many of us have been hurt, betrayed and wounded by life and by the actions of others. We have also hurt, betrayed and wounded others. The mercy of God changes the equation. God did not ignore our sin. Instead He poured out His wrath against it upon Jesus. God's mercy, forgiveness, healing and blessing were all purchased by the cross.

Truly happy Christians extend mercy to others because they've experienced the mercy of God. Mercy is more than sympathy or emotion. The Good Samaritan showed mercy through compassion that noticed someone in need and offered practical help.

Look around! Our communities are filled with desperate, broken people who need mercy. God has called us to be happy (merciful) church planters and to plant happy (merciful) churches.

Jesus, quoting the prophet Hosea, told us: "Go and learn what this means, 'I desire mercy, and not sacrifice.' For I came not to call the righteous, but sinners" (Mt. 9:13).

Father, Thank You for Your mercy to me in Christ. Teach me to receive, give and model mercy. Amen.

Jim Carpenter

The Happy Church Planter #6
Pure in Heart

Blessed are the pure in heart, for they will see God. ~ *Matthew 5:8*

READING: I Corinthians 6:9-11

If the non-Christian world were to write a beatitude, it might be "Happy are the promiscuous, for they will be fulfilled." Sadly, that reflects the values of many of the world's cultures. Such a sentiment is bankrupt of truth. It is the devil's lie. Only the prescription given by Jesus leads to true happiness.

New churches reach people whose lives are mired in sin and stained with impurity. The blood of Jesus frees and cleanses them, but they need ongoing training from God's word to learn how to walk according to the truth. And they need their pastoral leadership to model purity.

In the Bible purity means *clean from sin*, but also *sincerity* and *transparency*. Jesus promised that the pure in heart will see God. They will experience God's presence and blessing in ways that those who regularly succumb to temptation cannot.

So how can we fight for holiness in our own lives as leaders? First, live in God's justifying love. "… you were washed, you were sanctified, you were justified in the name of the Lord Jesus Christ and by the Spirit of our God" (I Cor. 6:11).

Second, immerse yourself in God's word (cf. Ps. 119:9, 11). Reading, memorizing, studying, and obeying the Bible is essential.

Third, flee sin and pursue holiness. "So flee youthful passions and pursue righteousness, faith, love, and peace, along with those who call on the Lord from a pure heart" (II Tim. 2:22).

And lastly, confess sin immediately and come back to God when you stumble (cf. I Jn. 1:9). As we learn to walk in purity, we will be able to lead our people in a deeper walk in holiness.

Lord, I want to have a clear vision of You; show me how to walk in purity. Amen.

Jim Carpenter

The Happy Church Planter #7
Peacemakers

*Blessed are the peacemakers, for they
will be called sons of God.* ~ *Matthew 5:9*

READING: Ephesians 2:13-21

I read recently that since the beginning of recorded history, the entire world has been at peace less than 8 per cent of the time! Something like 8,000 peace treaties have been made and broken during that time.

Peace in the Bible means more than the absence of conflict. Real peace starts with being right with God, which brings peace with other people. And Jesus is the Prince of Peace (Isa. 9:6).

Christ's peace is not the weak, temporary and compromising peace the world offers. His peace is strong, eternal, and founded in the holy love of God. Jesus said, "Do not think that I have come to bring peace to the earth. I have not come to bring peace, but a sword" (Mt. 10:34).

Because, the truth is, "There is no peace," says the LORD, "for the wicked" (Isa. 48:22). That's why the world needs new churches. Christ's peace comes because of the work of the cross. "For in him [Christ] all the fullness of God was pleased to dwell and through him to reconcile to himself all things…making peace by the blood of his cross" (Col. 1:19, 20).

So how do we "make peace?" First, before we consider ourselves peacemakers, let's make sure we are "peace-receivers" – that we have personally tasted, savored, and been comforted by the peace of God!

Second, pray for peace. Paul taught us to seek peace by praying for government leaders (cf. I Tim. 2:1, 2). But church planters must also be intercessors, praying for families, marriages and children in our churches, as well as the souls in our community.

Third, preach the gospel. It called the "gospel of peace" (Eph. 6:15). Only faith in Christ brings real peace!

Lord, Thank You for peace in Christ. Make me a peacemaker today. Amen.

Jim Carpenter

The Happy Church Planter #8
Persecuted

*Blessed are those who are persecuted for righteousness' sake,
for theirs is the kingdom of heaven.* ~ Matthew 5:10 (ESV)

READING: Acts 11:19, 21

A few years ago, I was talking to a Bible college student in India. His friends revealed to me that he had recently lost the hearing in one ear because of a beating he received when he was witnessing. While sharing Christ door-to-door he encountered some militant Hindus who reacted violently. The young man told me he was going back, even at the risk of his life.

Over 100 million Christians worldwide suffer interrogation, arrest and even death for their faith, with millions more facing discrimination and alienation.

Happy church planters will be prepared – not surprised – by persecution. "Blessed (truly happy) are you when others revile you and persecute you and utter all kinds of evil against you falsely on my account. Rejoice and be glad, for your reward is great in heaven, for so they persecuted the prophets who were before you" (Mt. 5:11, 12).

Persecution is part of God's plan for all Christians: "Indeed, all who desire to live a godly life in Christ Jesus will be persecuted…" (II Tim. 3:12).

God uses persecution to spread the gospel. Persecution scattered the early church all the way to Antioch, where a new church was planted (Acts 11:19 – 21). Persecution also reveals false believers (cf. Mt. 13:21), and confirms the identity of true Christians: *for theirs is the kingdom of heaven.* Persecution points us to eternity and the rewards that await us: "rejoice and be glad, for your reward is great in heaven."

Let's keep looking to Jesus for victory: "Consider him who endured from sinners such hostility against himself, so that you may not grow weary or fainthearted" (Heb. 12:2, 3).

Father, teach me to rejoice even in persecution, so that You may be glorified and the gospel may be spread! Amen.

Jim Carpenter

The Joys of Children and Grandchildren

Like arrows in the hand of a warrior are the
children of one's youth. Blessed is the man who fills
his quiver with them! ~ Psalm 127:4, 5a (ESV)

READING: Psalm 127

For most people, one of the greatest joys in life is having children. They require an immense amount of time, energy and money. Yet investing all of these only seems to make us love them more.

Now that our children are grown, my wife and I are excited to someday see our children have our grandchildren. We can envision why the writer of Proverbs 17:6a said, "Grandchildren are the crown of the aged." There is a great delight in a new life; in youthful curiosity, learning and growth.

On the other hand, watching our parents grow older, decline and die has been very painful. The aging process demonstrates the heavy cost of the fall and the curse. Likewise, watching churches Carolyn and I planted long ago grow older and decline has been painful. The church members are aging and declining and so are the churches.

Thankfully some churches are revived and have a sort of rebirth. But most churches go through a normal aging process and eventually pass away.

What's the solution? It's to give birth to baby churches which can in turn reproduce other churches so that there is continual regeneration of the body of Christ. Does it take time, energy and money to birth churches? Of course it does, just as it takes to raise children. But the joys of reproducing are worth it!

Dear Lord, thank you for the joys of church reproduction. Help me remember to invest resources to multiply, so that I can experience the joy of many generations of churches. Amen.

Mark Alan Williams

Fruit That Remains

*You did not choose me, but I chose you
and appointed you to go and bear fruit –
fruit that will last. ~ John 15:16*

READING: John 15:1-16

The first command in Genesis is fruitfulness. Then Jesus taught his disciples to remain in his love in order to bear fruit. Before Jesus ascended, he commanded his disciples to make other disciples, that is, to bear fruit. Fruitfulness, not mere activity, is the goal.

What does it mean for leaders and churches to bear fruit?

All throughout Scripture, good leaders, at some point in their ministry, usually in the very beginning, focused their attention on disciple-making. The succession plan was the plan. We see this all the way from Abraham (Isaac) to the apostle Paul (Timothy, Barnabas). Fruit that remains must of necessity force our attention onto disciple-making.

The very definition of leadership can be understood as investing in other leaders. The job of every church planter is to turn their attention to, invest in, and raise up other leaders. If we are not doing this, then are we leading at all according to the Biblical understanding of leadership?

In the same vein, every church that is planted is at once called to exist and to perpetuate that existence by planting other churches. The very health of the church plant demands that it crank its missional, reproductive gears from the onset as a way to define and legitimize itself as a church.

Blessed to be a blessing; saved to be a leader; and planted to become a planting church. This is the way and heart of God's kingdom.

Jesus, You are the first among many brothers and sisters. Your heart is not just for me and my world. I want to bear fruit. Help me to do so. Amen.

Peter Sung

Your Multiplication Legacy

*Then after fasting and praying they laid
their hands on them and sent them off. ~ Acts13:3*

READING: Acts 13:1-3

Recently I got to visit my granddaughter in the Philippines. It was so exciting to see that precious new baby – one of the greatest joys of my life. Carolyn and I have three unmarried sons, none of whom have any children. The "baby" I am referring to was a granddaughter church. Here's the story.

Eleven years before, the first church I founded in Vista, California, followed the Acts 13 model by laying our hands on a group of believers and sending them out to help start a daughter church in Oceanside, just 15 minutes away. (Since the church is the bride of Christ, churches are always female.)

That church has since led thousands to Jesus, one of whom was a Navy Corpsman, Edwin Samson. His life was dramatically changed. We met before he became a Christian and he was so new to the faith that for a long time he could not figure out what "church planting" meant when he read it on the business card I had given him!

Eventually, he graduated from seminary and two years later he arrived in the Philippines to begin a career of missionary ministry. So it was that I had the privilege to visit and preach in his first church plant there.

Spiritual offspring are a huge source of joy. Developing a church multiplication legacy is one of the greatest joys of ministry. Edwin's story really started over a decade before he even stepped into my daughter church. That's the way it is with a spiritual legacy. It often takes time and sacrifice, but when you look back, years later, you realize that the souls are well worth the sacrifice!

Dear Lord, Help me to think in terms of legacy and build that legacy by multiplying churches for your glory. Amen.

Mark Alan Williams

Recycled Faith

*...even we have believed in Christ Jesus, that
we may be justified by faith in Christ, and not by the
works of the Law; since by the works of the Law shall
no flesh be justified. ~ Galatians 2:16 (NASB)*

READING: Galatians 3:10-14

The practice of recycling is almost routine in the United States. There is somewhere to take everything that has lost its value and usefulness. Thrift stores receive clothes, toys, luggage and household goods. Recycling centers take discarded appliances, electronics and metal.

There are recyclers in Colombia, too. They are usually gaunt, disheveled men actually called 'recyclers.' Carrying large tarp bags, they walk through neighborhoods where trash has been put out. They devotedly collect their preferred scraps: cardboard, plastic, glass, etc. After a long day of work rummaging for their payload of recyclables, you see them walking the streets destined for an appropriate recycling center where they will be compensated a few pesos. Their tarp bag, filled to capacity, is tossed over their backs. Usually the only thing you can see from underneath their bulky bag of scrap is their feet!

As a church planter, Paul had to deal with Judaizers who pushed to recycle a commitment to the law. Paul explained to the Galatians that the law pronounces a curse on everyone who fails to keep the law in its entirety. All who hope to gain God's favor by keeping the law are exposed to a curse. The good news is that "Christ redeemed us from the curse of the law, having become a curse for us."

Some insist on carrying a hefty bag of garbage on their back that is nothing more than a curse of the law from whatever genre of belief system they left. But the gospel proclaims freedom from legalistic practices, a freedom that comes from the righteousness that is lived by faith.

Father, Help me to walk in my freedom in Christ. Amen.

Christine Cunningham

Setting the Precedent

*Nevertheless, I have this against you: You tolerate that woman
Jezebel, who calls herself a prophetess. ~ Revelation 2:20a*

READING: Revelation 2:18-29

I vividly recall the difficult days in our first church plant when my husband
Jim and the newly-installed elder board wrestled with the thorny problem of
dealing with a contentious couple who had been fomenting discord in the church
body. Jim had been scrupulous about following the guidelines found in Matthew
18, taking care to start one-on-one, then taking a witness before involving
the whole elder board. By God's grace, Jim and the elders all had humble,
compassionate hearts. They bent over backwards, extending chance after chance
for repentance and reconciliation in one exhausting meeting after another.

Eventually they came to a moment of decision that every new church
encounters sooner or later: Would they take the hard next step, the correct one,
even though they knew some people would misunderstand and some would
disagree?

Thank God, our board chose well.

Sadly, some churches can't bring themselves to make the tough choices.
They shrink away from appropriate church discipline out of a misguided
interpretation of what it means to "love one another." Or, because it's hard to
find competent teachers, they let it slide that their teachers are teaching heresy
or syncretism.

The identity of any church will be shaped, for good or ill, by how their
leaders choose to handle these tough choices. If done well, the church body
will be spurred to higher standards of love and holiness. If done poorly, the
church will sink into superficiality or legalism, at either extreme an easy target
for spiritual predators.

As you sense the solemn weight of this responsibility upon your shoulders,
take comfort that Jesus sees your heart and will honor the hard choice to
repudiate that which repulses Him.

*Father, Give us courage to step out in faith when we must make the tough choices.
Amen.*

Dionne Carpenter

Growth

*The company of the prophets said to Elisha, "Look,
the place where we meet with you is too small for us. Let
us go to the Jordan, where each of us can get a pole; and let
us build a place there for us to live." ~ II Kings 6:1, 2*

READING: II Kings 6:1-7

My vision of planting 1,000 churches in my native Middle Eastern country had a humble start. My first church plant had three attendees, no chairs and a budget of twenty rupees. It was hardly enough money for a handful of vegetables and some bread!

Through these initial days of uncertainty God significantly grew our small church in numbers and since then, by God's grace, we have seen tremendous growth, baptizing over 1,500 new believers last year alone! However it has often been the case that the body of believers has grown much faster than its resources. Such was the story of our first church plant where the growing numbers still had to deal with no building, no chairs and little or no money.

I have been greatly encouraged by the imagery of the iron axe head rising to the surface which illustrates how God can raise up the tools needed to build and provide for his Church.

In our experience of planting churches, oftentimes a lack of money and other resources has threatened to become a limitation for growth. The story recorded in II Kings 6:1 – 7 has been a constant reminder that the restrictions of our circumstances are no equal to the supernatural power of our God.

Dear Heavenly Father, Your love and Your provision for the Church has been seen through all generations. When we go through times of distress, help us to call on You, knowing that, like that axe that floated, You will raise up everything we need in ways that give You glory. Amen.

Saleem Sadiq

The Hummingbird

What do you have that you did not receive?
And if you did receive it, why do you boast
as though you did not? ~ I Corinthians 4:7

READING: I Corinthians 4:1-7

The tiny ruby-throated hummingbird harrumphed at our empty bird feeder and darted over to my window to twitter his displeasure. Oops! I quickly took down my feeder with its four plastic blossoms and refilled it with sugar water. That's better.

Within a few minutes the bantam warrior returned, taking up his favorite position on the azalea branch, and buzzed into action to chase away any other hummingbirds who happened by looking for a drink.

"That's *my* feeder! How dare you take what's mine! Mine! Mine!"

Although most birds remind me to trust God, hummingbirds usually remind me of my sin nature. And watching my pint-sized pirate defend "his" territory I thought of times I act as badly.

In I Corinthians 4:7, Paul asked those carnal Christians some very good questions.

How often have we prayed as fervently as my harrumphing friend for some gift from God, and then turned around to gloat when we received it? As church planters, how often have we hoarded our trained workers and other resources after our church plant has become established instead of freely sharing our supplies? It's so easy to forget that every blessing, every ability, every achievement comes from God's hand – even our next breath.

Our "feeders" would stay bone dry if God did not faithfully fill our lives with everything we need each day.

Father, Help me to remember how patient You are with me and how unfailingly good. And help me, with a humble heart, to share today the bounty You have given me with others who buzz around my azalea branch. Amen.

Dionne Carpenter

Train up Laborers for the Harvest!

*Then saith he unto his disciples, The harvest
truly is plenteous, but the laborers are few; Pray ye
therefore the Lord of the harvest, that he will send forth
laborers into his harvest. ~ Matthew 9:37, 38 (KJV)*

READING: John 4:27-38

Many books and websites remind us that there is a tremendous need to reach the unreached people groups and plant churches among them, especially into the 10/40 window. But, even outside the 10/40 window, there are thousands of small towns and villages that do not have the viable presence of a dynamic growing church. Those unreached villages should be the responsibility of the believers who are nearest in their vicinity. These more local believers often need training and motivating to do it.

Even though our current church plant can take up most of our own strength and energies, we ought to instill in our people the vision for others around the world who have much less opportunity to know and grow in Christ. We should expose our congregations to other church planters and give them a worldwide vision for reaching the needy nations around the world.

Every church is tempted to focus only its own needs. Therefore, missions visioning should be an integral part of our church planting strategy and the teachings that we give them. Do you invite missionaries in to give the vision for the nations? Have you considered a missions conference to motivate your people to reach out beyond the four walls of the local church? If not, why don't you pray about it and then do it?

Dear Heavenly Father, I believe that is never too soon to train my people to have a heart to reach other nations. Please give me your heart for the nations and the wisdom to organize our church to have an impact in the nations. Amen.

Ron Thiesen

Maximizing Your Missional Footprint #1
Taking an Audit

When I think on my ways I turn my feet
to your testimonies. ~ Psalms 119:59 (ESV)

READING: Psalm 119:57-64

Many people are considering how to reduce their carbon footprint. They are taking creative initiatives like installing rain barrels to gather rainwater from their roof for use in their garden. Recycling is becoming common practice. It can be both economical and friendly to the environment to reduce the amount of energy used to maintain a home or business. Many homeowners start by performing a home energy audit to discover energy wasters and to remedy problem areas. They may replace windows, install thermostats or add insulation.

But in the local church we have the opposite goal. We look for ways to increase our missional footprint because we want to have the widest possible kingdom impact.

A good first step is to do a missional audit to discover things in our 'house' that are unproductive, especially in this new world of technology, communication, commerce and transportation. What are we doing that is no longer having much impact on the Kingdom? What new opportunities for missional expansion are now available to us?

Perhaps the following questions and others like them will help you perform a missional audit so your ministry will have the widest missional footprint possible.

- Where are the pockets of people in our region not being reached by any church or ministry? How can we engage them with the gospel?
- How many churches are being started through our church?
- How are we multiplying church planting leaders?
- Why are we doing a particular activity? Should we keep doing it? Are there more efficient ways to achieve the same goals?
- Who can we partner with that we aren't currently?

Dear Heavenly Father, We ask for wisdom to more effectively reach the world for you. Amen.

Sean Pierce

Maximizing Your Missional Footprint #2
Multiplication

*The man who had received five talents went at
once and gained five talents more. ~ Matthew 25:16*

READING: Matthew 25:14-30

In the association of churches in which I serve we have defined a healthy, strong church as a "Reproducing community of Christ-followers." Size is not the defining issue, reproduction is.

The key issue for us is how are we helping churches multiply their disciples? Are we transforming lives, ministries, and leaders through church planting? How are we multiplying our efforts and the impact of our initiatives? As missions leaders, we maximize our missional footprint when we apply the concept of multiplication to everything we do. This is reflected in DCPI's 11th principle which says: "Healthy churches will reproduce and daughter church planting should be envisioned and planned from the new church's beginning."

Multiplication thinking is an important discipline in this rapidly changing world. To do it means giving up a measure of control and position because control tends to reduce multiplication. However, great reward comes from faithfully investing the time, influence and the resources God has given us for maximum return.

What will your ministry's missional footprint be in the world? What steps can you take today to increase your missional impact? Perhaps you should schedule a missional audit and ask yourself and other leaders some of the more difficult questions regarding your ministry.

We should do all we can to multiply our resources, and so hear our Lord say: "Well done, good and faithful servant! You have been faithful with a few things; I will put you in charge of many things."

Dear Heavenly Father, We want to be part of what You are doing. Keep us humble but allow us to see and experience a great work in the advancement of Your Kingdom. Take our ministry and mold it into a tool that can be used to change the world. Amen.

Sean Pierce

The Greatness of God #1

*Grace to you and peace from God our Father
and the Lord Jesus Christ. ~ Philippians 1:2 (ESV)*

READING: Philippians 1:1-6

We church planters need to encourage our congregations. They are filled with people who are exhausted, distracted, confused, grief-stricken, carnal, afraid, and just beat up by life. They need encouragement. And it seems there are only two kinds.

One kind of encouragement points to people and tells them they can do better, that they have hidden reserves of talent and energy that they have yet to develop. Keep on trying, keep on working, because things will get better.

The other kind points to God and says, our God is great, and He is in control no matter what comes. The Lord is good, all the time. He is full of wisdom and power, and whatever concerns Him, whatever it takes to accomplish His purposes, He will do. Trust Him, follow Him, obey Him, and He'll get you through.

Now the first kind of encouragement is good. It will help. We *should* try harder, not give up, and we *can* do more than we think.

But the second kind of encouragement is the kind Paul used when he wrote the book of Philippians. Rather than telling the Philippians they were a great people, he told them they had a great God. Instead of speaking of their great potential, he told them "I can do all things through Christ who strengthens me." And rather than telling them that if *they* just hung in there, things would get better for them, he told them that *Christ* was the only reason for living and dying, and that one day every knee would bow and every tongue would confess that Jesus Christ is Lord.

That's how he encouraged them. And that's the kind of encouragement we need to receive, and to give.

Father, Encourage me with a greater vision of Your glory! Amen.

Jim Carpenter

The Greatness of God #2

...I press on to make it my own, because Christ Jesus
has made me his own. ~ Philippians 3:12a (ESV)

READING: Romans 8:28-39

Sometimes people say, "Doctrine divides." But in church planting we need doctrine – fundamental truth from God's word – to build a lasting foundation. And nothing is as solid, or as encouraging, as the beauty and perfections, the plans and promises of our God.

Paul, the master church planter, modeled this when he wrote to the congregation at Philippi. After his opening remarks is this amazing statement about God: "And I am sure of this, that he who began a good work in you will bring it to completion at the day of Jesus Christ." Paul had come to a settled persuasion ("I am sure"): the believers in Philippi were going to make it. God would surely bring them to heaven!

Wrapped in this short statement are three wonderful truths about the greatness of our God. We'll cover one per day for the next three days.

First, *the good work of salvation begins with God.* "He who began a good work in you..." The fact that our salvation began in eternity, in the mind and heart of God, is meant to humble, comfort, and encourage us.

- "All that the Father gives me will come to me" (Jesus, Jn. 6:37).
- "So then it depends not on human will or exertion, but on God, who has mercy" (Rom. 9:16).
- "...he chose us in him before the foundation of the world..." (Eph. 1:4).
- "... God chose you as the firstfruits to be saved" (II Thes. 2:13).

Teaching the sovereign love, grace, and mercy of God will encourage and equip our new Christians through all the seasons of their lives.

Father, Teach me how to make much of You in all the training, counseling, and preaching I do, to Your glory. Amen.

Jim Carpenter

The Greatness of God #3

*I thank my God in all my remembrance of you always in every prayer
of mine for you all making my prayer with joy, because of your partnership
in the gospel from the first day until now.* ~ *Philippians 1:3-5 (ESV)*

READING: John 15:1-17

Early in my church planting ministry I saw many decisions but not many
disciples. I found myself wondering what happened to the people who "prayed
the prayer." Why weren't they following through? Sometimes I found myself
trying to assure people who had no evidence at all of conversion that they were
truly saved simply because they made a decision.

I've come to realize a hard, but encouraging truth: *The good work of salvation
always bears fruit.* Paul clearly believed this when he taught the Philippians that
"...he who began a good work in you will bring it to completion" (Phil. 1:6). That
"good work" was bearing fruit. He had observed their growth in grace over about
a dozen years. That's why he could be so encouraging.

John taught this lesson, too. "And by this we know that we have come to
know him, if we keep his commandments" (I Jn. 2:3). What about my "converts"
who were not following the Lord at all? John says it plainly: "Whoever says 'I
know him' but does not keep his commandments is a liar, and the truth is not in
him..." (I Jn. 2:4).

One of the ways we encourage our people and preserve the gospel is by
exalting God's greatness, and proclaiming salvation as a miracle-work of God.
Sure, we want anyone and everyone to accept Jesus! But repentance and faith
in Jesus are what we must proclaim. And God's grace will transform the true
convert. Fruit will appear eventually.

---

*Lord, Help me not to look for decisions, but to make disciples. Show me how to expect
the fruit of Your transforming grace. Amen.*

Jim Carpenter

The Greatness of God #4

*And I am sure of this, that he who began a
good work in you will bring it to completion at the
day of Jesus Christ. ~ Philippians 1:6 (ESV)*

READING: John 10:27-29

Paul was a great encourager. Even while awaiting possible execution in Rome, he encouraged his new churches. And one of Paul's favorite ways to encourage was to point people to the greatness and wisdom and kindness of God. That's what he did in his letter to the Philippians. The key verse for today lays out three wonderful truths. First, *the good work of salvation starts with God.* And then, from yesterday, *the good work of salvation always bears fruit.*

And for today: *God finishes what He starts.* Imagine how wonderful this promise would have been to those new Christians: "he who began a good work in you will bring it to completion!"

God will do that. Yes, you cooperate, you obey, you pursue holiness. But it's not ultimately in your hands, it's in His hands – the hands that have the nail-scars in them.

It's not based on your faithfulness, but on His. Not your power, but His. "[He] will sustain you to the end, guiltless in the day of our Lord Jesus Christ. God is faithful, by whom you were called into the fellowship of his Son, Jesus Christ our Lord" (I Cor. 1:8, 9).

Those who know Christ enjoy a living hope that is "kept in heaven for you, who by God's power are being guarded through faith for a salvation ready to be revealed in the last time" (I Pet. 1:3 – 5).

To equip and encourage people with the promises of a God this great is such a privilege!

Lord, Thank You for encouraging me, so I can encourage others. Let me point them to You today. Amen.

Jim Carpenter

Conflict in the Church

*I wrote a short letter to the church; but Diotrephes, who likes
to be their leader, will not pay any attention to what I say.
When I come, then, I will bring up everything he has done:
the terrible things he says about us and the lies he tells! But that
is not enough for him; he will not receive the Christians when they
come, and even stops those who want to receive them and tries
to drive them out of the church!* ~ *III John 9, 10 (GNB)*

READING: III John 1

Church planter, are you discouraged by conflict in your church plant? Be encouraged. Remember, if you are in church planting leadership, you will have conflict and will have to deal with difficult people just as Biblical leaders did:

- Despite God's miracles of protection and provision, Moses faced withering criticism as he led God's people out of bondage.

- David, relentlessly loyal to King Saul, was rewarded by Saul's trying to kill him repeatedly!

- The Apostle Paul, though suffering sacrificially for the Gospel, was deeply hurt by opposition from church members and was forced to defend himself.

- John, the Beloved Disciple, wasn't so beloved by some and had to defend himself as we see here in III John.

- Supremely, our Lord Jesus, the perfectly sinless one, faced opposition that led to his crucifixion. He was killed by his own people!

So don't be surprised when conflicts arise. We are in good company.

Lord, It is so good to know that it is not always me who is the problem. Please help me discern when it is and when it isn't. Help me apologize when the problem is me and to appropriately confront when it is not. Amen.

Mark Alan Williams

DECEMBER

The Joseph Principle

Attending to organizational and administrative matters will protect and stabilize the new church and enable it to grow in a healthy way.

Building a Good Foundation

*If any man builds on this foundation using gold, silver, costly
stones, wood, hay or straw, his work will be shown for what it is,
because the Day will bring it to light. ~ I Corinthians 3:12, 13*

READING: I Corinthians 3

Recently my husband was invited to help a local church plant that had struggled along for about ten years. Their pastoral staff was exhausted and their congregation befuddled and discouraged. Jim agreed, and our church mobilized with enthusiasm and goodwill. The more our pastoral staff investigated their situation, to revitalize and support their efforts, the more mess they uncovered.

No one there had set up any mechanism to train people to do basic ministry or established any guidelines for who could teach; so no wonder the pastors ran themselves ragged! Nobody set up simple ground rules for collecting, recording or depositing the weekly offering, or presented a budget to the church. In fact, the church had never in ten years held a business meeting. One or two people handled all the money from start to finish – inviting temptation and mismanagement.

Those involved in this church plant had a sincere heart for ministry. They loved Jesus and had a heart for the lost. They had won many precious converts. It might have seemed unspiritual to them to take time away from that important work to do humdrum things like set up financial rules and procedures, write job descriptions for teachers, and think through what they needed to set in place by way of classes or training or whatever to turn new converts into mature believers equipped to serve the Lord.

However, it is just such mundane details as these that transform a crowd of people into a functional church.

Dear Lord, Help me to see the eternal good that comes of such minutia and may I be faithful in small things. Amen.

Dionne Carpenter

Running the Race #1

Therefore, since we are surrounded by so great a cloud of witnesses, let us also lay aside every weight, and sin which clings so closely, and let us run with endurance the race that is set before us, looking to Jesus, the founder and perfecter of our faith, who for the joy that was set before Him endured the cross, despising the shame, and is seated at the right hand of the throne of God. ~ Hebrews 12:1, 2 (ESV)

READING: Hebrews 12:1-3

Church planting is not a sprint; it's a marathon. So we must learn to run the race with endurance. The author of Hebrews gives us three keys to a good race:

First, *choose the right heroes:* "since we are surrounded by so great a cloud of witnesses." These "witnesses" are the heroes of the faith listed in chapter 11 – the men and women who kept running their race with endurance, despite great obstacles. By their own examples they are cheering us on: Don't give up! Stay the course! Your reward is coming one day! Make sure your heroes are godly men and women who are running their own races with endurance.

Second, *give up anything that hinders:* "lay aside every weight, and sin which clings too closely." Successful runners strip off anything that could slow them down or cause them to falter.

One hindrance is called "weight" ("encumbrances," NASB) – anything that gets in the way of your pursuing God with a whole heart. Another is "sin which clings closely." Sin trips us up and causes us to stumble. Church planters must keep their lives clean.

Third, *keep your eyes on Jesus.* Keep looking to Jesus. Jesus is always the key to everything. The term "looking to" literally means turning away from other things to focus only on Him.

Lord, Teach me to run my race with endurance! Amen.

Jim Carpenter

Running the Race #2

Therefore, since we are surrounded by so great a cloud of witnesses, let us also lay aside every weight, and sin which clings so closely, and let us run with endurance the race that is set before us, looking to Jesus, the founder and perfecter of our faith, who for the joy that was set before Him endured the cross, despising the shame, and is seated at the right hand of the throne of God. ~ Hebrews 12:1, 2 (ESV)

READING: Hebrews 12:1-3

Jesus is our best role model in the race we run. Let's keep our eyes on Him!

Keeping our eyes on Jesus brings us security. Jesus is the "founder" (or "author") and "perfecter" of our faith. He is our leader, captain and hero. While we each must run this race, and must work and pray hard, in the end, the start and finish of our faith are in His hands.

Remember when Peter walked on water (Mt. 14)? As long as he kept his eyes on Jesus, he was fine. But when he looked at the storm around him, he began to sink.

Keeping our eyes on Jesus strengthens our courage. Jesus despised the shame of the cross. It was a shame He didn't deserve, but He faced it. As we follow Him, He gives us courage to carry our cross, however difficult it may be.

Keeping our eyes on Jesus reminds us of the goal. Jesus kept going "for the joy that was set before Him." The reward ahead is worth the long race we're called to run. There's joy set before us. Joy in bringing others to Jesus and helping them grow. Joy in finishing the race in faithfulness. Joy in the presence of the Lord one day.

Lord Jesus, Thank You for running Your race. Show me how to run mine in a way that brings You glory. Amen.

Jim Carpenter

He Fell Asleep

For David, after he had served the purpose of God in
his own generation, fell asleep… ~ Acts 13:36 (ESV)

READING: Acts 13:13-52

Scripture says David completed his mission and then went to be with the Lord. One day, all of us will "fall asleep." The question each of us must ask is this: Will we have served our purpose? Consider these situations:

Some leaders "burn out." They run hard and never take a break. It destroys their body and they die early.

Others "flame out." They burst onto the scene like a shooting star, here one moment but flaming out the next.

Still other leaders "rust out." They get old and crusty, losing their purpose and direction along the way.

Our goal should be to "run out" like David; we should serve God's purpose and finally run out of good works on that task-list that God has "prepared in advance for us to do" (Eph. 2:10). When will that be? Only the Father knows. I have known two church planters who planted multiple churches in their "retirement" years. Others maintained significant ministry in their retirement homes.

A few years ago, one of our Brazilian DCPI Certified Trainers traveled to Cuba to train church planters. He taught a lesson, sat down afterwards, had a heart attack and died. While the loss to his family was immense, he went home to Jesus serving faithfully. What a great way to go!

Lord, Help me not to burn out, rust out or flame out in ministry. Help me pace myself in order to serve your purpose in my generation and eventually run out of your work for me. May I then hear those words I long to hear: "Well done, good and faithful servant" and receive my heavenly reward. Amen.

Mark Alan Williams

The Vocabulary of Praise

When they had sung a hymn, they went out
to the Mount of Olives. ~ Mark 14:26

READING: Exodus 15:1-3; Psalm 118:13-24; Isaiah 12:1-3

Standing by the Red Sea, little did Moses know he would forever bless God's people. Sure, people had seen miracles before. Lots of them. But for the first time someone recorded a praise song about one. *"The Lord is my strength and my song; He has become my salvation"* (Ex. 15:2). Moses' song recounted how God saved them from dangers. *"The horse and his rider He has hurled into the sea."* It penned new names for God and celebrated God's glory.

Like waters from the Red Sea, this song rippled out to future believers, extending even to Jesus Himself, singing a hymn with His disciples. The hymn-writer of Psalm 118 told the story of a time he was *"about to fall, but the Lord helped me."* Searching for words, the psalmist borrowed the refrain from the Song of Moses – *"He has become my salvation."* Isaiah the prophet also quoted from the Song of Moses when he broke into song about the Messiah who *"has become my salvation."*

As we search for vocabulary to express what God has done for us, songwriters lend us phrases to articulate our feelings. Like the psalmists and prophets of old, we can add a church planter's stanza, making it our song, too. Other people need our songs. Praise songs can sustain believers when their hearts are too heavy to think up new words.

Tradition suggests that Psalm 118 might have been the hymn Jesus sang on the way to the garden that holy, awful night. I think about Jesus leaning on those ancient lyrics as He walked toward betrayal. And I think about Moses, offering those beautiful words to Jesus, our Messiah, who has *"become our salvation."*

Dear Father, Please fill my heart with a song of praise today. Amen.

Dionne Carpenter

About Jesus

"Ought not Christ to have suffered these things, and to enter into his glory?"
And beginning at Moses and all the prophets, he expounded unto them in all
the scriptures the things concerning himself. ~ *Luke 24:26, 27 (KJV)*

READING: Luke 24:13-35

I wonder what synagogue sermons are like. I bet they are filled with wisdom, truth, and principles. I bet lives are improved, relationships are healed, and money is managed better. And I bet synagogue sermons are even about God, filled with Scriptural verses and insightful theology.

We would do well to preach synagogue quality sermons.

On the road to Emmaus, Jesus interrupted two of his disciples and showed them how the whole of Scripture was about him. I bet they had never heard any sermon about Jesus in any synagogue.

Our call as Christian preachers is to work out our salvation with fear and trembling, to understand our Bible in such a way that every single verse is about Jesus, and not just about life. Life can and should be improved, but what humanity needs is more than help; we need salvation. And there is no salvation for us under heaven but in Jesus. Everything has been a prelude to Jesus and everything now is still about Jesus. He alone saves.

Truths, principles, rules, laws and wisdom are good things. And the primary role these play is to point us to Jesus who came not to destroy these but to fulfill them. And somehow, in him is life, life abundant.

In our consumer-driven, controlling world, it is tempting to preach things other than Jesus and to put power in human hands.

What are you planting: a church or a synagogue?

Jesus, Our alpha and omega, first and last, Take your seat, in my life, and in your church. Amen.

Peter Sung

Getting Out of the Way

The bride belongs to the bridegroom. The friend who attends the bridegroom waits and listens for him, and is full of joy when he hears the bridegroom's voice. That joy is mine, and it is now complete. He must become greater; I must become less. ~ John 3:29, 30

READING: John 3:22-31

The people we meet in the course of planting churches are often so hungry for someone to love them and pay attention to them, that it's fairly common for them to develop a personal attachment and loyalty to us as their leaders. Especially if we lead them to the Lord, they may look to us for general guidance and affirmation, not just in spiritual matters.

New believers need us to lead them. They're often spiritually ignorant, and don't know how to distinguish God's voice when they pray or how to recognize God's guidance. It is totally appropriate for us to provide godly guidance and to make ourselves available as a sounding board for our people as they begin to grow in their faith.

But eventually we must wean them off their dependence on us, after it has outgrown its usefulness, and steer them toward an un-mediated relationship with Christ. Otherwise, we will become a distraction or – worse – a competitor for their undivided loyalty.

In my experience, the Holy Spirit has spoken to my heart giving me a sense of when I should start getting out of the way. I begin withholding advice or comfort. Instead I gently suggest they take their dilemma or trauma to Jesus, giving them an opportunity to hear God's wonderful voice for themselves and receive His guidance and comfort directly.

It's not that we stop having any role. But they belong to Christ, not us. It's a joy when He takes center stage.

Father, Make me like John who pointed people to Jesus and then got out of the way. Amen.

Dionne Carpenter

The Lord is in the Details #1
Listen and Take the Problem Seriously

For God is not a God of confusion but of peace. ~ *1 Corinthians 14:33a (ESV)*

READING: Acts 6:1-7

There's an old saying: "the devil is in the details." But for church planters, it's far truer to say, "The Lord is in the details." For many church planters, administrative matters are dull and dry, and have little to do with the exciting business of establishing a church. But without attention to the details, without wise systems in place, church life can become haphazard and chaotic, and people will be hurt.

The new church in Jerusalem was a cultural blend of Hellenized (Greek-speaking) and traditional Jews. They all believed in Jesus, but their customs and language were very different. Though numerically large, the congregation was young and fragile. Its ethnic diversity made for a climate where misunderstanding could erupt into a crisis. That's exactly what happened. The church's "feed the widows" program somehow neglected the Greek-speaking widows. Understandably, the Hellenists were hurt and complained to the church's leadership.

If the apostles had not handled this first, major crisis with wisdom and sensitivity, the church might have been split, even destroyed. Christianity itself might have been permanently identified as an ethnic movement, rather than as a faith for all peoples. Thankfully, the apostles showed great skill and integrity. They handled things administratively, and the Lord was in the details!

All church planters can learn from their example. So for the next few days, let's look at five administrative principles from the apostles.

First, *they listened and took the problem seriously.* Sometimes spiritual leaders ignore trouble until it's too late. Or they may treat a problem as if it is an assault on God's vision, rather than an opportunity to minister to genuine needs.

Thank God for the administrative example of this first church's leaders!

Lord, Help me listen compassionately and plan wisely. Amen.

Jim Carpenter

The Lord is in the Details #2
Help Everyone "Own" the Problem

And the twelve summoned the full number of the disciples... ~ Acts 6:2a (ESV)

READING: Romans 12:3-8

My friend Tim worked as a computer repairman. People would come to his shop, plunk their laptop down on the sales counter, and start complaining. He learned to walk around the counter to stand with the customer. "Let's see what we can do to fix this," he would say. In a gentle way he demonstrated that he and the customer were on the same side; both wanted a solution to the same problem.

The apostles in Acts 6 handled the church's first crisis in much the same way. A dispute had erupted over a church program – feeding widows. But the Greek-speaking women were being neglected, and a rift in the church was in danger of developing.

The apostles were wise and spiritual men. Following their principles will help us handle the administrative details of our church plants with compassion and skill. Administration isn't so much about policies and procedures as about taking care of people. As we pointed out yesterday, they first listened and acknowledged the problem.

Here's the second principle: *they helped everyone "own" the problem.* By bringing everyone together, the congregation knew nobody was trying to hide the conflict and that no ethnic slur was intended. Instead of dividing the church, the crisis actually helped unite it. Of course we can't call congregational meetings for every problem. But with a wide-spread and potentially volatile issue, full-disclosure is needed.

The apostles didn't allow the crisis to separate them from the people who were hurting. They "stood on the same side of the counter." Though church planters are usually strong leaders, we must also have a humble heart and a gentle spirit.

Lord, Show me how to "stand on the same side" with people who are hurting, and to seek Your solution for every problem. Amen.

Jim Carpenter

The Lord is in the Details #3
Maintain Your Own Priorities

*It is not right that we should give up preaching the word
of God to serve tables…we will devote ourselves to prayer
and to the ministry of the word.* ~ Acts 6:2b, 4 (ESV)

READING: II Timothy 4:1-5

Have you ever had one of those weeks when unexpected problems and crises kept you from study and prayer, so that by Sunday you were not prepared to preach? All pastors have weeks like this. But being careful about organizational details, systematically training and deploying people, having back-ups – these are the administrative details that over time will help us keep our balance so we won't be thrown off course when emergencies hit.

It's a principle we can learn from the leaders of the Jerusalem church. When the "widow crisis" surfaced, they might have been tempted to deal with the problem themselves. But here's the third principle from their story: *they reaffirmed their own priorities.*

They saw the problem had to be fixed, and they knew it was urgent. But they also knew their ministry of preaching and prayer could not be delegated. It was God's call for them as leaders, shepherds, and equippers.

The church planter often has to do everything in a new church. He arrives early on Sundays and sets up chairs, leads worship, teaches children, plans picnics, chaperones youth events, drives others to appointments – a multitude of good, godly activities. But if he doesn't recruit, train, and delegate soon, he will ruin his health and neutralize his effectiveness as an intercessor and preacher.

Church planter, administrative attention will save your true priorities! It will keep you from exhausting yourself with important, but non-essential, tasks, and allow you to stay true to your calling – preaching and prayer.

Father, Protect me from getting so busy with things others should do that I neglect what you've called me to do: pray and preach. Amen.

Jim Carpenter

The Lord is in the Details #4
Select and Deploy the Right People

...pick out from among you seven men of good repute, full of the Spirit and of wisdom, whom we will appoint to this duty. ~ Acts 6:3 (ESV)

READING: I Timothy 3:8-13

In our first church plant music was a problem. We did our best, and God was praised, but I often cringed at the lack of quality. It wasn't anybody's fault. We just didn't have the right worship leader. Then God sent us Bill. He was a gifted musician, but even more, he was good at helping others develop their musical gifts. Several of our vocalists blossomed under his mentoring. Worship became a strength rather than a liability under his leadership.

Effective church planters organize and administrate. What that often means is they find the right people for the right job. That's the fourth principle we can see in the Acts 6 story. A crisis that threatened to split the Jerusalem church was averted and unity was strengthened because the apostles *selected and deployed the right people.*

Notice how they did it. They set the parameters for the job of overseeing the widows' program: how many leaders were needed, and what their qualifications needed to be. More than anything, they had to be men of proven character.

But then they gave the task of actually selecting the men back to the congregation. This plan "pleased the whole gathering" (v. 5). The church knew this wasn't a "rubberstamp" of the apostles' preferences. It was an administrative partnership.

The names of the seven men show they were from the Hellenists' group. What better way to correct the inequity than to put men from that group in charge! Crisis averted, unity restored, congregation strengthened – all by wise administration.

Lord, Grant me the wisdom to see the right people for the right jobs, and help me find them even before I need them. Amen.

Jim Carpenter

The Lord is in the Details #5
Celebrate the Solutions

*These they set before the apostles and they prayed
and laid their hands on them. ~ Acts 6:6 (ESV)*

READING: Nehemiah 12:27-43

The apostles were so wise. They were not only visionary leaders but calm administrators. New churches need both. The visionary sees where God wants the church to go; the administrator charts a course to get there. The visionary excites and mobilizes; the administrator plans and organizes. Most church planters cannot be both. But every visionary leader must be convinced that organizational attention is crucial, and must find a way to attend to it.

The "widows" crisis in the Jerusalem church is a case study in good crisis management. The apostles not only averted disaster, but strengthened the unity of the church and increased the number of godly leaders.

The fifth principle: *they celebrated the solution* that God brought to the crisis. Like Nehemiah before them, they chose to spotlight the accomplishments of God's people in working together, solving problems and strengthening community.

The seven "deacons" chosen by the congregation were publicly commissioned. There must have been great joy among both the Hellenists and the Hebrews. Joy that unity was restored, that godly solutions were found, and that their church had wise and unselfish leaders who humbly shared the credit and joined hands in celebrating the solution.

The conclusion? "And the word of God continued to increase, and the number of the disciples multiplied greatly in Jerusalem, and a great many of the priests became obedient to the faith" (Acts 6:7). It's a great illustration of a key church planting principle: Attending to organizational and administrative matters will protect and stabilize the new church, and enable it to grow in a healthy way.

Jesus, Help me share the credit and celebrate the solutions You provide to whatever problems arise in the church You've given me to lead – and administrate. Amen.

Jim Carpenter

Learning to Trust
When I Don't Understand

*Trust in the LORD with all your heart and lean not
on your own understanding; in all your ways acknowledge him,
and he will make your paths straight. ~ Proverbs 3:5*

READING: Hebrews 11

When assessing a potential church planter we always look for someone who "walks by faith" and not by sight. When a new church planter ventures out by faith, there is so much that is not seen, understood or predictable. Yet, learning to trust the Lord when the path is not plainly visible is an essential quality of a church planter.

There have been MANY times when I have stood on the back porch of my house during my quiet time and I have cried, shouted, and wept... "God, I don't understand...." He has replied, "Just trust me." I have responded, "But I don't..." His firm reply, "Just trust me." He doesn't always explain everything and He does not owe me an explanation.

As a church planter, when key leaders have left the church, offering receipts were down, plans have gone awry, doctors reports were not good, or when my wife was killed in an auto accident leaving me with three children in college and one in high school, I cried, "I don't understand!" He said, "TRUST ME!!"

One older pastor reminded me, "Don't doubt in the darkness what you knew to be true in the light." Over the years He has proven that He is trustworthy, even when I don't understand.

Lord Jesus, I choose to trust you even when I don't understand. Today, I have a lot of unanswered questions, but I trust you, the omniscient One who sees the BIG PICTURE. Thank you for being my patient loving Heavenly Father who protects me even when I don't understand. Amen.

Sam Douglass

Problems

But he told me: "My kindness is all you need. My power is strongest when you are weak." So I will brag even more about my weaknesses in order that Christ's power will live in me. Therefore, I accept weakness, mistreatment, hardship, persecution, and difficulties suffered for Christ. It's clear that when I'm weak, I'm strong.
~ II Corinthians 12:9, 10 (GW)

READING: II Corinthians 12:1-10

This passage came up on my Bible reading schedule at a perfect time. It was during a prolonged fast when I had encountered challenges and was feeling like it just wasn't fair – that God owed me special favor for fasting and praying.

The heroic church planter, Paul, could have felt the same way, and much more so. But the remarkable "visions and revelations" God gave Paul (v. 1) did not mean he never again had problems. In fact, challenges came (including a recurring "thorn in the flesh") because he had such incredible revelations and, as he put it, God needed to "keep me from being conceited" (v. 7).

God would not take the difficulty away, despite Paul's pleading, (v. 8). Instead, God told Paul that He was strongest when Paul was weakest, and verse nine says Paul therefore "bragged" about his weaknesses!

Verse 10 reveals that because of this truth, he rejoiced in weakness, challenges, persecution, mistreatment, hardship, etc. Church planting leaders experience the same problems today. We, too, can rejoice because "when I'm weak, I'm strong." God is strongest when we are weak.

We oftentimes think that weakness means Ichabod (the glory has departed). But, instead: Weaknesses = strength in the Lord. Hallelujah!

Lord, Please help me remember that problems are not the enemy, but instead they are friends which can help me lean upon you and become strong. Amen.

Mark Alan Williams

This Side of Heaven

*My soul yearns, even faints, for the courts of the Lord; my heart and my flesh
cry out for the living God… Blessed are those whose strength is in you,
who have set their hearts on pilgrimage. ~ Psalm 84:2, 5*

READING: Philippians 2:12-21

Although human beings are made by God and for God, on this side of
heaven, we will find ourselves in want for more and other. We are plagued with
perpetual "if only" thoughts, caught in an endless cycle of hope to disappointment,
trapped in "arrival thinking." But scripture testifies that nothing and no one will
ever take us there, save Jesus.

Many good churches and preachers have slipped into arrival thinking,
making false promises of health, wealth, moral righteousness, relational harmony
and perfect peace. But on this side of heaven God calls us to pilgrimage.
Whatever joy and satisfaction we find will be found in the journey; all of the life
and joy is in the process, for now. And I imagine that even in heaven, there will
always be tension as we grow in the knowledge of our infinite God. I believe our
"Holy, Holy, Holy" will be based, not just on what we have come to know, but on
what we will discover for all of eternity.

So find your strength in God and put your trust in him. Nothing we obtain
will ever suffice. This puts things in their proper place and we no longer need to
extract completion from them. Peace and joy can be had even now.

Pastor, find your joy in the journey and your people will learn to embrace
this world loosely as they build home and church with you.

---

*Jesus, My knuckles are white from gripping so tightly to this world. Are you really
enough? Are you really what I have always longed for? Create in me a clean heart and
take not thy Holy Spirit from me. Amen.*

Peter Sung

Giving

Give and it will be given to you. A good measure, pressed down,
shaken together and running over, will be poured into your lap.
For with the measure you use, it will be measured to you. ~ Luke 6:38

READING: II Corinthians 8

Times are tough economically. Pastors are telling me that giving is down in many churches. The economy of this world is selfish and self-centered. It says, "You need to keep everything for yourself, especially during tough times."

But that is not what Jesus said. The picture that Jesus paints is of a person having the lap of his robe filled to overflowing with grain. The trigger is giving.

God's economy is based on faith expressed in God through giving. The Lord says "Give and it shall be given. As you give to me in faith, I will provide for you. You will be blessed! Trust me!"

Many pastors are afraid to teach about giving. My conviction is that pastors should be afraid NOT to teach about giving. Why? When we do not teach what the Bible says about giving, we keep our people from being blessed. We neglect teaching our people about a great way to glorify God. Our church remains impoverished.

In my fourth church plant, I taught four consecutive Sunday messages on giving from II Corinthians 8 and 9. I was afraid. How would my people respond? Would they feel like the church just wanted them for their money? Would some people leave the church?

It turned out to be one of the best received message series I ever taught. People gave spontaneous testimonies about how God was blessing them as result of their giving. They were discipled in giving. They glorified God. The church was strengthened financially.

Consistently teach your people to give to God. God will bless.

Father, Give me courage to teach my people about giving so we can all enjoy your provision. Amen.

Paul Becker

To Live Is Christ

For to me to live is Christ… ~ *Philippians 1:21a*

READING: Philippians 1:12-26

How would you complete this sentence: "For me to live is _____."? Suppose your spouse, children or a close friend were to answer for you. What would they say is your reason for living?

Most church planters are driven by a vision to win people to Christ, plant a great church, or start multiple churches. So the honest answer to "for me to live is _____," might be "church planting" or "serving Jesus" or "evangelism."

The Apostle Paul, the greatest church planter who ever lived, spelled out his philosophy of life: *For me to live is Christ*. So how is his answer different than that of many church planters?

For Paul, living was about Christ Himself – not just serving or working for Him, but knowing *Him*. Even more than evangelism or church planting or *doing* anything for Him, it was intimacy with the Lord Himself.

So what does that mean – to live is Christ? I think it means at least five things:

1. *Christ is the Lord of my life.* He is, and always will be, the most important Person in my life.

2. *Christ is the hope of my life.* I'm trusting only Him for my eternal destiny. It's never what I've done for Him but always what He's done for me that counts.

3. *Christ is the strength of my life.* I am weak without Him and it is His strength that enables me to live with joy in every circumstance.

4. *Christ is the meaning of my life.* Knowing, loving, serving and glorifying Him is my highest goal and ambition .

5. *Christ is the love of my life.* I love Jesus more than anyone, including even my family or myself.

Jesus, I love serving You, but teach me to love knowing You even more. May I be able to say, "To live is Christ." Amen.

Jim Carpenter

To Die Is Gain

For me to live is Christ and to die is gain. ~ *Philippians 1:21*

READING: Acts 7:54-8:8

A few years ago I was shocked to read the story of a young pastor who was electrocuted during a baptismal service. He left a wife and small children, and a growing church. Most of us church planters don't think about our deaths, but we are all going to die. The exact length of our earthly life is established by God, not by us (Ps. 139:16).

The Apostle Paul was beheaded in Rome. Sensing his departure was close, he made this amazing statement: "to die is gain."

You can't understand "to die is gain" without first understanding "to live is Christ," our theme from yesterday. And obviously death is not "gain" for everyone. To die without Christ is to lose everything forever.

But for us who love Jesus, how is death gain? Death is gain because…

It means victory over sin. In heaven we'll be able to live without that old, nagging struggle with our sin nature. We'll serve the Lord in holiness and innocence and perfection.

It gives us one last witness. We have the opportunity to bring glory to Christ in our death. That was Paul's desire: "…it is my eager expectation and hope that I will not be at all ashamed, but that with full courage now as always *Christ will be honored in my body,* whether by life or *by death*" (Phil. 1:20, my emphasis).

We'll be in Christ's presence. This is most precious of all, and what Jesus prayed for us: "Father, I desire that they also, whom you have given me, may be with me where I am, to see my glory…" (Jn. 17:24).

May our new churches teach people how to live and how to die to God's glory.

Father, Show me how to bring You glory in my life and in my death. Amen.

Jim Carpenter

Priceless

Instruct them to…be generous and ready to share, storing up for themselves the treasure of a good foundation for the future, so that they may take hold of that which is life indeed. ~ I Timothy 6:18, 19 (NASB)

READING: Philippians 3:7-21

Bernie Madoff was a financial assets manager who was convicted of embezzling millions of dollars. At an auction of his personal possessions, held to pay off his debts, some bidders paid inflated prices to take home a piece of criminal history. A Steinway & Sons grand piano, expected to sell for $16,000, went for $42,000. A leather footstool brought in $3,300, almost ten times the estimate. Collectors who paid extravagant prices for memorabilia considered their cache priceless.

Church planters invest their lives and resources in spreading the gospel and establishing viable growing communities of believers. They risk everything for the sake of God's call to glorify His name in the earth. But, when we step out on nothing in faith, we always find something there that is abundantly more valuable than a piece of criminal history!

After a furlough, we returned to a church plant in a little enclave of Colombian indigenous homes made of discarded material found in dumps. Twelve-year old Camila was helping her mother clean a fresh catch of fish. She did not notice we were there. Bounding around the corner of the house after she was done with her chore, she finally saw us. With a jubilant pre-teen squeal she rushed toward us and hugged us, giggling with delight that we were back! This is priceless! This is worth the sacrifice of laying down our own dreams to accomplish the will of God for the world. Need I say more?

Lord, Help us keep our eyes on the real treasure of life. Remind us that true joy comes from seeing your life in those to whom we are sent. Amen.

Christine Cunningham

Every Tribe and Language and Tongue and Nation

And they sang a new song, saying, "Worthy are you to take the scroll and to open its seals, for you were slain, and by your blood you ransomed people for God from every tribe and language and people and nation." ~ Revelation 5:9

READING: Revelation 5:1-14

One Easter Sunday morning our worship service began with greetings and Scripture readings in five languages. As we sang about Christ's Resurrection, pictures of precious people from around the world, from Africa to Asia to Latin America, scrolled across the screen.

I preached from Revelation 5, maybe an unusual text for Easter Sunday. But it is John's vision of a great celebration in heaven. The four living creatures, twenty-four elders, and a numberless throng of angels all worship the Resurrected Lamb!

Their thunderous cries of "WORTHY, WORTHY IS THE LAMB WHO WAS SLAIN," unveil a preview of church planting's reward. "You ransomed people for God from *every tribe and language and people and nation.*"

Church planter, wherever you are, the Lamb has ransomed people by His blood. One day your tears and toil and trials will be transformed into a vast chorus of people from every ethnicity, nationality, and mother tongue.

Imagine when we'll all be together before the throne, singing in the greatest choir ever known, to the Only Worthy One, the One we love the most. Imagine the faces of those who came to faith because of your new churches. Faces of every race and color, radiant in reflected glory, exalting the One you served to bring them there. Worthy is the Lamb, we'll all sing together.

Don't give up! The Lamb is worthy. His blood has bought a people for God, and He's using you to reach them.

Worthy Lord, Guide me, use me and lead me to that day when all your ransomed children will be home. Amen.

Jim Carpenter

Shaking Off the Dust

If anyone will not welcome you or listen to your words, shake the dust off of your feet when you leave that home or town. ~ Matthew 10:14

READING: Matthew 10:1-16

When Jesus sent out the Twelve on their first preaching tour, He gave them sound instruction that can free us from much angst about rejection or failure when we plant churches. In keeping with the ancient customs of hospitality, He told them to find a worthy person to lodge with while preaching and ministering in each town. Their blessing would rest on that home. But if the host or the town rejected their message, Jesus instructed His disciples to shake off the very dust of that place as they left. He solemnly warned that it would be more bearable for Sodom and Gomorrah on Judgment Day than for those unreceptive towns.

There is a right way and a wrong way to shake off the dust. Unfortunately, I've seen bad examples of how to do this. Perhaps a well-intentioned but harsh Christian will do a bad job of sharing the gospel and alienate people by his ham-handed and insensitive behavior. When the local folks finally get fed up and kick him out, he curses them with a vindictive and dramatic flourish, announcing that he is "shaking off the dust!"

That is NOT the Spirit of Christ (Lk. 10:51 – 56).

We have totally missed the point if we take any pleasure in shaking off the dust. Even if people have treated us shabbily, the love of Christ should constrain us (II Cor. 5:14). Our hearts should grieve their pitiable condition and be quick to release any leftover bitterness regarding them.

We don't have to labor under a burden of failure or rejection. Jesus invites us to shake it off, and find joy in following Him.

Dear Father, Thank You for granting us grace to experience the fellowship of Your suffering. Amen.

Dionne Carpenter

Despising Small Things

For whoever has despised the day of small things
shall rejoice… ~ Zechariah 4:10a (ESV)

READING: Matthew 13:31, 32

Church planting often starts small. Most new churches do not grow to become "megachurches." There's a danger in measuring God's blessing by the scale of attendance or conversions or baptism. Is not every work of God a miracle?

Some churches have an attendance of 50,000. Does that mean that God has withheld His blessing because your new church has an attendance of 85, and that "only" 27 people were saved last year?

When Jesus healed the blind man, was that a lesser miracle than the parting of the Red Sea? Did Christ's turning water into wine for a small wedding deserve less praise than when He fed the 5000? Was the raising of Lazarus less praiseworthy than the "many" Matthew reports (28:52, 53) who were raised when Jesus died on the cross?

Every true conversion displays the infinite power and sovereign grace of God. Measuring a miracle only by the size of the human response will create a man-centered standard, and deprive God of glory due Him.

We really don't know what God is up to. One soul converted may lead to multitudes saved in future generations. One small church may become the mother of a cluster of daughter churches.

As Zechariah led the rebuilding of the Temple, some despised the small beginnings of the project. But God was in it. Jesus said one small mustard seed would one day become a large bird sanctuary (Matthew 13:31, 32).

Don't despise the "small things" God is doing. Bigger numbers will always be reported somewhere. But let's rejoice that the seed of the gospel is being planted, and that the true size of the harvest is known to God alone!

Lord, Teach me not to despise small things. May I recognize and rejoice in the miracles You are doing every day. Amen.

Jim Carpenter

The Lord Is My Support

They confronted me in the day of my disaster,
but the LORD was my support. ~ Psalm 18:18

READING: Psalm 18:1-19

Those of us who raise support to fund church planting projects find ourselves in a curious position of depending on the faithfulness of many people to sit down every month and write a check, or hand us money, or send money that gets collected and disbursed by our sending organization. I don't know about you, but for Jim and me, it was always a small drama to open our paycheck envelope each month to see whether or not we had a full check.

It's easy to begin to rely heavily on these many, mostly very good people and to feel anxious or upset if some who promised to support us are sporadic in follow through. Although we should always be grateful for their support, we run into a snare if we begin to place our main trust in those supporters or those charitable organizations.

The fact of the matter is that "the LORD is my support" – not my main support or my biggest support but simply and only *my support*. (The Hebrew word David uses here is *mish'an* [Strong's - H5472] meaning "support of every kind." It's clear from cross referencing Isaiah 3:1, the other place this Hebrew word is used, although in a negative connotation, that *mish'an* includes basic supplies like bread, water and military re-provisioning.)

To the degree that we know in our bones that every good and perfect gift comes directly from God's hand, through whatever intermediary supporter's purse, to that degree we will be free from anxiety and fear about finances.

Dear Lord, Help me today to rejoice in the assurance that You are my support. Thank You for blessing me through wonderful supporters. Amen.

Dionne Carpenter

The Birth of Hope

And she shall bring forth a son, and thou shalt call his name JESUS:
for he shall save his people from their sins. ~ Matthew 1:21, (KJV)

READING: Matthew 1:18-25

During the Christmas Eve service we sang "Hark! The Herald Angels Sing," the classic Christmas melody. One of the verses penned by Charles Wesley touched the core of my spirit:

Hail the heav'n-born Prince of Peace! Hail the Son of Righteousness!
Light and Life to all He brings, ris'n with healing in His wings.

Earlier that day we had brought my wife Carolyn's mother home from the hospital. The doctors had predicted a short time for her to live and, indeed, she died a month later. On Christmas that year we were also hosting a family whose mother unexpectedly lay comatose in a hospital.

Yet, as the advent passages were read and we sang that carol, the hope of Christmas flooded my heart. Wonderful hope is found in the clear statements of Scripture: "For unto us a child is born, unto us a son is given: and the government shall be upon his shoulder: and his name shall be called Wonderful, Counselor, The mighty God, The everlasting Father, The Prince of Peace" (Isaiah 9:6 KJV).

"In him was life, and the life was the light of men. The light shines in the darkness, and the darkness has not overcome it" (John 1:4, 5 ESV). Without Jesus, none of us is in a very hopeful situation. Illness, pain and physical frailty are around the corner. But in Jesus we have eternal life and eternal joy.

Christmas is the birth of hope!

Lord Jesus, I thank you from the bottom of my heart for coming to earth to die for my sins and the sins of the world. Thank you for the blessed hope! Amen.

Mark Alan Williams

You Shall Call His Name Jesus

She will bear a son, and you shall call his name Jesus, for
he will save his people from their sins. ~ *Matthew 1:21 (ESV)*

READING: Matthew 1:18-25

The children sang in an impromptu choir. One of the young men played the guitar, and the rest of us joined in on the familiar Christmas carols. Mrs. John's house echoed with our voices, and I thought how wonderful it was to be so far from home at Christmastime, and still celebrate His birth.

That December was the first time I felt the connection between Christmas and church planting. I was 9,000 miles from home, in Bangalore, India. I sat with people whose culture, mother tongue, and life experience were very different from mine. But because someone had planted a church, we were brothers and sisters together, rejoicing in the birth of our Savior.

Church planting was born when Jesus was born. The Christmas story brings to mind images of the Baby of Bethlehem, of shepherds and stars and wise men. But it should also always remind us of people that need saving and churches that need planting.

When the angel appeared to Joseph in a dream, he set the stage and outlined the reason for church planting. His words were prophetic: *you shall call his name Jesus, for he will save his people from their sins.*

Church planting is the inevitable result of Christ's birth. The name Jesus, in Hebrew Joshua (*Yeshua*), means Savior. Every time we speak His name – Jesus! – we acknowledge humankind's helpless need for a Savior. Every time we preach the gospel, we are calling out the people he came to save. Every church we plant is a fulfillment of his mission, and the best Christmas present of all.

Father, As I celebrate the birth of Jesus, grant me a renewed love for those He came to save. Amen.

Jim Carpenter

Your Father Knows

*When you do good deeds, don't try to show off. If you do, you won't
get a reward from your Father in heaven. ~ Matthew 6:1 (CEV)*

READING: Matthew 6:1-4

Wouldn't it be nice if people recognized our efforts, valued our sacrifices
and honored our church planting accomplishments? But if we pin our hopes on
expecting honor and recognition when we sacrificially serve Christ, we may be
sorely disappointed.

I remember a business meeting in my first church plant. That church
was birthed in large part by my blood, sweat and tears. Yet people publically
questioned my motives and compensation. I was surprised, but I shouldn't have
been.

Sometimes those who serve most sacrificially, who are most dedicated, who
deserve the greatest awards, not only don't get the credit they deserve, they get
persecution and even martyrdom.

What will enable us to bear up under the lack of well-deserved credit,
blessing and encouragement? We must remember, first, that the greatest leaders
of our faith suffered greatly for it, just as Jesus said they would. Our Lord
Himself willingly bore the most extreme agony.

Rather than trying to impress people and be recognized, we must remember
that Jesus warned us not to do things just to receive the praise of men. In fact,
He said that doing so robs us of our reward from the Lord. We should live only
to please Him and perform our best for an audience of One.

Most importantly, we must remember that our Heavenly Father knows
what we are enduring and He will faithfully reward us for it at the right time.
If we do receive recognition from time to time, we can be grateful and perhaps
even surprised.

---

*Dear Lord, Help me not to seek recognition from anyone but You. Thank you that You
will faithfully reward my service. Amen.*

Mark Alan Williams

Using Perception
to Encourage the Faithful

*Therefore, encourage one another and build each other up,
just as in fact you are doing. ~ I Thessalonians 5:11*

READING: Acts 4:13-31

As a co-leader of a local prayer group, I arrived early and noticed that forty chairs had been set up for our group of twenty people. I instantly saw there were too many chairs, so I removed and stacked fifteen chairs before the other leader arrived.

She was curious about how I had "known" so emphatically that we had too many chairs. I laughed in reply: "Oh, I guess it just triggered all my instincts as a church planter. I'm so used to thinking about what will encourage the core group." I explained that when twenty people see forty available chairs, it feels to them as if they are few, isolated, somehow daunted. But the same twenty people, sitting in fewer chairs, tend to feel encouraged: "Great, we're all here and I can speak up in this intimate and friendly group."

This principle comes into play when our church plant sets attendance goals. If our core group (of forty) sets a goal for sixty to attend a special event, and then eighty show up, that's shouting time! Hallelujah! But if those forty set a goal for 100 to show up, and the same eighty come, that identical outcome feels like a massive failure. It's all a matter of perception.

I've often seen this same principle at work. When the established church where we currently serve held prayer meetings, they would feel discouraged when only a few ladies came. But after hearing the 5% statistic about the number of prayer warriors in a typical church, we (and our prayer team) feel wonderfully encouraged and emboldened because our group regularly far exceeds that percentage.

Our core group is precious. Sometimes we encourage best just by taking away the extra chairs.

Father, Make me a perceptive encourager. Amen.

Dionne Carpenter

Positive Attitude

Rejoice in the Lord always. ~ Philippians 4:4

READING: Philippians 4

Recently, I was with a fellow minister, a man whom I love and respect. He had been going through some hard times in his family life and in his ministry life. As we talked, I began to notice that most of what he said reflected a negative attitude toward life and ministry.

A negative attitude is a great danger. Our attitude reflects whether we really believe that God loves us and wants the best for us. There are certainly times in our lives when God disciplines us. That is never fun. But it is always ultimately for our best. He doesn't hurt us just to hurt us. He allows pain to come into our lives to shape us into stronger people and more effective servants.

The Apostle Paul was under house arrest in Rome when he wrote the book of Philippians. His circumstances were not good. He endured a loss of freedom, filth and abuse. And yet, if you had to summarize Paul's attitude with just one word it would be JOY. His positive attitude overcame his circumstances.

God's promise to supply all our needs, found in verse 19, does not give us a blank check to do anything we want to do. This passage is in the context of our circumstances and God's providence. The Apostle Paul had learned the secret to contentment, no matter what his circumstances. He had learned that he could handle any circumstance because God was with him.

God has given me, too, the strength I need to overcome anything. I learned this lesson through the four year cancer battle and ultimate death of my first wife.

Hold on to a good attitude. Never let it go, no matter what your circumstances. YOU can do everything through our Great God who gives you strength!!!

Lord, Help me to maintain a positive attitude. Amen.

Paul Becker

Twelve Stones

And Joshua set up at Gilgal the twelve stones
they had taken out of the Jordan. ~ Joshua 4:20

READING: Joshua 4

The twelve stones at Gilgal were the first of seven stone memorials that Joshua set up, as recorded in the Book of Joshua. (See Josh. 7:26; 8:28, 29; 8:32; 10:27; 22:34; and 24:26, 27.) Each one provided a witness, a reminder or a warning of some momentous event in the conquest of the Promised Land. They helped the Israelites to remember God's past blessing or discipline.

I happened to be reading through this portion of Joshua right after our church weathered a particularly difficult church crisis. Limp with relief at how God protected and guided us through, it suddenly struck me that I should set up a "Twelve Stones" kind of reminder about this most recent victory.

Biblical memorials took many forms, including such things as celebratory parties, jewelry, written accounts or just plain piles of rock. The best ones were designed to provoke conversation – to re-tell "the story."

Because I'm a weaver, I wove a tapestry depicting twelve stones on a grassy knoll. I've hung that weaving in our house ever since. And, for years, on the anniversary of the pivotal meeting that ended our "Twelve Stones" crisis, we took the elders out to eat who had stood so courageously with us. We would praise God for watching over us and thank them once again for the part they played.

It's curious; we've had dozens of wonderful milestones in the churches we planted. But the ones I remember best are those with a tangible reminder, maybe hanging on the wall, written down in a journal or memorialized in a photograph.

It's no coincidence that the land Joshua conquered was positively littered with memorials. Courageous faith goes hand in hand with remembering all God has done for us.

Father, Show me creative, tangible ways to remember Your many kindnesses. Amen.

Dionne Carpenter

The Planting of the Lord

...every tree that does not produce good fruit
will be cut down and thrown into the fire. ~ Luke 3:9

READING: Isaiah 61:1-3

In the synagogue, Jesus read this to the Jews who were present (Lk. 4:18, 19). His twist on the passage is that the time of the Lord's favor has come. Isaiah said, "that they may be called oaks of righteousness, the planting of the Lord, that he may be glorified."

The Lord's favor has come to oaks of righteousness: the poor, the brokenhearted, the captives, and those who are bound who mourn in Zion. They receive beautiful headdresses instead of ashes, the oil of gladness instead of mourning, the garment of praise instead of a faint spirit. They are the planting of the Lord for the purpose of glorifying Him!

Greatly offended, the synagogue crowd took Jesus out to a cliff intending to throw him to his death. Miraculously, he passed through the angry mob to continue the story of his glory with power and authority. His followers continue, to this day, bringing the story of his glory and establishing oaks of righteousness in the earth.

'Planting churches' is the planting of the Lord. We are the oaks of righteousness, dead and fallen to the earth where new life can sprout for the purpose of the kingdom of God. Oak is strong and resists disease. Its products are enduring and beautiful. Furniture is made from oak. Oak barrels are preferred for aging wine. Oak wood chips bring a uniquely rich flavor to smoked fish, meat and cheese. May we continue to plant more oaks of righteousness with the articulate and accurate conveyance that the Lord would be planted and glorified!

O Sovereign Father, Make us oaks of righteousness, an eternal investment of life entrenched in the earth forever extending toward heaven. Keep us continually multiplying and growing with strength and endurance. Amen.

Christine Cunningham

The Sacrifice of Good Works

*Through Jesus, therefore, let us continually offer to God a sacrifice of praise –
the fruit of lips that confess his name. And do not forget to do good and to share
with others, for with such sacrifices God is pleased. ~ Hebrews 13:15, 16*

READING: Hebrews 13

I was once asked to speak to a women's group in another church. I prepared
well after making every aspect of the presentation a matter of prayer. Nobody
bothered to mention that the ladies were all quite elderly. They grazed from a full
buffet and then, well-fed, settled in for my talk. Most of them fell sound asleep!
I was devastated. Why had that happened? Hadn't I heard correctly on what to
say and how to present it?

In response, the Lord tenderly brought this passage to mind, commenting:
"The sacrifice of good works can be given twice." The first time we give God
this sacrifice by working hard to be as obedient and as prepared as possible. Our
sacrifice is the good deed, done well.

Sometimes that's the end of it.

But if our thoughts return to that good deed, either to dwell pridefully on
how well we did, or to second-guess all the mistakes we made, then it's time to
give it to God a second time. I gave that "good deed" to God again when I prayed
this prayer:

"Father, I have no idea why You led me to give a talk to a room full of
snoring ladies. But I give You that presentation again. Please use it – or don't use
it – however You choose. I leave it with You. Help me to forget about it, one way
or the other."

The safest place to keep those memories is in God's hands.

---

*Father, Help me to regularly dump the baggage of past ministry and move forward
with simple trust in You. Amen.*

Dionne Carpenter
Adapted from *Trust Training* ©2008

OUR CONTRIBUTORS

Paul Becker. A veteran church planter, Dr. Paul Becker is the president and founder of Dynamic Church Planting International (DCPI) in Oceanside, California.

John Bond. A church planter and senior pastor, Dr. John Bond is the founding director of Sonlife Ministries and the South Asia Pacific World Zone leader for DCPI.

Dionne Carpenter. A church planter with her husband, Jim, in Southern California, Dionne Carpenter is a writer and editor, and author of *Trust Training: A Field Manual for Confident Trust in God Before, During and After Life's Battles.*

Jim Carpenter. Dr. Jim Carpenter planted multiple churches, pastors a church in California, and is a writer and editor.

Ross Chenot. Dr. Ross Chenot has been a pastor, church planter and church planting mentor, and serves on the staff with Transformation Ministries in Covina, California.

Christine Cunningham. Christine Cunningham serves with her husband, Kevin, as a church planter and missionary with Faithworks, International in Colombia, South America.

Kevin Cunningham. Pastor Kevin Cunningham serves with his wife, Christine, as a church planter and missionary with Faithworks, International in Colombia, South America.

Sam Douglass. A church planter in multiple plants in North America, Dr. Sam Douglass is founder of *Just Coach Me* and is the North American World Zone leader for DCPI.

David Godoy. A church planter in Uberlandia, Brazil, Rev. David Godoy serves as the Latin America World Zone Leader for DCPI.

R. Jayakumar. Along with planting multiple churches in Bangalore, India and throughout Asia, Dr. Jayakumar is the founder of Bible Believing Churches and Missions and serves as the Asia Indian Ocean World Zone Leader for DCPI.

Buddy Johnson. A church planter in Mexico for 27 years, Rev. Buddy Johnson is the Hispanic Coordinator with the Baptist Missionary Association of America. He serves as a Senior Master Trainer with DCPI.

Scott Last. Rev. Scott Last was a church planter and church planting mentor in Italy and Portugal and serves as the HQ Europe World Zone Coordinator and International Staff Pastor with DCPI.

Del Loy. Rev. Del Loy has served as a senior pastor and has planted churches in Oceanside, California and Natchez, Mississippi.

Chris McKinney. Rev. Chris McKinney was a missionary in the Philippines for 24 years, planting churches and training Christian leaders. Chris is currently the Director of Research & Analysis as well as the Headquarters World Zone Coordinator for Asia at DCPI.

Sean Pierce. Rev. Sean Pierce is an experienced church planter and serves as the Director of Associational Development for the Hudson Baptist Association in Schenectady, New York. He helps churches and church planters in leadership development and church planting strategy.

Saleem Sadiq. Pastor Saleem Sadiq is a pastor and church planter, and founder of Gospel Outreach in Lahore, Pakistan.

Hal Seed. Dr. Hal Seed is founding pastor of New Song Community Church in Oceanside, California. Hal is the author of *The God Question, Future History, Jonah,* and *The Bible Questions.*

Eitan Shishkoff. Pastor Eitan Shishkoff is a church planter in Israel.

Peter Sung. Dr. Peter Sung helped plant multiple churches before becoming Director of Church Planting with the Evangelical Covenant Church.

Ronald Thiesen. Pastor Ron Thiesen is a church planter along the Amazon River in Peru with the Association of Faith Churches and Ministries.

Hendrik Vorster. Dr. Hendrik Vorster is a pastor and church planter who has served in South Africa and Australia. He is a Master Trainer with DCPI.

Amir John Williams. Pastor Amir Williams has planted multiple churches in Pakistan and now pastors a church he planted in Seattle, Washington.

Mark Alan Williams. A veteran church planter and daughter church mentor in California, Dr. Mark Williams serves as Vice President of Global Church Planting Materials and Partnerships for DCPI.

DYNAMIC
CHURCH
PLANTING
INTERNATIONAL

Experience the Vision... Empower a Movement!

THE VISION... *Equipping leaders to plant five million dynamic churches to reach the world for Christ!* God is giving favor to DCPI church planting training in the nations of the world. He has presented this mission with a wide open door to equip leaders to plant dynamic churches worldwide.

THE NEED... Nearly half the world's population does not have access to a dynamic church! People worldwide come to Christ but have no church to attend, no one to disciple them, no one to minister to their needs and no one to teach them to share their faith—they've become spiritual orphans!

THE CHALLENGE... In keeping with the Great Commission to go and make disciples of all nations, DCPI understands that effectively reaching people for Christ requires disciple-making as well as introducing people to the gospel. Disciple-making requires the presence of healthy, sustainable, and dynamic churches within easy access for people. While we hear of multitudes coming to Christ around the world, there is a shortage of healthy churches. A primary factor in the shortage of churches is the lack of trained leaders who are equipped to establish new churches and disciple new believers. There is a church planting 'training famine' in many nations.

THE SOLUTION... That is why Dynamic Church Planting International (DCPI) does what we do—find and train indigenous leaders to plant dynamic churches. Then, we equip these leaders to teach others. These trained leaders will go places we can never go, reach people we cannot reach, train in languages we cannot speak and relate to their "people groups" as we cannot.

THE OPPORTUNITY... There are leaders waiting to be sent. As the body of Christ, we can work together to equip them. Let's bring God's message to all the nations.

PROVEN EFFECTIVENESS... Since its inception in 1995 DCPI has:

- Trained tens of thousands of church planting leaders
- Certified National Trainers in over 80 countries
- Our research projects that more than 100,000 churches have been planted resulting in over 5 million new believers in Christ
- Developed five tracks of church planting training materials
- Produced 13 church planting-specific publications

IMPACT... As the ministry of equipping church planters is multiplied through indigenous leaders, there will be a fresh infusion of the gospel throughout the nations of the world, resulting in eternal life for millions and bringing us closer to the completion of the Great Commission.

"And the things you have heard me say in the presence of many witnesses entrust to reliable men who will also be qualified to teach others." ~ 2 Timothy 2:2

www.dcpi.org
For more information, email: service@dcpi.org